# ATLAS OF UNIDENTIFIED FLYING OBJECTS

To my wife and children, for whom I try my best.

# ATLAS OF UNIDENTIFIED FLYING OBJECTS

and Unidentified Anomalous Phenomena

ANDY MCGRILLEN

Foreword by D.W. Pasulka

IVY PRESS

1 ROSWELL
2 KINGMAN
3 KECKSBURG
4 VARGINHA
5 COYAME
6 THE BASS STRAIT
7 SNOWFLAKE
8 PASCAGOULA
9 DEVIL'S DEN STATE PARK
10 LANCASTER
11 NEAR KINGSTON
12 NEAR SAN DIEGO
13 WASHINGTON DC
14 RENDLESHAM FOREST
15 SHAG HARBOUR
16 BELGIUM
17 TEHRAN
18 COLARES
19 SAN CARLOS DE BARILOCHE
20 TRANS-EN-PROVENCE
21 XIAOSHAN
22 MOUNT RAINER
23 STEPHENVILLE
24 BROAD HAVEN
25 NEW DELHI
26 DALNEGORSK
27 GWANGJU
28 DAYTON
29 MELBOURNE
30 RUWA
31 VORONEZH
32 DECHMONT
33 SOCORRO
34 KOFU

32
14
16
31
20
17
25
26
27
34
21
30
29
6

# CONTENTS

# **FOREWORD** BY. D.W. PASULKA

I first met Andy McGrillen a few years ago, just as he was launching his podcast dedicated to exploring the intriguing world of unidentified flying objects. I was fortunate to be a guest on his show and was impressed by his genuine curiosity, careful research and his sincere commitment to illuminating this enigmatic subject for a broader audience. Andy approaches this field not merely as an enthusiast but as someone dedicated to bringing clarity, objectivity and thoughtful analysis to a topic often clouded by speculation.

*Atlas of Unidentified Flying Objects* is a much-needed contribution to the field. The book provides a clear entry point into the fascinating and sometimes perplexing phenomenon of UFOs. Andy has meticulously curated a collection of both iconic and lesser-known cases from around the globe, presenting them with clarity and balance. The detailed accounts in this atlas are accompanied by compelling visual elements, including photographs, maps and insightful illustrations, enhancing the reader's understanding and engagement.

What distinguishes this work is Andy's thoughtful approach – he neither sensationalizes nor dismisses the topic. Instead, he invites readers to explore the evidence, ponder the possibilities and appreciate the complexities inherent in the UFO phenomenon. The diverse range of cases featured in this atlas underscores the global scale and enduring mystery surrounding these events.

Whether you are new to the topic or have long been intrigued by it, *Atlas of Unidentified Flying Objects* is an invaluable guide, thoughtfully compiled and engagingly presented. It is my pleasure to introduce this work, confident that it will enlighten, provoke thought and deepen appreciation for one of the most captivating mysteries of our time.

# INTRODUCTION

My fascination with the world of UFOs goes way back to my childhood. I would spend hours in the local library looking at books on aliens, the Loch Ness monster, who built the pyramids and other strange phenomena. I can pinpoint my lifelong interest in the UFO topic, though, to a particular incident, which happened late on a cold, dark winter's night in Knightswood, a busy suburban area of Glasgow. Being young at the time, maybe eleven or twelve years old, exact dates are fuzzy but it was around November in the mid 1990s. There was a group of five us, including my mum, leaving a small church where I attended the Boys' Brigade. As we waited to cross the busy road with houses lined up along either side, we looked up and down the single lanes of traffic, waiting for our opportunity to cross. However, at the end of the road, around a kilometre (half a mile) away, something caught our eye. At ground level, low enough that some houses and trees blocked the view of the bottom of it, was a huge spinning string of lights. Imagine a Ferris wheel at a carnival, but tilted and spinning incredibly fast, like a washing machine in its spin cycle. These lights must have been 9–15m (30–50ft) high. We were in awe, all five of us, adults and children stunned. All I remember is that we stood looking at this object hovering there at a strange angle and my mum and another parent quickly exchanged a quick 'That's odd!' conversation. As quickly as that we decided to just cross the road and continue our walk home, in a slightly different direction away from the object. No camera phones, no evidence, just our five sets of eyes seeing something we couldn't explain.

Ever since then, I've wondered what it was we saw that night. There was no carnival in the local area, no fairground ride that would have explained what we were looking at and it wasn't your typical UFO sighting high up in the night sky it was low to the ground and in a busy area. We didn't report it – indeed, most sightings aren't reported, and who would we even have called? I do regret that we didn't even try to get a bit closer and walk towards it. It was, however, enough to really light the fire of my interest in UFOs and it's stayed with me for life.

In 2020 I started my own podcast during the early days of the coronavirus pandemic lockdown, and between working my fulltime job and family life, I got to speak to people from all around the world, from all different sides of the UFO conversation. The podcast gave me the opportunity to write this book. It includes just a small number of UFO cases from around the globe, some famous, some less well known, but all giving a glimpse into a world filled with mystery, intrigue and incredible possibilities. Whether you thumb straight through to some particular events or you read all of the entries in depth, I would like you to keep an open mind and consider the number of witnesses all describing encounters of different kinds. I want you to think to yourself that if this represents only a tiny percentage of all the UFO incidents across the world, then a truly staggering number of encounters are likely happening on an even bigger scale than we can imagine. My hope is that this book informs, entertains and inspires others to go and do their own research, lending new ideas, new approaches and fresh thinking to the UFO conversation in an ever-changing landscape.

From civilians to military personnel, farmers to pilots, cross-generational encounters haunting entire families, there are mysteries here that could shake our entire understanding of our place in the universe.

The UFO topic has changed, perhaps forever. It has gone from a fringe topic to one that is now being discussed year on year in the US Congress and US Senate. The highest levels of government are now talking about extraterrestrials, non-human biologics and anomalous craft. In Brazil, there have been open hearings held in its Senate, discussing cases from its own unique history. Politicians are trying to bring forward first hand whistleblowers who have worked on alleged 'UAP Crash Retrieval Programs', for many the 'holy grail' of the subject, the recovery of downed alien craft. Are we at a turning point where as a species are getting ever closer to finally being told that, not only are we not alone, but life is far more incredibly complex and wonderful than we have ever dared to imagine.

RIGHT: UFO sighting in Riverside, California on 23 November, 1951.

Chapter 1

# CRASH RETRIEVAL

| *New Mexico, USA* | 33.5754° N, 105.1850° W |
|---|---|

# ROSWELL

Where it all began: the infamous 1947 Roswell Incident

Many places around the world evoke particular thoughts when mentioned. Hawaii makes us think of sunshine and beaches, Paris is romance and fine dining, Egypt is the pyramids. Roswell, a small city in southeast New Mexico, USA, conjures up particular thoughts and emotions, as the mention of the name worldwide brings up conversations of UFOs, alien bodies, crashed flying saucers and more. It is, for many, where the UFO conversation entered the public realm, inspiring generations of thinkers, writers, researchers, authors and lecturers. An event that seems to have outlasted so many others, starting in 1947, but as powerful now as it was then. I couldn't have put this book together without highlighting an incident that for many has been the launching pad for their own journey into the world of UAP (Unidentified Anomalous Phenomena).

In July 1947, in the searing heat of the New Mexico desert, where temperatures often reach the high 30s Celsius (around 100 degrees Fahrenheit), one of the most well-known UFO incidents in history occurred. Roswell, a city with a humble population of around 26,000, was primarily an agricultural hub, producing crops such as cotton, alfalfa and pecans. Cattle ranching was also a substantial industry in the area, which we will shortly see is significant. This agricultural scene played a vital role in the community of Roswell, its people and its economy.

In addition to its agricultural significance, Roswell had a newly established military presence. In 1947, just two years after the Second World War ended, Roswell Army Air Field (RAAF) was operational. The base trained crews who would fly bombers and was considered an important installation for strategic operations during the Cold War era. This additional infrastructure brought more money and development to the area.

It's an eerie coincidence that shortly after the establishment of this military infrastructure, an incredible event, potentially involving one of the biggest military cover-ups of all time, took place.

At the beginning of July 1947, a rancher, William 'Mac' Brazel, discovered something incredible on his ranch located around 120km (75 miles) north of Roswell: scattered across a wide area, he found debris containing parts of 'something' including, reportedly, metallic rods, chunks of plastic-like material and, most famously, very thin metal sheeting.

Albuquerque
Roswell
Crash site
NEW MEXICO
Trinity
Test Site
Roswell
Roswell Army
Air Field
Holloman Air
Force Base
Alamogordo
UNITED STATES
OF AMERICA
TEXAS
N
Ciudad Juárez
MEXICO
50 miles
100 kilometres

This sheeting would become infamous around the world and go on to influence many science-fiction books, series and movies. The sheets were astonishingly light, like paper, but when crumpled by hand, would then fold back out into a perfect sheet again. Brazel, clearly taken aback by the discovery, collected some of the material and took it home. The incident was then reported to sheriff, George Wilcox, who forwarded the report to the RAAF base

On receipt of the report from the sheriff, the RAAF, under the command of Colonel William Blanchard, got involved. Major Jesse Marcel, unknowingly about to write his name into the history books, was dispatched to the ranch to help recover the material. Upon arrival at Mac's home, he too, seeing that the sheets of metal, feather-light to hold, and which could be crumpled and unfolded back to a perfectly flat sheet, was amazed by the strange material and its incredible properties.

This is where the story of cover-ups begin! There are not many reported or well-known incidents of UFOs being recovered before 1947, so it's fair to say this was the first time the US government and the US Air Force were flexing their crash-retrieval muscles. It is likely they had no real procedure for recovering anything otherworldly but used their experience of retrieving fallen aircraft or other atmospheric junk like weather balloons.

On 8 July 1947 the RAAF issued a now-famous press release, perhaps its biggest mistake in all of this. It reported that from the ranch of Mac Brezel they had recovered,

LEFT: In 1947 Roswell was primarily an agricultural and cattle ranching hub.

BELOW: The 8 July 1947 edition of the *Roswell Daily Record* announces the capture of a flying saucer.

OVERLEAF: Major Jesse A. Marcel holding foil debris from the UFO crash site in Roswell, New Mexico.

Roswell Daily Record

RECORD PHONES

Business Office 2288
News Department 2287

ablished 1888 — Roswell, New Mexico, Tuesday, July 8, 1947 — 5¢ PER COPY

RAAF Captures Flying Saucer On Ranch in Roswell Region

Claims Army Is Stacking Courts Martial

Indiana Senator Lays Protest Before Patterson

House Passes Tax Slash by Large Margin

Defeat Amendment By Demos to Remove Many from Rolls

Security Council Paves Way to Talks On Arms Reductions

No Details of Flying Disk Are Revealed

Roswell Hardware Man and Wife Report Disk Seen

The intelligence office of the 509th Bombardment group at Roswell Army Air Field announced at noon today, that the field has come into possession of a flying saucer.

According to information released by the department, over authority of Maj. J.A. Marcel, intelligence officer, the disk was recovered on a ranch in the Roswell vicinity, after an unidentified rancher had notified Sheriff Geo. Wilcox, here, that he had found the instrument on his premises.

Major Marcel and a detail from his department went to the ranch and recovered the disk, it was stated.

After the intelligence office here had inspected the instrument it was flown to "higher headquarters."

The intelligence office stated that no details of the saucer's construction or its appearance had been revealed.

Mr. and Mrs. Dan Wilmot apparently were the only persons in Roswell who have seen what they thought was a flying disk.

They were sitting on their porch at 105 South Penn. last Wednesday night at about ten minutes before ten o'clock when a large glowing object zoomed out of the sky from the southeast, going in a northwesterly direction at a high rate of speed.

Wilmot called Mrs. Wilmot's attention to it and both ran down into the

Ex-King Carol Weds Mme. Lupescu

Former King Carol of Romania and Mme. Elena Lupescu relax aboard the S. S. America bound for Cuba and Mexico in May, 1941. A member of Carol's household in Rio de Janeiro said the ex-king and his companion for 23 years in reign and exile were recently married at their hotel Copacabana Palace suite. (AP Wirephoto)

Miners and Operators Sign Highest Wage Pact in History

t Satellites
ris Meeting

not a weather balloon or junk, but a 'flying disc'. This was a time before the internet, before immediate international news media, instant social media reaction and commentary. However, the press release managed to funnel through to national news outlets and gained the story some unwanted traction and attention. It didn't last too long, as the following day, Brigadier General Roger Ramey of the Eighth Air Force in Fort Worth, Texas, in a hastily arranged press conference explained that the material recovered was simply from a weather balloon that had broken up over the ranch. This seemed enough to appease the press and public, and the story disappeared as quickly as it arrived.

In fairness, at a time when the public and press didn't have social media on which to read an immediate opinion, the weather balloon explanation was reasonable. It could also be argued that people nowadays are more aware of technology, the likelihood of the cover story being true, and there is a more-developed distrust of government. While balloons were used for weather and atmospheric research, one could fairly assume that experienced military personnel and even a rancher would be able to distinguish basic materials from the incredible properties being described. It would later come out in various reports that a secret project at the time, Project Mogul, was the explanation for the retrieved material. The new, official explanation over forty years after the event was that Project Mogul involved high-altitude balloons, which were carrying equipment for long-distance eavesdropping to detect, among other things, Soviet nuclear tests. It could be argued that the secrecy behind this is logical and it would mean some material would look strange to be associated with the then weather balloon conclusion. However, at no point since has the technology developed for a sheet metal, light as air with a glowing aura about it, that can be contorted and crumpled, and then straightened back out to its original shape. Even if it now existed, it certainly did not in the late 1940s.

Other notable witnesses to the event include Roswell mortician Glenn Dennis, who claims that the day after the crash happened, he was contacted by RAAF, about ordering some small 'child-sized caskets', and asked about preserving bodies that had been outside and exposed to the elements for several days. Dennis noted in interviews that he had travelled to the RAAF hospital shortly after the event and that he had seen wreckage he believed not to be of human origin, but was warned against speaking of what he had seen. A nurse he knew allegedly confided in him that she had been involved with the examination of small, alien bodies with large heads, huge black eyes and they had been recovered at the crash site.

The Roswell case was in large part forgotten about until the late 1970s when UFO researchers began to dig into the topic. In 1978, one of the most respected names in UFO lore, researcher Stanton Friedman, interviewed Major Marcel, who had handled the materials at the Brazel property. Major Marcel was steadfast in his opinion that not only was the material he handled at the ranch that day not a weather balloon, as per the official explanation, but that it was material of a crashed extraterrestrial spacecraft. This interview lit a fire under the Roswell case and it rose back to public prominence.

So, what was it that was recovered on that day in Roswell in July 1947? The missteps and back peddling in various explanations by the US Air Force over the decades have certainly done nothing to put out the fires of conspiracy and cover-up. Many witnesses from the days close to the findings on the ranch and afterwards have come forward to state that not only was material recovered, but also bodies of non-human entities – or aliens in everyday language. There are so many differing opinions and theories for what happened at Mac Brazel's ranch: maybe the bodies were of crash test dummies, or even deformed human skeletons suffering from radiation poisoning., For many interested in the UFO topic, one thing is clear: it wasn't a weather balloon.

The legacy of Roswell right now is still an incredibly positive one. For people like me, it helped spark childhood wonder in the UFO topic, watching early movies and TV series dedicated to the topic; taking books out from the local library and reading about the recovered bodies, the rumour, the speculation. This has shaped popular science-fiction culture, bringing on the next group of UFO researchers, writers and influencers.

It may be that the original records no longer exist. Stories of where the bodies and materials were stored after (Wright Patterson Air Force Base) to where they are now is anyone's guess. It's a case that if and when Disclosure happens, we may get the answers to some of what happened back in the wilds of New Mexico all those decades ago.

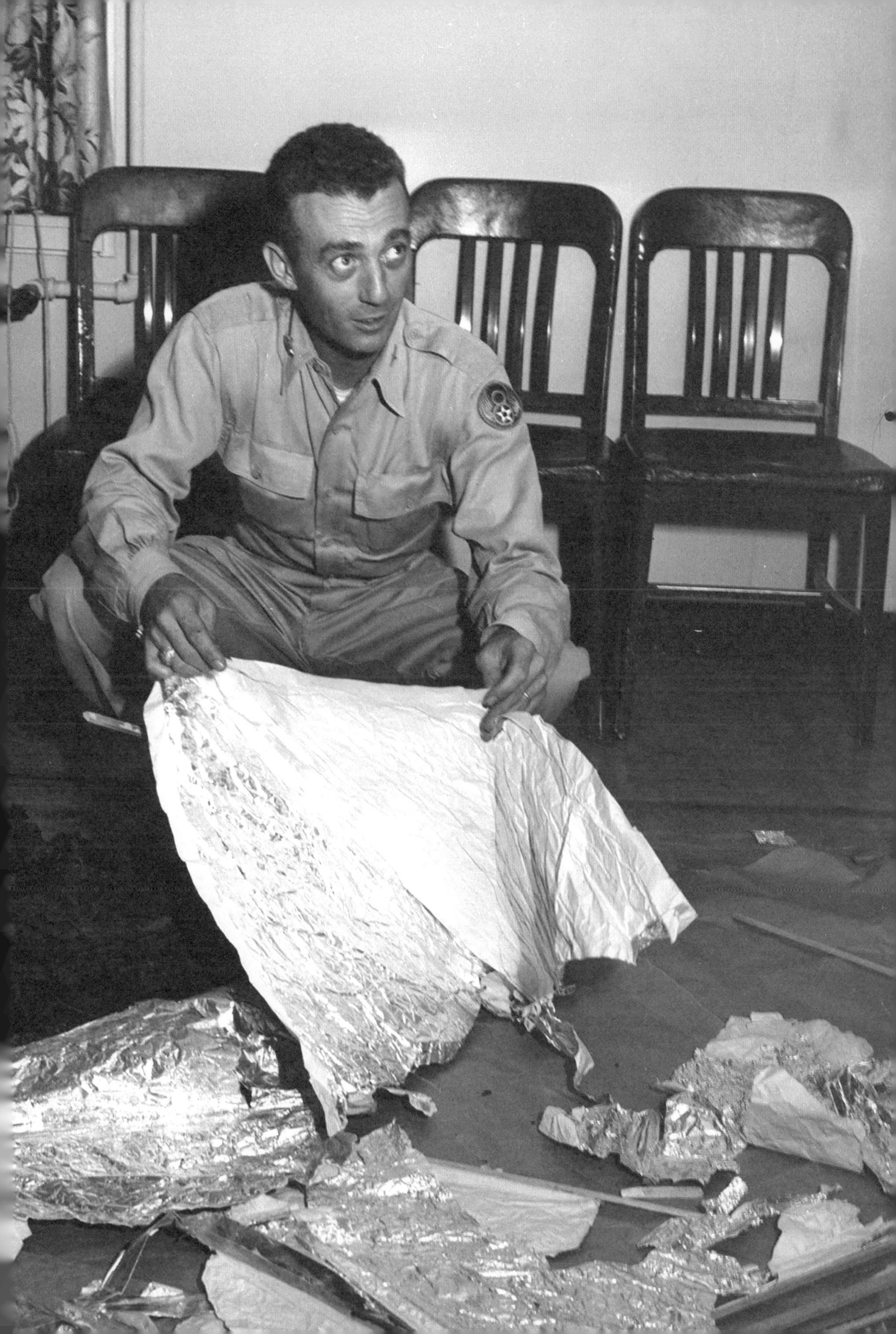

| *Arizona, USA* | 35.1403° N, 113.5625° W |
|---|---|

# KINGMAN

Alleged notable UFO crash retrieval

Kingman, Arizona is a small town situated along the famous Route 66, which makes it a popular stopping point for truckers, travellers and anyone else making the long journey that way across the United States going from California to Chicago, or heading towards Las Vegas, Nevada.

In 1953, it was an even smaller town than it is now, reportedly with a population of little more than two thousand. Unlike today where there are modern facilities and a focus on passing tourism and retail, it was a pretty humble town, with only a few schools, churches and businesses.

The story of what happened in May 1953 didn't come out until many years later, in 1973, when UFO researcher Raymond Fowler, while interviewing a Wright-Paterson Air Force engineer who went by the pseudonym 'Fritz Werner' (later revealed to be one Arthur Stansel Jr) gave Fowler some incredible testimony. Stansel was working on a top-secret project, known as Operation Upshot-Knothole, and his job was to measure blast effects on various types of buildings constructed for nuclear tests. During these tests, eleven nuclear test shots were carried out in the Nevada proving ground, with some of the worst nuclear fallout ever recorded on record. On the evening of 20 May 1953, Stansel received a phone call from Dr Edward Doll to say he would be required on a special job the following day. He was flown to Phoenix, then placed on a bus with blacked-out windows, and during a four-hour journey to a remote area of desert near Kingman, the members of the task force were told that a 'super-secret' air force vehicle had crashed, and their expertise was required.

By the time, they arrived at the crash site, it had been locked down and was swarming with military personnel. Bright spotlights were shining down on something embedded into the desert. There, sticking out of the ground, was an object described by Stansel to Fowler as two saucers, one inverted on top of the other, around 9m (30ft) in diameter. The material appeared to be a dull, silver-like metal, resembling aluminium, and there was a light that appeared to be coming from an open hatch on the craft, though Stansel does say that the light could have come from a source installed by those who had been working on the craft once they found it. His job on site was to determine the angle from which the object had impacted the sand, and some sources say that he was there to determine the vessel's speed

UTAH
NEVADA
St George
Kanab
Groom Lake and Area 51
Kingman
Las Vegas
Boulder City
Grand Canyon
Landing site
Kingman
Bullhead City
Crash site
Flagstaff
R66
Winslow
R66
Needles
Prescott
Lake Havasu City
CALIFORNIA
UNITED STATES OF AMERICA
Phoenix
ARIZONA
Gila Bend
Casa Grande
Yuma
BAJA CALIFORNIA
N
Tucson
50 miles
50 kilometres
SONORA

upon impact, which he worked out had been nearly 2,000km/h (1,200 mph). Amazingly for these velocities, there was no sign of debris, damage or even scratch marks on the object. Impossible, surely? While on site, Stansel also told Fowler that he had noticed a tent with a bright light inside, and lying on a table there appeared to be the body of a being, and not one that he could convince himself was human. The being was described by Stansel as around 1.4m (4ft) tall, wearing a skull cap and silver suit. It had a dark brown complexion and large eyes. Stansel himself never saw inside the craft, but claims he spoke to someone who had been in, who mentioned that inside were two swivelling seats and multiple strange screens and instruments.

Stansel reported that the object was taken to a military installation for further investigation and analysis. He and the rest of the crew had to swear an oath to not discuss any of their work on the site. He didn't, until interviewed years later.

In Raymond Fowler's book, *Casebook of a UFO Investigator*, published decades later, Stansel, under his pseudonym Fritz Werner, gave the following statement:

*I, Fritz Werner, do solemnly swear that during a special assignment with the U.S. Air Force, on May 21, 1953, I assisted in the investigation of a crashed unknown object in the vicinity of Kingman, Arizona. The object was constructed of an unfamiliar metal which resembled brushed aluminum. It had impacted twenty inches [50cm] into the sand without any sign of structural damage. It was oval and about 30 feet [9m] in diameter. An entranceway hatch had been vertically lowered and opened. It was about 3½ feet high and 1½ feet wide [1 x 0.5m]. I was able to talk briefly with someone on the team who did look inside only briefly. He saw two swivel seats, an oval cabin and a lot of instruments and displays.*

*A tent pitched near the object sheltered the dead remains of the only occupant of the craft. It was about 4 feet [1.2m] tall, dark brown complexion and had 2 eyes, 2 nostrils, 2 ears and a small round mouth. It was clothed in a silvery, metallic suit and wore a skull cap of the same type [of] material. It wore no face covering or helmet.*

Let's go back to the forty-eight hours before Stansel was taken to the crash site, which reveal some interesting additions to the story that may support its legitimacy.

On the morning of 21 May, 10 a.m., multiple witnesses, including ordinary civilians and law-enforcement and military personnel, reported seeing groups of disc-shaped 'craft' hovering in the sky above their town. Some reported that they appeared to be in a formation, with as many as eight disc-shaped objects being mentioned. It's one thing having an event where there is a mass sighting of objects, but it's not often that one of these objects reportedly crashes into the local area. What makes this even more interesting, is that we now know that on that same day there were nuclear blasts happening not that far away from the area. UFOs are commonly reported in and around nuclear test sites, storage facilities and even modern-day nuclear-powered navy fleets. So, were the objects seen hovering above Kingman observing the tests that had been carried out in the Nevada proving grounds from a suitable safe distance? Furthermore, is it possible that one of these highly advanced

RIGHT: The 14 January 1979 edition of the *Arizona Daily Star* alleged that the CIA covered up a multitude of UFO sightings, including the 1953 encounter in Kingman.

OVERLEAF: Kingman is a small town which sits in the centre of Route 66, on the edge of the Mojave Desert.

# 30-year cover-up on UFO findings charged to CIA

© 1979 The New York Times

PHOENIX — Documents obtained in a lawsuit against the CIA show that the agency is secretly involved in the surveillance of unidentified flying objects and has been since 1949, an Arizona-based UFO group said yesterday.

The CIA has repeatedly said that it investigated and closed its books on UFOs during 1952, according to Ground Saucer Watch, a nationwide research organization of about 500 scientists, engineers and others who seek to scientifically prove or disprove the existence of UFOs, but 1,000 pages of documents obtained under a freedom of information suit show "the government has been lying to us all these years," it said.

"After reviewing the documents, Ground Saucer Watch believes that UFOs do exist, they are real, the U.S. government has been totally untruthful and the cover-up is massive," William Spaulding, head of the group, said.

Spaulding, an aerospace engineer with AiResearch, one of the largest producers of specialized aerospace components, said the documents show that U. S. embassies are used to help gather information on UFO sightings and that the information "seems to be directed to the CIA, the White House and the National Security Agency."

A CIA memo of Aug. 1, 1952, recommends continued agency surveillance of "flying saucers," saying, "It is strongly urged, however, that no indication of CIA interest or concern reach the press or public, in view of their probably alarmist tendencies to accept such interest as 'confirmatory' of the soundness of 'unpublished facts' in the hands of the U.S. government," the document said.

Among the documents are several detailed reports of Air Force attempts to either intercept or destroy UFOs.

In a 1976 incident in Iran, one report says, two F-4 Phantom jet fighter-bombers pursued a large UFO, which seemed to send out smaller craft. One of the smaller craft "headed straight toward the F-4 at a very fast rate of speed," the report said. "The pilot attempted to fire an AIM-9 missile at the object but, at that instant, his weapons-control panel went off and he lost all communications." The pilot eluded the craft, then watched as it "returned to the primary object for a perfect rejoin," the report continued.

A major point of concern, a CIA document of Oct. 2, 1952, shows, is that UFO sightings could mask Russian air attacks or "psychological warfare." The report — to the director of central intelligence from the assistant director for the Office of Scientic Intelligence — recommends that the National Security Council be advised of the "implications of the 'flying-saucer' problem," that the matter be discussed with the Psychological Strategy Board and that the CIA help "develop . . . a policy of public information that will minimize concern and possible panic resulting from the numerous sightings of unidentified objects."

A document dated November 1975, directs against acknowledging any pattern in sightings. "Unless there is evidence that links sightings, or unless media queries link sightings, queries can best be handled individually at the source and as questions arise," it said. "Response should be direct, forthright and emphasize that the action taken was in response to an isolated or specific incident."

Spaulding says the documents show that there are links and patterns in the sightings. From that evidence, he says, he believes UFOs are here on surveillance missions.

"We find a concentration of sightings around our military installations, research and development areas," he said. "The UFO phenomenon is following what our own astronauts are doing on other planets — we send a scout ship, we take soil samples and then we land."

Spaulding said he has sworn statements from retired Air Force colonels that at least two UFOs have crash-landed and been recovered by the Air Force.

One crash, he said, was in Mexico in 1948 and the other was near Kingman in 1953. He said the retired officers claimed that they got a glimpse of dead aliens, who were in both cases about 4 feet tall, with silverish complexions and wearing silver outfits that "seemed fused to the body from the heat."

craft had been knocked out of the sky by a blast, or even had its instrumentation or power source fail because of the fallout? These are popular theories for how the object, seemingly technologically infallible, somehow ended up buried in the desert sand.

Some sceptics would argue that much of the information around this event comes from one source, Arthur Stansel Jr, and there is a lack of any other evidence. While his testimony is certainly the main driver of this particular event, some others have added weight to his testimony. Uhouse, a former military engineer, came forward in the mid 1990s and shared the story that he was actually asked to work on a flight simulator a decade after the crash in Kingman, and that it was the Kingman recovered craft that was used as the basis for the simulator. This was not only to replicate the Kingman event, but to help train pilots using other recovered extraterrestrial vehicles in future. Bill Uhouse learned that the recovered craft from 1953 had no seat belts, saying that it created its own gravitational field, so that the pilots operating the craft, regardless of the incredible speeds and manoeuvres, wouldn't feel the extreme movements. He added more detail, going as far as saying that he was aware of four beings being recovered at the site, two of which had died, but two survived and were

taken to a laboratory in Los Alamos, New Mexico for treatment to injuries sustained in the crash (Uhouse claimed he had contact with one of the live ones named J. Rod).

Much more recently, the former Deputy Assistant Secretary of Defence for Intelligence for the Clinton and Bush administrations has been a champion of the UAP subject for many years, adding that he had spoken to senior government officials who had accessed a classified programme that related to the recovery of the craft in Kingman in the 1950s. More senior officials lent their credibility to this story.

It's hard to be sure of what happened in that remote desert outside Kingman, Arizona. Fritz Werner (a.k.a. Arthur Stansel Jr) either fabricated a story that made its way into UFO lore, via the US government, or, he was indeed involved in a rather remarkable event, one of the first reported crash recovery events of the last century. Noted historian Michael Schratt has discussed the crash multiple times, stating: 'The Kingman incident stands out as one of the notable UFO crash retrievals, supported by various testimonies and evidence that point to the plausibility of the event.'

| *Pennsylvania, USA* | 40.1110° N, 79.2746° W |
|---|---|

# KECKSBURG

Giant acorn crashes in Pennsylvania woods

In 1965, the town of Kecksburg, Pennsylvania was a quiet, unremarkable place. It hadn't yet caught up with sweeping industrialization and economic growth taking place across other parts of the United States. Focused mainly on agriculture, it was the sort of close-knit community where everyone knew each other's names. Its scenery was quite breathtaking, with stunning views across rolling hills, farmland and picturesque woodland. If it was then fairly anonymous on the map, that would change on the evening of 9 December 1965.

As the winter night drew in, a spectacular display would be seen across the sky, not only in Kecksburg, but much further afield. Witnesses across six states, including Michigan, Ohio, Indiana, New York, Pennsylvania and even parts of Canada reported that a fireball was streaking across the skies. Those filing reports included pilots, police officers and others. The object, described by many as a 'dazzling orange ball with trailing smoke plume', with reports also of sonic booms, then appeared to crash into a wooded ravine, just off a road in Kecksburg. Within hours of the reported crash, reporters, firefighters and more scrambled to get to the scene. By the time ordinary people reached the site, the military were already on hand, securing the area, setting up perimeter barriers to stop anyone catching a glimpse of what was embedded in the dirt. Well, at least the military *believed* that they had reached the site first.

In fact, one of the first to arrive was eighteen-year-old local volunteer firefighter, James Romansky. He described what he'd seen come down, saying that it appeared to be a large metallic bronze-coloured acorn-shaped object, partly buried into the ground due to the impact. Several witnesses said it was big enough to accommodate an adult human inside at around 3.5m (12ft) high and 7.5m (25ft) in diameter. The outside was said to have been a seamless, metallic material like it had been moulded, with no signs of construction joins or rivets. Interestingly, Romansky believes he could see writing, or symbols, on the object. Research by Stan Gordon, pointed to the closest resemblance being Egyptian hieroglyphics. Randy Overly was another local who saw the craft in detail before it hit the ground, and he described the object as moving slowly overhead, at a speed stable enough to see that it was indeed shaped like an acorn, its colour a sort of golden-brown. His account was very similar to what Romansky had reported.

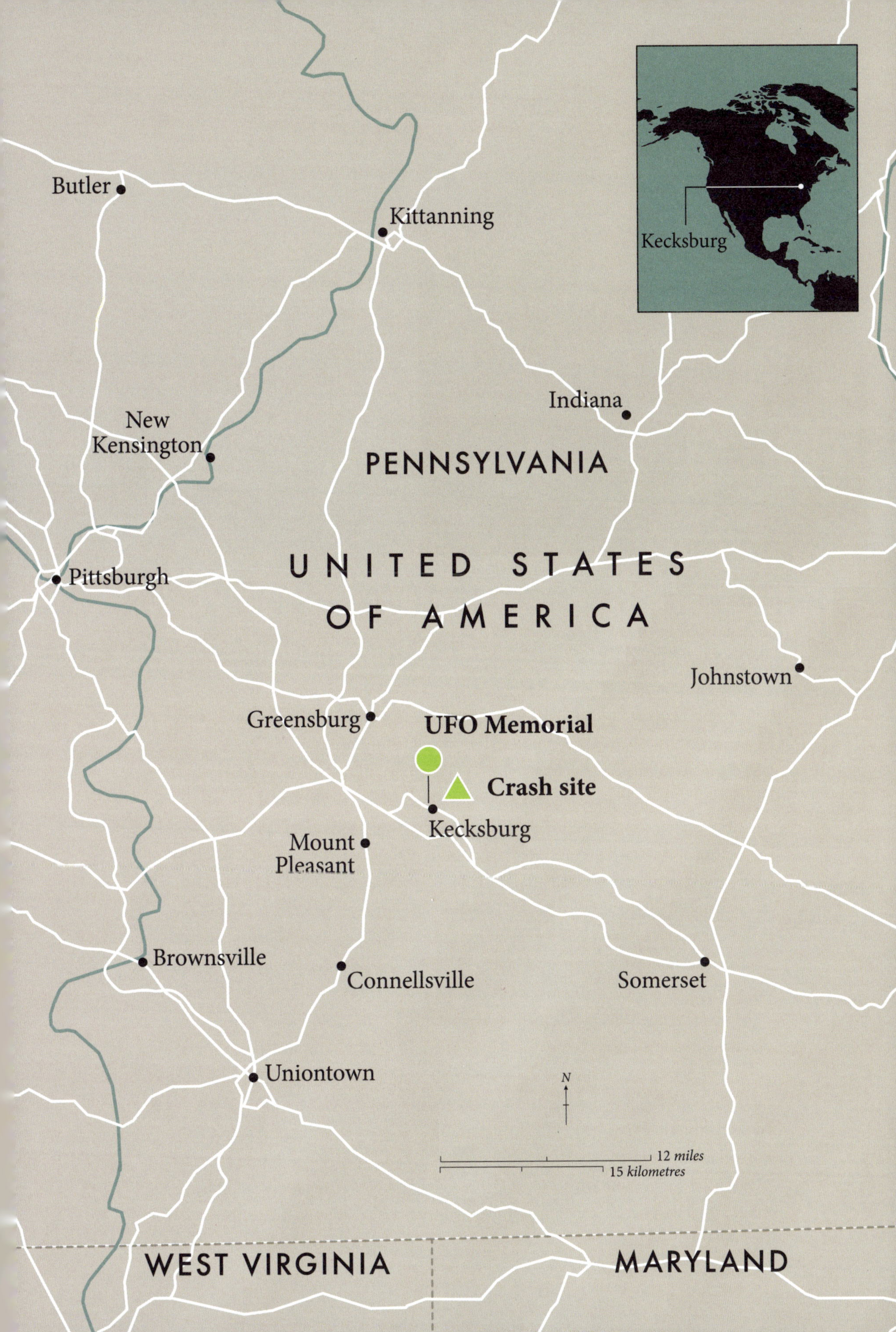
Butler
Kittanning
Kecksburg
Indiana
New Kensington
PENNSYLVANIA
Pittsburgh
UNITED STATES OF AMERICA
Johnstown
Greensburg
UFO Memorial
Crash site
Kecksburg
Mount Pleasant
Brownsville
Connellsville
Somerset
Uniontown
N
12 miles
15 kilometres
WEST VIRGINIA
MARYLAND

LEFT: A replica of the large, metallic acorn-shaped object that crashed into the woods now sits on display in Kecksburg.

RIGHT: Stan Gordon, a local investigator of the Keckshurg incident, points to the location of the sighting.

The first reporter on site was John Murphy from WHJB Radio, a local station in Kecksburg, who not only conducted interviews around the area, but reportedly took photographs of the site. This was confirmed by his widow, who also said these were confiscated before they could be made publicly available. Murphy played a key role in the early reporting of the incident, broadcasting a special news bulletin on the 'object in the woods' on WHJB and following this on later with additional material. After getting nowhere with the men heading the search on the scene, Murphy contacted the State Police HQ at Greensboro and was advised to travel there to find out what was happening. On arrival, he was given the following statement: 'The Pennsylvania State police have made a thorough search of the woods. We are convinced that there is nothing whatsoever in the woods.'

Reporting in general was confusing at the time, as with many UFO events. What was reported initially by newspapers quickly became a different story; one would assume due to the influence of shadowy figures in government or military pressure being applied to control the narrative. One such reporting outlet, the *Greensburg-Tribune Review*, had initially featured witnesses who had seen a fireball, and stated that the object had come down in the woods. The article quoted witnesses who described the acorn-shaped object, made of a strange, seamless metal being stuck in the dirt, and went on to share that the military had arrived, taking over control of the scene. It was only a short time after this that official military reports began to trickle in, downplaying the incident. They concluded that this was a downed aircraft, or some sort of space debris, that the initial sightings had been a simple case of a meteorite catching the attention of locals.

It is usual practice, though, to come in, dismiss any witness accounts, focus on the prosaic, the mundane. Had all those witnesses who describe objects lied? Had they mistaken what they had seen in the woods so badly? After being informed that the officers were about

to head back to the site for a second sweep, Murphy was allowed to participate in another search, but his group was soon prevented from going any further into the woods.

Researcher Stan Gordon is the foremost investigator of the Kecksburg UFO incident, and he has spoken to hundreds of people over the years who witnessed the event. Some reportedly returned to the area while the military cordon was still in place. What they say isn't that the military found nothing, but that the recovered object was placed on the back of a large truck, covered with tarpaulin to conceal the 'craft' and taken to Lockbourne Air Force Base (AFB), near Columbus, Ohio. There, armed guards kept watch, with an alleged shoot-to-kill order for any unwanted trespassers who tried to get near the recovered acorn. It remained there for a short time, before being moved to the famous Wright-Patterson AFB, famed as an apparent storage site for non-human craft, to be examined and studied.

What exactly came down is hard to say. John Murphy's photographs were confiscated, and there is no other known evidence, other than the town statue of the craft. Some folks say that it could have been a fallen satellite or Russian probe; given this was only a few years after the Cuban Missile crisis, the tensions of the Cold War were very much at a high point.

It really is a classic UFO case. On one hand, there are hundreds of witnesses, with diverse backgrounds, professions and disciplines, all describing an incredible event with details of a crashed craft, and multiple testimonies over decades that just won't go away. On the other hand, there is an ongoing military presence for an event where they allege nothing happened and there was nothing to see.

What crashed in Kecksburg in 1965 may forever be a mystery, but what is almost certain is that something was found in those woods, something was recovered by the military, and it wasn't the first, and it won't be the last. If you're travelling nearby, you can now look out for the famous site, which has been re-named 'Meteor Road', in honour of the incident.

| *Minas Gerais, Brazil* | 21.3721° S, 45.1436° W |
|---|---|

# VARGINHA

A UFO crash with fatalities, including one human

The city of Varginha, located in southeast Brazil and with a population of around 130,000 residents, is steeped in rich culture. It is famed for its coffee production, musicians, artists and, like many South American cities, its love of sports. However, the nature of its notoriety changed in 1996 after an incident occurred that has become known as the 'Brazilian Roswell' (see page 14).

On 20 January 1996, three girls aged between fourteen and twenty-two, Liliane Fatima Silva and her sister, Valquiria, along with friend Katia Andrade Xavier, reported coming across a non-human being while making their way home through a local park. This wasn't a late-night encounter in dark fields with obscured vision and a glimpse of something strange. No. This was in the middle of the afternoon, and they came within feet of the creature they described as having a smell of ammonia coming from it. It was cowering, brown-skinned and its skin seemed oily. In follow-up interviews, Valquiria said after making eye contact it seemed fragile, vulnerable, scared, not unlike how they felt in that moment themselves. The girls reported that the creature had telepathically communicated with them, asking for help without making a sound.

Military Police Officer Marco Chereze was on duty at the time, and allegedly apprehended the being and took it into police custody. During his capture of the entity, Chereze was scratched and later became severely ill. As he lay dying, his sister Marta Tavares asked him about his involvement with the case, and she firmly believes he died after contact with a being not of Earth. After his death, the on-call doctor requested that Marco Chereze be buried as quickly as possible due to the presence of toxins in his system. The doctor was clearly scared this was something that could spread to others if the body was left. The cause of death was given as indeterminate, but the doctor who treated him at the time will say that there were extra-terrestrial beings in the city at the time.

The following day, a local farmer reported finding a dead creature on his property, that resembled the one the girls had come across the previous day. The farmer noted that it looked like the devil, with horns on its head, brown oily skin and smelled strongly. Local authorities, including the police and the military, arrived at the scene to take it away.

What followed was an attempted cover-up, but what was, in fact, a full-scale takeover

BARCELONA
BOM PASTOR
Rua Venceslau Braz
Avenida São José
Rua Santa Cruz
Police Station
SANTA MARIA
Rua Delfim Moreira
CENTRO
Rua Presidente Antônio Carlos
Precinct Civilian Police
VILA PINTO
Rua Resende Xavier
VARGINHA
Nave Espacial de Varginha
Avenida Benjamin Constant
Rua Wellington Pereira
VILA FLORESTA
CATANDUVAS
BRAZIL
Al. Otávio Marquês de Paiva
Avenida Francisco Navarra
JARDIM ANDERE
Sighting
CANAÃ
SANTANA
VALE DOS IPÊS
N
Varginha
500 yards
500 meters

of the City of Varginha. Witnesses report to this day that whole streets were closed off and military convoys became a common sight as 'something' was going on. The military and other officials were looking for something, but they wouldn't say what. Within days of the initial reporting, military vehicles were spotted transporting an unknown object through the streets, covered from view.

James Fox, one of the world's pre-eminent researchers and documentary filmmakers, stated at the beginning of his documentary, *Moment of Contact*, that North American Aerospace Defence Command (NORAD) had alerted days earlier that an object had entered the atmosphere around Brazil, lending further credence to the theory that an Unidentified Object had crashed around the City of Varginha at the time. About this event, Fox said, 'How many cases can you think of where you have an alleged UFO crash, the beings survive, they are walking through a town in broad daylight. You get the military who block off large swathes of the town, they threaten the media with jail if they ask more questions. Threaten civilians who are just walking home, this is three o'clock in the afternoon! I've never heard anything like it.'

To this day, rumours are rife that not only was a being found, but it was taken to a local medical facility and studied by Dr Ubirajara Franco Rodrigues, who claims that the being was certainly not of this earth.

Of course, no military cover-up is complete without a poorly orchestrated press conference. And one took place a little over a week after the initial incident on 29 January 1996. The Brazilian army claimed they knew nothing of crashed alien craft or non-human bodies, and that the claims made by those involved were simply misidentifications. The Air Force would also weigh in, admitting that it had recovered an object in Varginha, but it was simply debris from a weather balloon.

When all the evidence is taken into consideration, the crash, recovery of bodies, mysterious illnesses, mass cover-up and ultimately accusations of misidentifications and weather balloons, it's easy to see how this incident has come to be known as 'The Brazilian Roswell'.

RIGHT: The Nave Espacial de Varginha, a water tower in the shape of a UFO sits in the centre of Varginha's central park as a monument to the sighting.

BELOW: James Fox's documentary, Moment of Contact, features firsthand accounts from witnesses and descriptions of the craft.

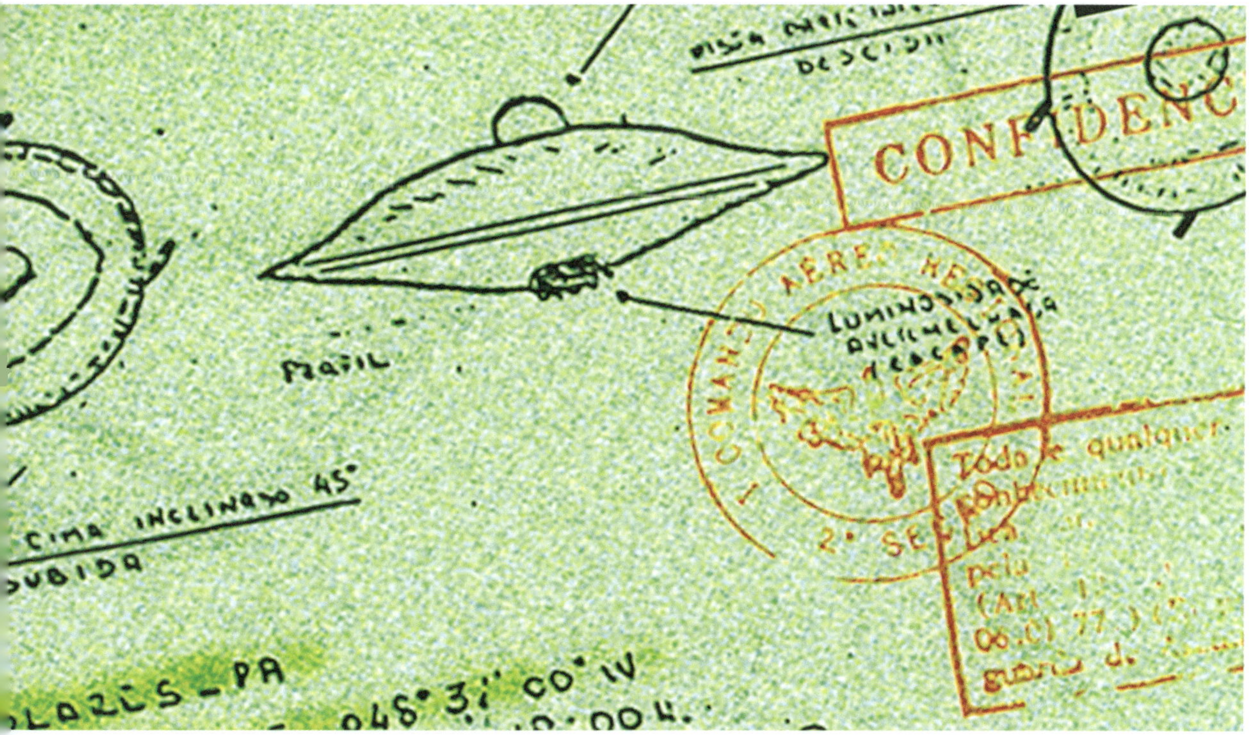

| Chihuahua, Mexico | 29.3031° N, 105.0915° W |
| --- | --- |

# COYAME

A UFO crash with fatalities, including one human

Just over an hour's drive from the US–Mexican border is the small town of Coyame. Hot summers, mild winters and little rainfall are all staples of the climate you could expect to find if you travelled through the area. Like many rural areas everywhere, the local economy relies on a mix of agriculture and livestock farming to bring in the resources to keep its people going. The Coyame area is historically significant, as in pre-Columbian times it was inhabited by indigenous groups, and during the Spanish colonisation it became known as an important strategic location for trade routes. The town boasts a wealth of natural beauty and wonders too, with the Coyame Caves, or *Grutas de Coyame*, a popular tourist attraction that many with an interest in spelunking come from near and far to explore.

Our interest in the town, however, is to do with an event that many would call the 'Mexican Roswell'. It was a quiet summer night on 25 August 1974 when US Air Defence systems picked up an object on radar, entering the Gulf of Mexico and moving at high speed. With a speed of 4,000km/h (2,500mph) at 23,000m (75,000ft), it was first suspected of being a meteor. Initially on a course for Corpus Christi, Texas, it changed direction and headed for Mexican airspace where it descended to nearly 14,000m (45,000ft) and slowed to 3,200km/h (2,000mph). Being a meteor was ruled out, as the object's movement was not that of an arc one would expect with a meteor, and its changes of pace, slowing and speeding up, along with a change of direction indicated something under intelligent control. At the same time, a small aircraft was readying itself for take-off from El Paso airport, bound for Mexico City, where tragically, it would never make its expected landing. The monitored object showed up again around this time, near the US-Mexico border, its nature, origin or intent still unknown, and also now being monitored by Mexican radar. The light aircraft disappeared from radar screens, alarmingly around the same time the UFO dropped off radar. It was at this time that locals report hearing a loud noise like an explosion and also seeing smoke coming from the desert. Had the worst-case scenario really happened? Had the UFO collided with the aircraft, a genuine mid-air collision of a human aircraft and something of unknown origin? The mood changed as those monitoring the situation were pressed into action.

The following morning, the US military keeping tabs on communications between

Caballo Reservoir
WHITE SANDS NM
Alamogordo
Brantley Lake
NEW MEXICO
Las Cruces
UNITED STATES OF AMERICA
Carlsbad
Fort Bliss
El Paso
Ciudad Juárez
TEXAS
CHIHUAHUAN
CHIHUAHUA
Van Horn
Villa Ahumada
MEXICO
UFO flight path
DESERT
Ojinaga
Coyame
Landing site
Coyame Caves
N
30 miles
30 kilometres
Coyame

the Mexican military intercepted a message to say they had located the wreckage and were moving in to recover it. Reports are that the US contacted Mexican officials to ask if they required assistance in any operation, but the Mexicans, not wanting to give much away, denied any knowledge of any unknowns, and said that it was simply the debris of a light aircraft they were going to retrieve. Both sides were aware that the other knew what was going on, but a game of chess was being played, with the US officials readying to go in if needs must. Out in the desert, the Mexican team came across what appeared to be a downed metallic disc, measuring approximately 5m (16ft) wide, around 1.5m (5ft) thick with the appearance of polished steel. No distinguishing marks could be made out; no windows, no exhausts, no bodies present. There were two indentations where it seems the object had sustained some sort of damage, either from the impact of hitting the ground, and/or the collision with the small aircraft. Some accounts suggest there was a tear in the side of the object which exposed its insides to our earthly elements. Mexican officials declared radio silence across all search activities: this was to be done as quietly as possible. The Mexican team began work to recover and move the crashed saucer. Perhaps inexperienced in this sort of work compared to its US counterparts, more tragedy was to unfold. The US team, keeping close watch through various spy capabilities, noticed on the following day, 27 August, that while the Mexican team had moved the object onto the back of a large flatbed truck, the bodies of the team appeared lifeless next to the truck. The US team, consisting of helicopters and other specialised teams move in from Fort Bliss, on the location over the border. The American soldiers were taking no chances and were dressed in bio-hazard suits. They were wary that perhaps exposure to the craft or some sort of substance-leak sustained in the crash had caused the deaths. Given the nature of crash retrievals, hard evidence and

documentation of these events are rare, if not completely non-existent. However, rumours and reports suggest that the US team dealt with the site, the dead bodies and the remaining equipment with explosives, potentially with the help of Mexican officials who understood that this was a mission perhaps beyond their capabilities. Further reports suggest the saucer was taken to either Fort Bliss or Wright-Patterson Air Force Base for study.

A resurgence in UFO reports in the 1990s brought the story from 1974 back to the forefront with a re-ignited public interest. This was after a mass sighting during a solar eclipse. Many cameras, camcorders and pairs of eyes picked up what looked like a certified metallic looking saucer hovering in the sky. Sceptics say it was the planet Venus, shining brightly in the sky. But many UFOlogical researchers and civilian witnesses argue that the sheer volume of reports and sightings negate the likelihood of this being a misidentification. From there, Mexicans began to explore the UFO topic again, with the Coyame incident coming back to prominence. Given the nature of the event, it will likely remain highly classified, with little to go on in terms of public evidence. Information about the impact of the initial two craft colliding, with a loss of a human pilot, then the deaths of the team tasked with recovering the vehicle would worry the general public and could cause panic. This would certainly suit the information gatekeepers wanting to keep this incredible technology to themselves, and away from the hands of hostile nations.

ABOVE: Coyame is a small town that sits close to the US-Mexico border and is known as the 'Mexican Roswell' due to the UFO sightings in 1947.

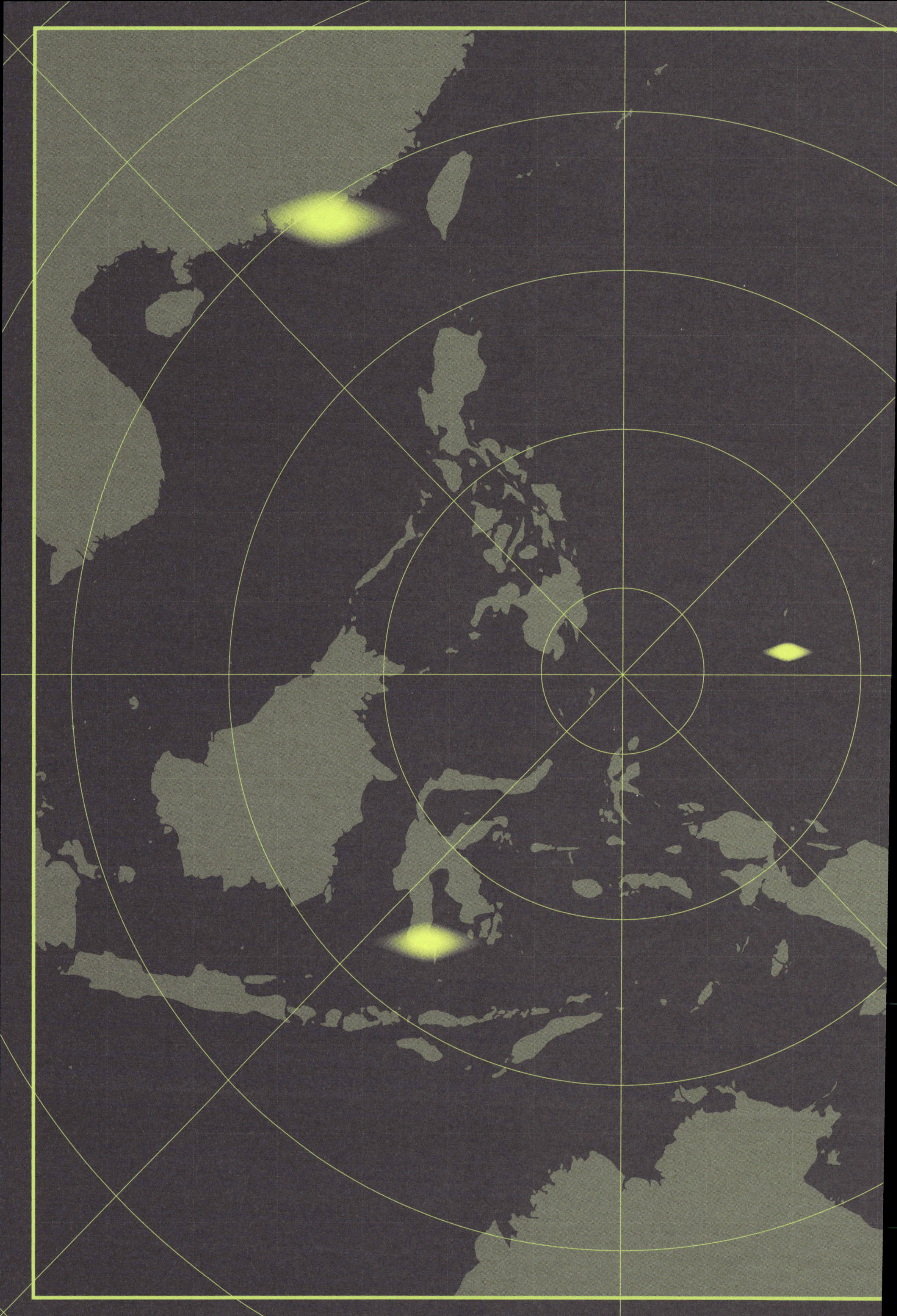

Chapter 2

# ABDUCTION

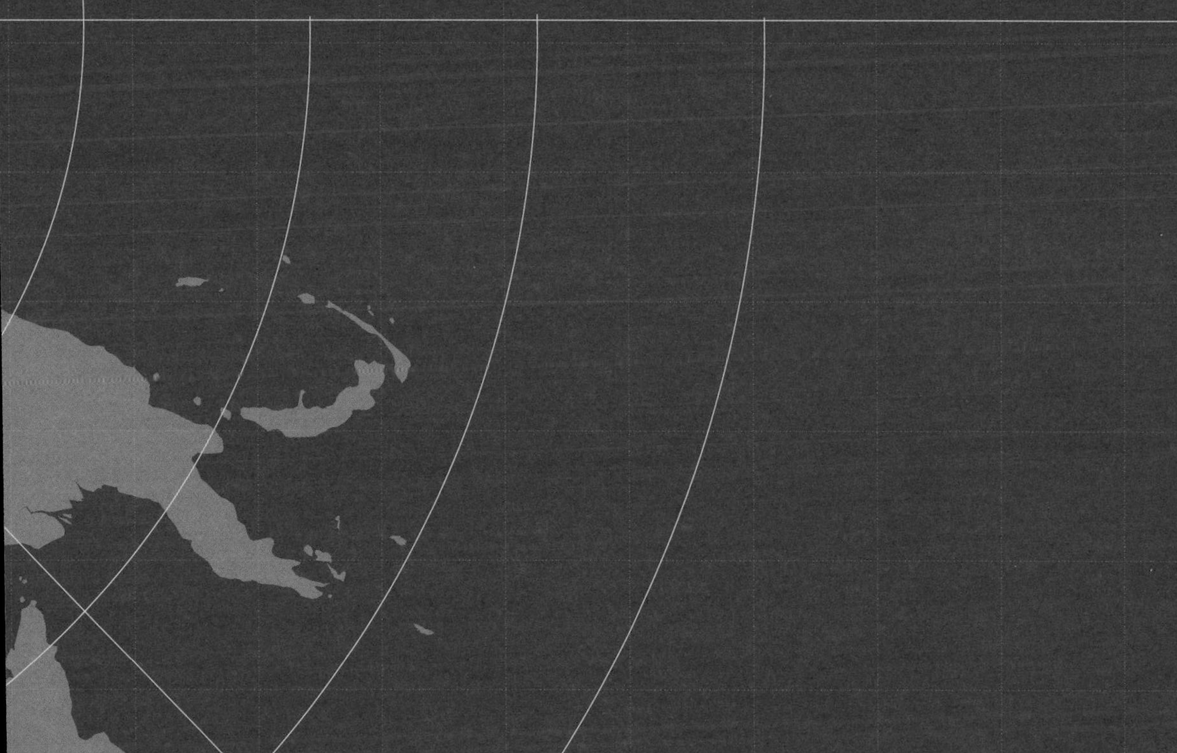

| Victoria, Australia | 39.2400° S, 143.4500° E |
|---|---|

# THE BASS STRAIT

## The disappearance of Frederick Valentich

Between the state of Victoria on the Australian mainland and the island of Tasmania lies the Bass Strait, a 500km (310 mile) stretch of water. It was named after George Bass, a British naval surgeon and explorer who in the eighteenth century mapped the coastline with his colleague Matthew Flinders. It's a major shipping route, one of huge local importance, too, with commercial fishermen catching scallops and rock lobster among many species found in the waters. Alongside the abundance of sea life, is a region found rich in oil, with natural gas deposits being exploited with many offshore drilling platforms and production facilities located in the waters.

In UFOlogy, the strait is famous for a rather tragic event, namely the disappearance of a young pilot on 21 October 1978, Frederick Valentich, at the time only twenty years old. Events began to unfold a little after 7 p.m. on that fateful Saturday as Frederick radioed Melbourne Flight Service with an alarming transmission: he was being followed. An unidentified craft was tailing him.

Earlier that day, Frederick had hired a Cessna 182 VH-DSJ, and after attending a meteorological briefing, he submitted his flight plan for that evening. He would keep below 1,500m (5,000 ft), with the intent to fly to King Island for crayfish. There was another reason given for his flight: he told others he was going to collect some friends. At 7.06 p.m., the doomed pilot radioed in and this is the communication between him and the flight service at Melbourne:

**19:06:14**

Valentich: *Melbourne, this is Delta Sierra Juliet. Is there any known traffic below five thousand feet?*

Melbourne: *No known traffic.*

Valentich: *I am . . . seems to be a large aircraft below five thousand.*

Melbourne: *What type of aircraft is it?*

Valentich: *I cannot affirm. It is four bright . . . it seems to me like landing lights.*

Melbourne: *Delta Sierra Juliet.*

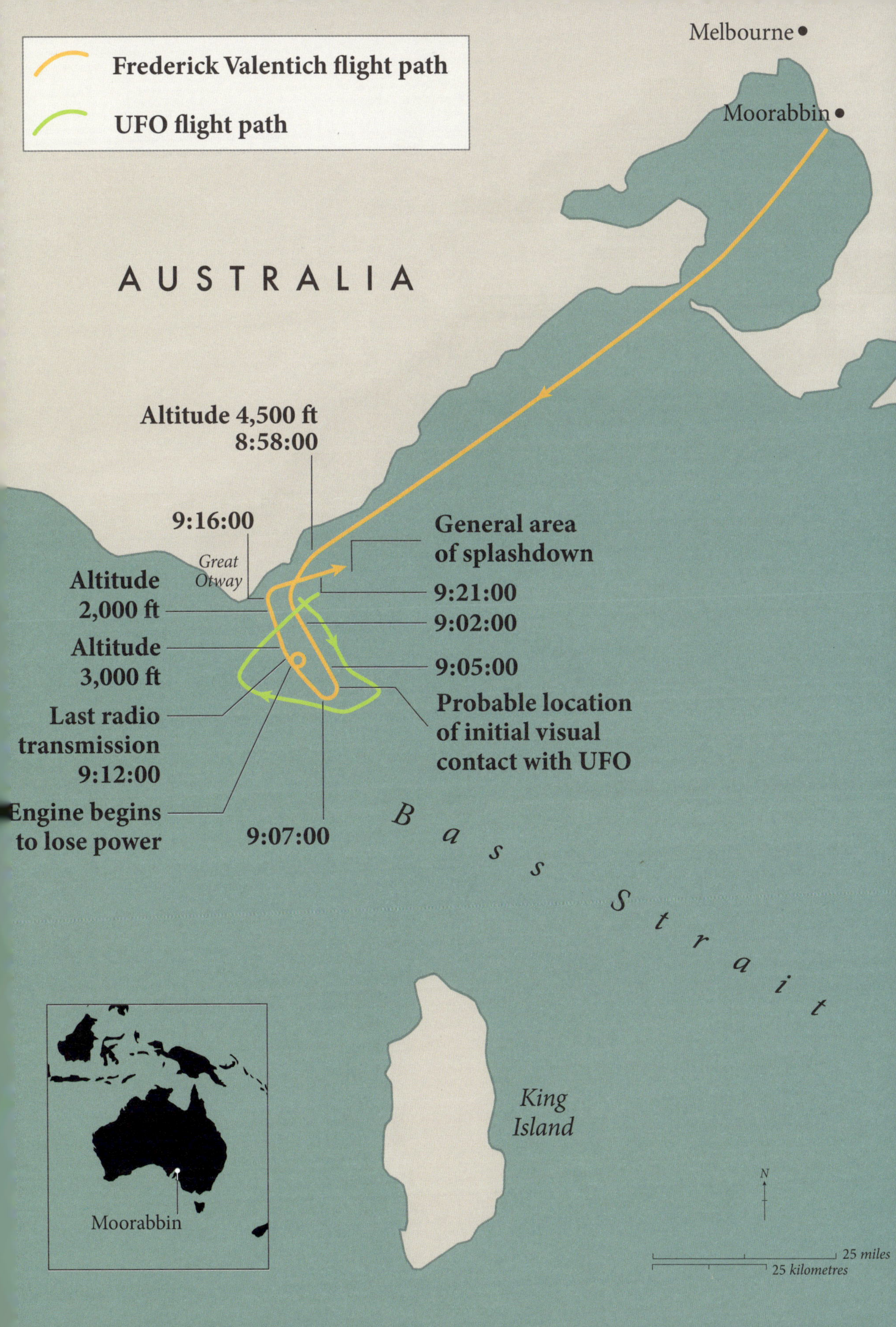

Frederick Valentich flight path
UFO flight path
Melbourne
Moorabbin
AUSTRALIA
Altitude 4,500 ft
8:58:00
9:16:00
Great Otway
General area
of splashdown
Altitude
2,000 ft
9:21:00
9:02:00
Altitude
3,000 ft
9:05:00
Probable location
of initial visual
contact with UFO
Last radio
transmission
9:12:00
Engine begins
to lose power
9:07:00
Bass Strait
King
Island
Moorabbin
N
25 miles
25 kilometres

Valentich: *Melbourne, this is Delta Sierra Juliet. The aircraft has just passed over me at least a thousand feet above.*

Melbourne: *Delta Sierra Juliet, roger, and it is a large aircraft, confirmed?*

Valentich: *Er, unknown, due to the speed it's travelling. Is there any air force aircraft in the vicinity?*

Melbourne: *No known aircraft in the vicinity.*

Valentich: *Melbourne, it's approaching now from due east towards me.*

Melbourne: *Delta Sierra Juliet.*

Valentich: [open microphone for two seconds] *Delta Sierra Juliet, it seems to me that he's playing some sort of game, ah, he's flying over me two, three times at a time at speeds I could not identify.*

Melbourne: *Delta Sierra Juliet, roger. What is your actual level?*

Valentich: *My level is four and a half thousand, four five zero zero.*

Melbourne: *Delta Sierra Juliet, and confirm you cannot identify the aircraft.*

Valentich: *Affirmative.*

Melbourne: *Delta Sierra Juliet, roger, stand by.*

Valentich: *Melbourne, Delta Sierra Juliet, it's not an aircraft, it is . . .* [open microphone for two seconds]

Melbourne: *Delta Sierra Juliet, can you describe the . . . er, aircraft?*

Valentich: *As it's flying past, it's a long shape.* [open microphone for three seconds] *Cannot identify more than that. It has such speed.* [open microphone for three seconds] *Before me right now, Melbourne.*

Melbourne: *Delta Sierra Juliet, roger. And how large would the . . . er, object be?*

Valentich: *Delta Sierra Juliet, Melbourne, it seems like it's stationary. What I'm doing right*

LEFT: Frederick Valentich and his Cessna 182 VH-DSJ disappeared on 21 October 1978.

RIGHT: A UFO was photographed at Crayfish Bay on 21 October 1978, shortly before Frederick went missing.

*now is orbiting, and the thing is just orbiting on top of me also. It's got a green light and sort of metallic-like. It's all shiny on the outside . . . it's just vanished.*

Melbourne: *Delta Sierra Juliet.*

Valentich: *Melbourne, would you know what kind of aircraft I've got? Is it a military aircraft?*

Melbourne: *Delta Sierra Juliet, confirm the . . . er, aircraft just vanished.*

Valentich: *Say again.*

Melbourne: *Delta Sierra Juliet, is the aircraft still with you?*

*Valentich: Delta Sierra Juliet; it's* [open microphone for two seconds] *now approaching from the south-west.*

Melbourne: *Delta Sierra Juliet.*

Valentich: *Delta Sierra Juliet, the engine is rough idling. I've got it set at twenty-three twenty-four, and the thing is coughing.*

Melbourne: *Delta Sierra Juliet, roger. What are your intentions?*

Valentich: *My intentions are to go to King Island. Ah, Melbourne, that strange aircraft is hovering on top of me again.* [two seconds open microphone] *It is hovering, and it's not an aircraft.* [open microphone for seventeen seconds]

The final transmission came six minutes after the first, with some final noises of metallic scraping sounds before the eerie static silence was all that remained on the line.

After he failed to arrive at his destination on King Island in the Bass Strait, halfway between Australia and Tasmania, an extensive search was carried out of the surrounding land and sea. Nothing was ever found.

Do planes go missing? Yes, it can happen. But there are a few outstanding issues here that strongly suggest this is a real mystery. Of course, there is the report of the unknown craft in the chilling final exchanges between Frederick and the flight controllers. And on the night itself, there were ideal flying conditions: it was clear with minimal cloud, ruling out the weather as a likely problem.

Let's look back though at the inconsistencies in the story. There was the pilot's conflicting reasons for flying: he had told friends and family he was flying out there to collect crayfish, yet told the operator and briefing officer where he rented the plane from, he was going to collect friends. The investigation showed that there were no passengers waiting to be collected, and nor had any orders for crayfish been placed on King Island. It seems likely that there was an ulterior motive for the flight, one which we will never find out. And on that evening, there were reports of mysterious lights being seen out in the direction of the Bass Strait by people on the mainland.

Various theories have arisen over the years. Was it the case that a UFO interfered with the plane, potentially causing it to crash or even abducting it and its pilot? Did the pilot go off course and for reasons unknown, crash the craft in a different location, which could explain the lack of any wreckage being recovered? We will probably never know, but the final chilling transmission of young Frederick Valentich will continue to be discussed in the lore of UFOlogy.

LEFT: The Bass Strait is a 500km (310 mile) stretch of water that sits between the mainland of Australia and Tasmania.

| *Arizona, USA* | 34.1808° N, 110.3834° W |
| --- | --- |

# SNOWFLAKE

The story of Travis Walton who was taken into an alien spacecraft for five days

Some stories in UFO lore have such an impact that for decades they stay at the forefront of the topic. One such story is that of Travis Walton, whose incredible abduction on the 5 November 1975 has become the subject of multiple movies and documentaries, and influences many more forms of media whenever the UFO narrative is being discussed.

It was a late afternoon, and Travis, twenty-two years old at the time, was working as a logger as part of a crew out in Snowflake, Arizona.

Snowflake, Arizona is a small, unremarkable town with a population now of around 6,000 people. However, in 1975, there were only a little over 2,000 living in the town. It was formed in 1878 by Mormon pioneers and boasts one of the most stunning Mormon temples outside Salt Lake City, the Snowflake Temple, renowned for its architecture. The surrounding area is a mix of desert, grasslands and natural bush, with the Apache-Sitgreaves National Forest near Heber serving as the site of Travis Walton's abduction.

At the end of a long day logging, Travis and his crew packed up their work equipment and were heading home for the day. While on the road, they noticed in the sky up ahead a light settling into the forest off the dirt road. Curiosity got the better of them, and pulling off of the road, the men went to investigate. Often with any sort of UFO event, witness numbers can be low; sometimes only one person sees anything. Not on this occasion when there were a crew of seven men on the scene of what was about to happen. As well as Travis, the crew was made up of Mike Rogers, the crew foreman, and also a close friend of Travis, and Ken Peterson, John Goulette, Steve Pierce, Allen Dalis and Dwayne Smith.

The trees were still thick in this area (though part of the logging contract, they hadn't reached it yet). A clearing up ahead, however, held an incredible sight; one that was about to change the life of Travis Walton forever. As the men approached the clearing, Travis decided to take a closer look and left the truck; as he moved through the thick trees into a wider space, the clearing was lit up by an unearthly glow, one Travis has said many times that has been difficult for any artist or CGI impression to replicate: a golden colour, with a softness to it that was not so brilliant he couldn't make out the craft. It was the surface of this craft that seemed to be creating the glow. A metallic object, a disc-shaped craft that has become synonymous with UFO sightings, sat there in front of Travis. He was awestruck, as were

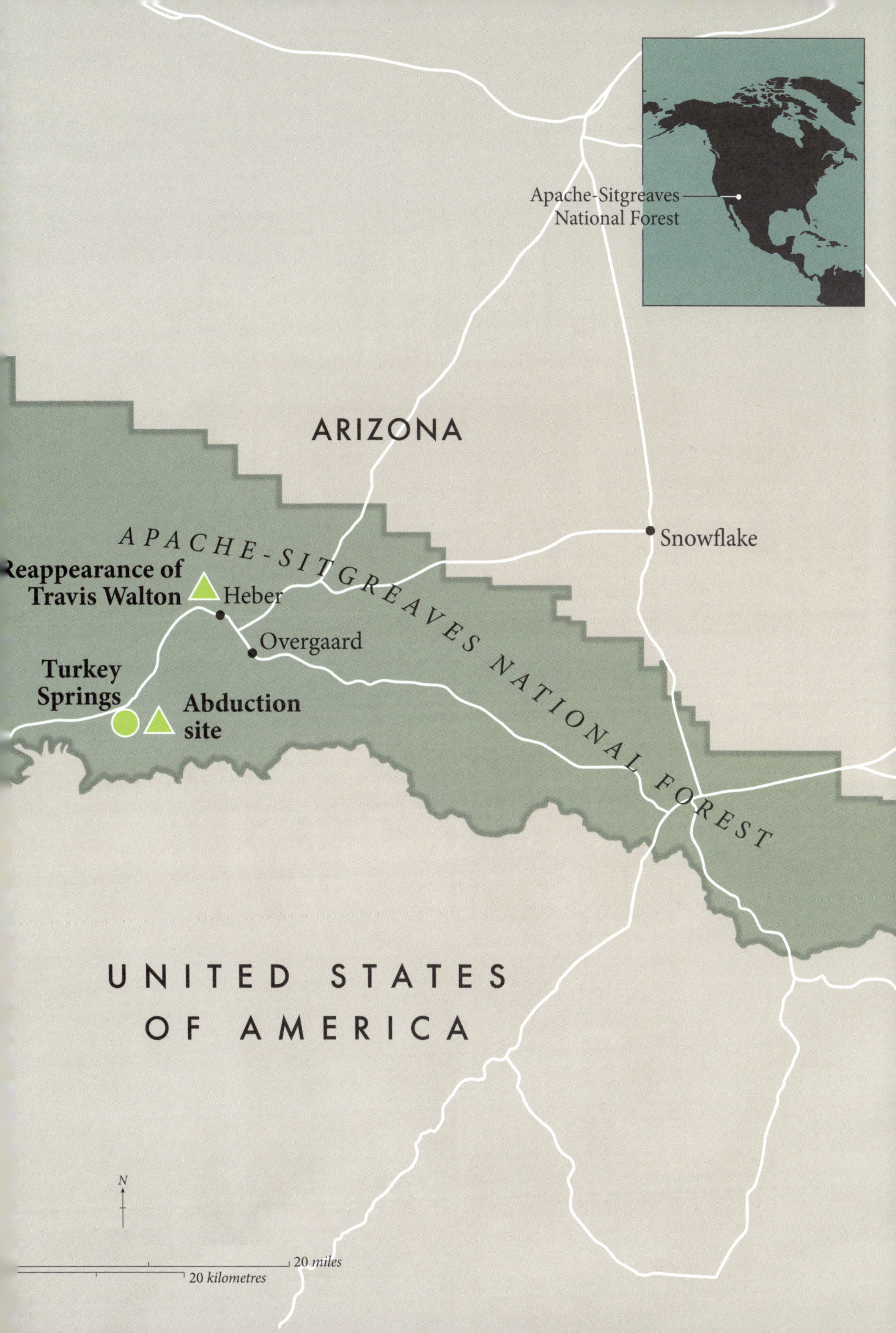
Apache-Sitgreaves
National Forest
ARIZONA
APACHE-SITGREAVES NATIONAL FOREST
Snowflake
Reappearance of
Travis Walton
Heber
Overgaard
Turkey
Springs
Abduction
site
UNITED STATES
OF AMERICA
N
20 miles
20 kilometres

ABOVE: Snowflake, Arizona, was formed in 1878 by Mormon pioneers and is notable for its temple.

RIGHT: Travis Walton's crew all observed the craft in the clearing.

Michael Rogers

Allen Dalis

John Goulette

Kenneth Peterson

Steve Pierce

Dwayne Smith

the other members of the crew who stayed further back, fear freezing them to their seats in the truck. It was then the craft began unexpectedly to move. A low thunderous rumble filled the air, one that could be felt almost more than it could be heard, in the same way that electricity in the air can be sensed. As it moved, this noise got louder.

Travis was startled at the movement, and his concerned crew mates were screaming urgently 'Let's go, let's go!' He didn't think as he jumped for cover behind a log, a move that still left him less than 3m (10ft) away from the craft. Travis speaks of an energy discharge towards him happening at this point: a brilliant blue-green light struck his body and his now confused and terrified colleagues could only watch on in terror, as one of them shouted out in horror 'It got him!' Whatever this energy beam was, it had had an incredible effect on Travis. Was it to stun him, was it a consequence of his proximity to the craft, was it a warning or an accident? To this day, Travis isn't entirely sure.

After seeing Travis being struck, instinct kicked in and the rest of the crew fled the scene. As things calmed a few minutes later, some of the crew declared they had to go back and try to rescue Travis, whether he was alive or otherwise. However, when they returned to the scene, both the craft and Travis were gone.

There are conflicting reports about what happened next. According to the Aerial Phenomena Research Organization (APRO) account of the incident, Rogers drove to Heber, the closest town around 25km (15 miles) from the site and reported it to the sheriff there. Other reports are that from Heber, Rogers called Deputy Sheriff Chuck Ellison, from the Navajo County Sheriff Department, who after listening to this wild story, got in touch with Sherriff Martin Gillespie. From there Gillespie, Ellison and a third officer, Coplan, drove to meet the logging crew.

This kicked off days of searching. With time marching on and no sign of Travis or his body, people started to believe the logging crew had murdered him themselves, perhaps disposing of the body in the thick woods or even in the stacked logs that Mike Rogers and his crew had been working on. Days passed, with no evidence being found to suggest what had happened.

Then, five days after Travis encountered this incredible craft out in the clearing, on 10 November he re-appeared at a gas station near Heber, Arizona. He did not look well, he was dehydrated, disorientated and wearing the same clothes as when he had gone missing. However, he was making the most incredible claim: that he has been on board an alien spacecraft.

After various medical and psychological evaluations, despite the length of time he had been gone and the claims being made, those investigating the events could find no holes in his, or the crew's, story. What he and the others said remains consistent. Polygraph (lie detector) tests were administered not just once, but multiple times, and the seven men were interviewed and asked about what had happened to Travis. Following initial mixed results, all tests showed the men were indeed telling the truth.

This leaves the question, what did Travis Walton experience after that beam of energy hit him in the clearing? It wasn't five days of darkness, it wasn't a bump on the head with no memories. What Travis remembers is incredible.

When he awoke, he was no longer out in that clearing, but indoors. Inside, but inside what? He was aware he was lying on a surface like a bed or a table, with a bright light hanging above his head; the height of the light indicated the ceiling wasn't all that high above his head. He was in intense pain, all over his body; it stopped him being able to move. As he regained consciousness his vision was still blurry, but he could make out three figures leaning over him. At first he thought they may have been human men, but he soon came to realise these were not human. Speaking in an interview immediately after the event in 1975, he said '. . . They aren't really men. They were a lot like men, but they weren't quite human. What they physically looked like, they were, they had kind of underdeveloped features, and no hair, of any kind. They were dressed in kind of brownish orange. . . they were slightly shorter than myself. . . (the clothing) was sort of a loose cover off, I didn't see any buttons or anything like that.' Writing on his website, Travis-Walton.com, he says the following:

*I looked at the vague but reassuring forms of the doctors around me. Abruptly my vision cleared. The sudden horror of what I saw rocked me as I realized I was definitely not in a hospital. I was looking square into the face of a horrible creature . . . with huge, luminous brown eyes the size of quarters! I looked frantically around me. There were three of them! Hysteria overcame me instantly.*

In his book *Fire in the Sky*, Walton writes:

*They stood still, mutely. They were a little under five feet in height. They had a basic humanoid form: two legs, two arms, hands with five digits each, and a head with the normal human arrangement of features. But, beyond the outline, any similarity to humans was terrifyingly absent. Their thin bones were covered with white, marshmallowy-looking flesh. They had on single-piece coverall-type suits made of soft swedelike material, orangeish brown in colour. I could not see any grain in the material, such as cloth has. In fact their clothes did not appear even to have any seams. I saw no buttons, zippers or snaps. They wore no belts. The loose billowy garments were gathered at the wrists and perhaps the ankles. They didn't have any kinds of raised collar at the neck. They wore simple pinkish tan footwear. I could not make out the details of their shoes, but they had very small feet, about a size four by our measure.*

With his pain becoming unbearable, Travis recalls lashing out at the beings, and jumping into the corner of the room he was in. He hit the beings with the back of his arm, noticing they didn't have a lot of weight to them as they fell back easily. Light-headed and still disorientated, Travis struggled to stand properly. Frantically reaching for whatever he could, he grabbed a piece of what he thought was glass and the beings didn't approach, but motioned for him to stop. Travis says the beings then left the room urgently, and he tried to regain his breath for a few minutes, not knowing if or when the beings would return. He moved through the open doorway, into a curving hallway, where he entered another doorless room, some 10–12m (30–40ft) down the narrow corridor.

Remarkably, Travis remembers seeing through the walls to the stars outside; no windows, but a transparency to the stars outside. A man suddenly appeared through the entrance,

NATL. ENQUIRER DEC. 16 '75

**5 Witnesses Pass Lie Test While Claiming . . .**

**Arizona Man Captured by UFO**

**In one of the most baffling cases ever recorded, a young laborer was taken aboard a UFO — in full view of six terrified co-workers — and held for five days.**

The stunned witnesses readily agreed to take lie-detector tests. Five passed, proving they were telling the truth. The sixth was so nervous that the results of his test were inconclusive.

By TONY BRENNA, JOHN M. CATHCART, CHRIS FULLER, PAUL JENKINS, NICK LONGHURST, ROBERT G. SMITH and JEFF WELLS

The abducted man, 22-year-old Travis Walton of Snowflake, Ariz., suddenly disappeared when struck by a dazzling ray from the strange hovering, saucer-shaped object, his fellow workers told police and The ENQUIRER.

In gripping detail, the witnesses described the chilling incident:

Dwayne Smith, 21: "It was a spaceship, there's no doubt of that — and Travis went on it. He got out of our truck, walked toward it — and just vanished!"

Kenneth Peterson, 25: "I saw a bluish light come from the machine and Travis went flying — like he'd touched a hot wire."

Alan Dalis, 21: "It sent out a blue ray, and the last we saw of Travis was his silhouette outlined, arms outstretched. We couldn't believe what was happening — the horror was unreal!"

**SKETCH** of hovering UFO drawn by Mike Rogers and Dwayne Smith.

tree trimmers were heading home at dusk along an isolated mountain road. Crew member Dwayne Smith said they were about 12 miles from Heber when they suddenly spotted the saucer hovering in a clearing beside the road.

"I was numb with disbelief

just vanished! Mike Rogers, who was driving the truck, screamed 'Shut the door!' and gunned past the saucer.

"When we could see the saucer wasn't following us, Mike stopped the truck and we all got out, shouting and screaming at each other with fear in our faces and terror in our hearts. Then we saw a flash in the trees, and figured the saucer was leaving.

"We went back to the spot where the saucer had been . . . but Travis was gone. He went on the spaceship, there's no doubt of that.

"We went and reported what had happened. We didn't expect anyone to believe us, and nobody did — until we took lie detector tests."

Because Walton wasn't able

**EXPERTS QUIZ** abducted man, Travis Walton (center). At left is Dr. Jean Rosenbaum, at right Dr. James Harder.

Dr. Harder that as he approached the craft for a closer look, he was hit by something and suddenly everything went black.

"When I woke up, there was a strong light in my eyes and I had problems focusing. I was panicked because there was a terrible pain in my head and chest," he told Dr. Harder.

"My mind cleared a little and I thought I was in a hospital. I was lying on a table on my back, and these figures were standing over me.

"It was weird. They weren't human — they were creatures.

"They looked like well-developed fetuses to me — they were about 5 feet tall and wore tight-fitting tan-brown robes. Their skin was white like a mushroom and they had no clear features. They made no sounds.

"Their faces had no texture or color, and there was no

**SHERIFF** Marlin Gillespie: "I'm sure they saw UFO."

ing aboard the craft — and his description of the creatures he

LEFT: The 16 December 1975 edition of the *National Enquirer*'s report on the abduction of Travis Walton.

not like the other beings, it was a human-looking man, wearing some sort of helmet. 'He was a man about six feet two inches [nearly 2m] tall. His helmeted head barely cleared the doorway. He was extremely muscular and evenly proportioned. He appeared to weigh about two hundred fifty pounds [113kg] . He wore a tight-fitting bright blue suit of soft material like velour. His feet were covered with black boots, a black band or belt wrapped around his middle. He carried no tools, or weapons on his belt or in his hands; no insignia marked his clothing.'

Travis began to ask questions, babbling and mumbling, but the figure just led him by the arm down the corridor and through another door. It led him to a sort of airlock room, with a ramp leading down and out of the craft, where he noticed a cool wind in his hair. He started to feel better and the burning in his chest had begun to ease. Trying to get any information from the human figure leading him proved useless, the man would only gesture for Travis to keep moving. It seemed he was being moved into a second building or ship, directed down more hallways until he was finally facing three other human-looking figures, similar to the man who had accompanied him from the first ship. These three figures, two males and a female, stayed quiet and two of them led Travis to a table. Travis co-operated, feeling more at ease than he had previously.

They attached some sort of oxygen mask to his face and he lay down facing another light on the ceiling as he felt himself drift off.

That moment was the last he recalls, as when he awoke, he was on the roadway, it was dark and cold and above his head he noticed a light on the bottom of a flying saucer as it ascended off into the night sky.

While he felt weak, dehydrated and confused, the pain felt in the ship when he first came round was gone. Travis believes whatever damage had been done to him from the beam that hit him was undone by the beings, they repaired him on that second ship and returned him home.

RIGHT: The phone box that Travis Walton used to call for help after his abduction has been decorated to commemorate the event.

The theory is that time passes differently on board these ships, that a few days on such ships can be mere minutes on earth. However, it seems that Travis was away for those five days as his facial hair had grown in that time, and his level of dehydration would indicate a lack of water and nutrition in that time too.

While the core story has remained the same over the near fifty years since it first came to prominence, it must be acknowledged that there are some details which have caused a sceptical eyebrow to be raised at times. As mentioned earlier, the polygraph tests initially yielded mixed results. Many observe that polygraph tests aren't entirely reliable as indicators of the truth, so neither result should be used as damning evidence. There are other nuances that have changed, such as Travis thinking as time passed that the beings were actually trying to help him, rather than harm him as he believed early on. This is fair, as with any

self-reflection on a traumatic incident over time, it's perfectly reasonable to think differently about an event, even to start to mis-remember some details. Whether you believe Travis Walton and his crew's version of events or not, undoubtedly this remains one of the most well-known events in the history of the UFO subject, and it is one which has left its mark.

UFO historian Richard Dolan has investigated and researched this case over the years, and he does not doubt its validity. 'The Travis Walton case remains one of the most compelling and well-documented UFO abduction cases to date. Despite ongoing scepticism, the consistency of the witnesses' testimonies and the impact of the incident on their lives lends credibility to the event. Walton's account of being taken aboard a craft, encountering non-human entities, and his subsequent return five days later has withstood numerous investigations and scrutiny over the decades.'

| *Mississippi, USA* | 30.2212° N, 88.3352° W |
|---|---|

# PASCAGOULA

Two men went fishing and got caught themselves

Just along the Gulf Coast of the United States is the small city of Pascagoula, Mississippi. It experienced considerable growth due to its contributions to the Second World War, most noteworthy its shipbuilding, which will play its part in our story here. One of the largest employers in the area is Ingalls Shipbuilding Corporation. Established in the 1930s, it is still building US Navy ships such as amphibious assault vehicles and destroyers. A Chevron oil and gas refinery is another source of income for the people of Pascagoula. Aside from that, the prime coastal location is home to many fishermen, seafood processing facilities and other industries taking advantage of the locale. With hot summers and mild winters, it is vulnerable to hurricanes and flooding, and the city sustained considerable damage in 2005 after Hurricane Katrina. In the 1970s where our focus is, the shipbuilding boom was well underway, the oil refinery had boosted the local economy and local food festivals, Mardi Gras and other community events were on the calendars of many locals in the tightknit community.

On 11 October 1973, it was the end of a long day at work for Calvin Parker, who had finished his first day at the shipyard, a job he had got through a friend of his father, Charles (Charlie) Hickson. Charlie asked Calvin if he would enjoy going fishing after work. Calvin, who had no equipment with him, was honoured when Charlie offered his equipment – no small offer for a man in the South to share such prized possessions with anyone. They set off and cut through an abandoned shipyard, secluded and out the way of any potential law enforcement. Calvin noticed 'No Trespassing' signs all around. It took around fifteen minutes to make their way to a quiet spot on the back of the Pascagoula River, and pulling up a log to sit on, they were ready to try and catch some fish. It was dark and quiet and Calvin looked out across the river, noticing a coastguard ship moored on the other side, wondering the sort of random thoughts that come in serenity when sitting with a rod next to peaceful water. However, panic set in when as the pair caught sight of some blue lights reflecting on the water: it was the police, it had to be, and they were trespassing. They thought they could be in trouble here, and they were, but not the kind they were expecting. As they both stood up, expecting to see a sheriff's vehicle behind them or at least making its way toward them, they were bathed in a bright light; it surrounded them.

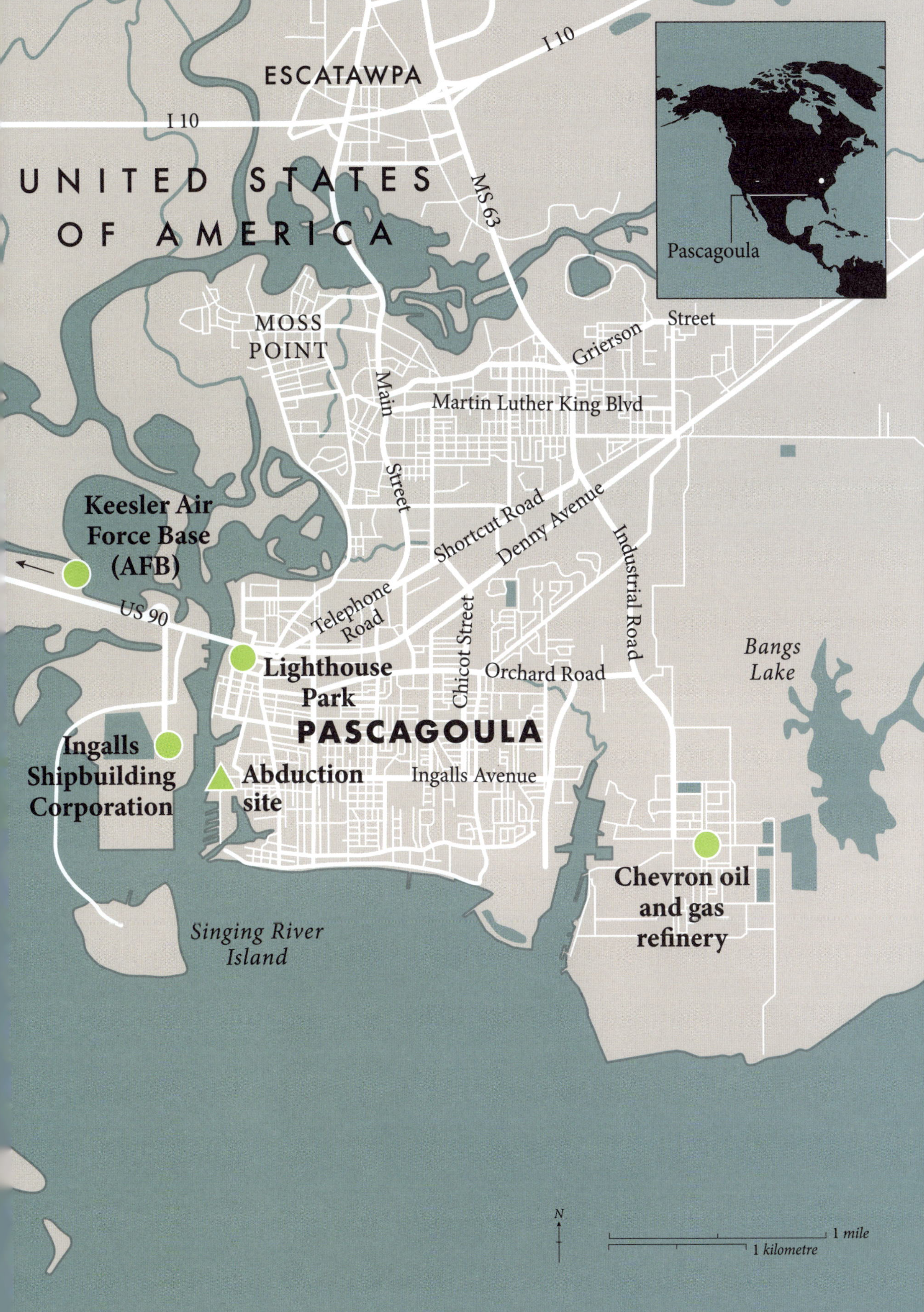
ESCATAWPA
I 10
I 10
UNITED STATES OF AMERICA
MS 63
Pascagoula
MOSS POINT
Grierson Street
Main Street
Martin Luther King Blvd
Keesler Air Force Base (AFB)
Shortcut Road
Denny Avenue
Industrial Road
Telephone Road
US 90
Chicot Street
Lighthouse Park
Orchard Road
Bangs Lake
PASCAGOULA
Ingalls Shipbuilding Corporation
Abduction site
Ingalls Avenue
Chevron oil and gas refinery
Singing River Island
N
1 mile
1 kilometre

ABOVE AND LEFT: The Ingalls Shipbuilding Corporation is one of the largest employers in Pascagoula and is close to where Calvin Parker and Charlie Hickson were abducted.

There was no car, no law enforcement. In the light, they could make out the shape of three bodies coming towards them. These were strange figures, difficult to make out in detail in the dazzle of the lights but enough to see that these did not look like ordinary human beings. Before they could react, the figures were on them; two grabbed Charlie, while the other one grabbed Calvin by the arm. Before he could fight his way out of the grip, he felt a sharp sting, like a needle had punctured the skin on his arm. Then, nothing, he was unable to move, other than slight roll of his head and eyes; he was paralysed, confused, defenceless. Speaking to me when interviewed on *That UFO Podcast*, Calvin Parker said:

*When it got me, I wanted to run away, we were surrounded by water. When it grabbed me by the arm, I felt this injection . . . I didn't care if I got away or not. I could only move my head a little bit or roll my eyes.*

He could tell he was being moved closer to the light, the source of which was unclear, but as he approached a doorway he managed to glance at the light and noticed that it wasn't coming from a bulb or spotlight of any kind, but the material of the object itself. Calvin was carried inside the object, aware he was being taken down a long hallway, turning left, then right again, which gave him a sense this was a sizable structure. He was taken into a room that he described as being an examination room and laid on a glass table, on his back, facing the ceiling. Still unable to move much at all, he could see the entity that had carried him into the room moving off into the corner of the room and appearing to 'power down'. This made Calvin think that perhaps it wasn't a living being at all, but some sort of robot. He couldn't make out many features, but in many he interviews refers to it as 'the big ugly one'. A small object on the ceiling above him then got his attention, as it began to move. Speaking to me in our interview, he recalls:

*I could see something on the ceiling about the size of a deck of cards, kinda blueish on the bottom. It came down about a foot and a half [0.5m] from my head and started clicking. Click. Moved to the side. Click. Moved behind me. Click. Then it shot back up into the ceiling.*

It had scanned him, for what reason he was unsure, but it had done its job and moved back to the ceiling. His senses were still a bit confused, but he got a sense that something or someone else had entered the room. It wasn't Charlie – he hadn't seen or heard Charlie since they had been grabbed. Rolling his head to the side, still on the table, he could make out a female-looking creature, almost as he describes it 'a little redneck girl', that could have come from his own town; however, some features appeared off or skewed and her middle fingers were elongated. Perhaps these beings were trying to mimic a human to make him feel more at ease , but they failed to achieve perfection. This hadn't calmed Calvin, though. She raised a hand to his cheek, gently feeling his skin, then pushed his chin down and stuck her fingers into his mouth, curving them up into his nasal passage. This was incredibly uncomfortable for Calvin, but he couldn't defend himself. He recalls that at this point the being stopped and tried to communicate telepathically with him, a message 'We are not trying to hurt you', although the pain in his throat, the scratching from the fingers that had violated his airways, made this hard to believe.

The female entity then made a noise, one similar to that of an alligator's communication, sounding like a vibrating or deep bellow. With this sound, the robotic entity in the corner sprung to life, and made its way back over towards the stricken Calvin Parker. He felt another sharp sting in his arm, another injection, but then a wave of calm; he assumed some sort of sedative had been administered. He was then picked up by the large robot, taken back outside the craft and placed on the same spot he had been taken from only minutes earlier. As his senses started to come round, he could hear a familiar voice, a friendly one, saying: 'Calvin, are you ok?' It was Charlie, he was there beside him. Of course he wasn't ok, how could you be, how could either of them be? They turned back to the light, to see the craft lift up and off the ground and shoot off at speed into the dark night sky. It was over.

Charlie motioned to Calvin to sit, telling him they should talk about what had just happened, that they should let someone know they had just been abducted. Calvin didn't want to and didn't like the idea of sharing this story with anyone else at all. He wanted to go home, go to bed, get up and go to work, forget this had ever happened. After a few minutes they got themselves together and got up, making their way wearily back to the car. As they got to the vehicle, they noticed it seemed to be magnetised: their keys stuck to the metal outside and a glass window shattered and fell out of place when they opened the door. They didn't care, they just wanted to get away. A little way along the road, they pulled over into a convenience store. Charlie wanted to make a phone call – this was a time before cell phones, social media or internet. What had just happened could have easily remained a secret between those two men forever, but Charles Hickson had other ideas. Calvin hadn't asked who he was calling but heard him on the phone to the local Keesler Air Force Base (AFB), in Biloxi, Mississippi, not far from where they were. Calvin would be told afterwards that the AFB was not interested in, nor were they investigating UFOs. They recommended that the men call the local sheriff's department in Jackson County, so Charles dug a few more coins out and made the call. Concerned for the state of the men and the claims being made by Mr Hickson, the officer who took the call told them to stay where they were and they would send someone along. Calvin was annoyed that Charlie had decided to alert people to this, even though he had been adamant they should keep it private. The officers came and asked Calvin, not Charlie, to complete a sobriety test, checking his driver's licence and for signs of intoxication. There were none. Satisfied that Calvin was fit to drive, they asked the two men to follow them along to the sheriff's office for further comment. When they arrived at the station, they asked the two men to sit in two separate rooms for interrogation about what had happened to them. They were also put into a room together with, unknown to them, a secret tape recorder which picked them up talking about the incident. This at least gave Sheriff Fred Diamond enough of an indication that something had happened to them. He asked them both to return home and come back in the morning.

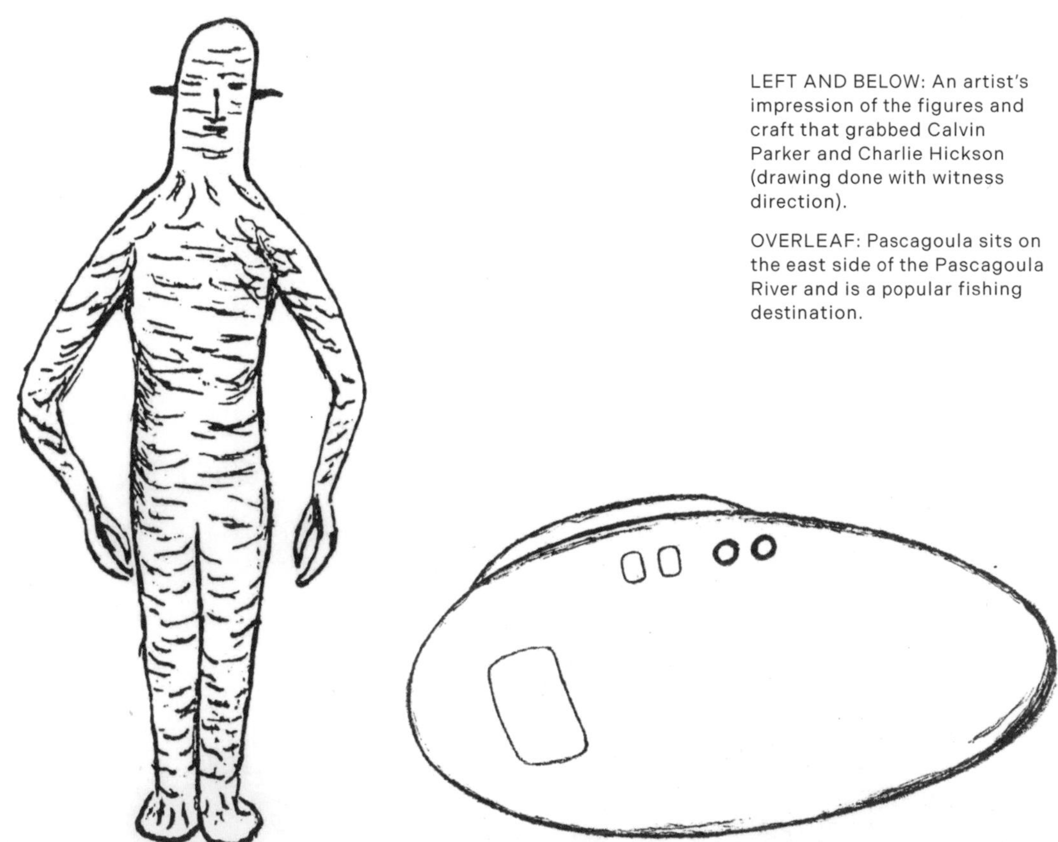

LEFT AND BELOW: An artist's impression of the figures and craft that grabbed Calvin Parker and Charlie Hickson (drawing done with witness direction).

OVERLEAF: Pascagoula sits on the east side of the Pascagoula River and is a popular fishing destination.

The following morning, they both went to work, having had little sleep after the frightening experience. They weren't in the building long when over the intercom their names were called to head to the main office. There, they were informed that the media had picked up the story and that they were to put together a statement to put a stop to the situation. Amid concerns about them being contaminated or that they should be in some kind of quarantine like the Apollo astronauts, the pair were taken to see a physician, Dr Bosquez. He examined them and, while both men appeared emotionally distressed, they showed no signs of physical harm, but he did confirm that Calvin had been injected with something. They were then informed they had to travel 50km (30 miles) to Keesler AFB to be checked there. Military Police met them there, and after being checked over for radiation levels by men in hazmat suits, they were escorted down a long hallway. Calvin felt uneasy, unsure as to what they wanted, who was going to be there and what they were going to be asked. He wanted the whole ordeal to be over with, to go home, get on with living as boring a life as possible after this. In the conference room they were taken to, Calvin Parker says there were officials from the US Navy, the air force, three local mayors and three local police chiefs, all expecting to be told exactly what had happened to them on the night of 11 October. Charlie did the talking, telling them the version of events personal to him: being examined by a lens-like device rather than something resembling a deck of cards, that two entities had taken him, not one like Calvin.

When they left, the sheriff informed them they had one more stop to make, to see the famed UFO researcher and head of the US Air Force Project Blue Book, Dr J. Allen Hynek. Hynek would find the two gentlemen credible and the case itself a fascinating one.

Calvin later said he stayed in touch with Dr Hynek up until he passed away.

Afterwards, Calvin Parker returned home, and never spoke to his family about it after a few appearances on a limited number of media outlets, deciding it best it wasn't discussed. Charles Hickson released a book about the encounter the following year in 1974, and was much happier to discuss the event until his own passing in September 2011. Calvin tried to distance himself as much as he could from the story until, more than four decades had passed and at the funeral of a neighbour, he signed the book of condolence and some attendees, curious to know if it was the same Calvin Parker, approached him to ask about the event. Afterwards he and his wife finally spoke about the event, and she convinced him that maybe it was time to tell his version of events, time to open up and let people know what had happened. Researcher and publicist Philip Mantle worked to bring Calvin's story to life in print. When asked about the event for this book, Mr Mantle said:

*When it comes to the 1973 Pascagoula alien abduction case it is almost the perfect case. It has more than one percipient, both of those involved (Calvin Parker and Charles Hickson) were interviewed in person by the local sheriff within hours of the encounter. The next day they were at the hospital and then Keesler AFB. They were then interviewed in-person by Dr James Harder and Dr J. Allen Hynek. Added to this there are countless independent first-hand eyewitnesses to*

*UFO sightings that night in and around the location. Last but not least, there were two others on the opposite side of the Pascagoula River that night who saw what was happening to Parker and Hickson and who had their own encounter as well. I could go on but just compare this case to that of Betty and Barney Hill and Travis Walton [see pages 70 and 46] and neither of them come close to having this much supporting evidence.*

What did happen on that evening to Charles Hickson and Calvin Parker? Some sceptics argue that there is a complete lack of physical evidence, that likely explanations would be hoaxes to profit from the event or hallucination of some kind. If it was profit, then Calvin certainly waited many, many decades before deciding to cash in, but many who have heard his story believe there is a genuineness to him and what he says. Whatever the case, other witnesses have come forward over the decades to confirm they had seen lights on the night from different vantage points, perhaps of the same craft that took the men away from their planned night's fishing. Neither of the two are still alive, as Calvin Parker passed away after a long illness in 2023. The true events of what happened that night have gone with them, but they left their stories as a legacy, and for many, these are among the very best testimony for proof that we are truly not alone.

| *Arkansas, USA* | 35.3805° N, 94.0340° W |
|---|---|

# DEVIL'S DEN STATE PARK

A camping trip takes on an extraterrestrial dimension

Devil's Den State Park is located in northwest Arkansas and was established in 1933, as part of then President Franklin D. Roosevelt's New Deal Program, which was a set of economic and social reforms as a response to the Great Depression. The park is well known for stunning scenery and it attracts a diverse range of people wanting to take part in many recreational activities in the surroundings, such as hiking, camping, rock-climbing and many more. Lee Creek is a substantial waterway running through the park, popular for fishing, and along its way there are many small caves and other natural rock shelters to hide from the elements when required. The park hosts many events throughout the year, attracting people from not only the US but much further afield. It's not far from Fayetteville, Arkansas, from where day trips to the park are possible. But it was the allure of a night's camping under the stunning night sky of the park that would bring this story to being.

Terry Lovelace and his friend Toby were air force medics stationed at Whiteman Air Force Base and had cleared a four-day holiday with their employer. Their plan was to drive for six and half hours south to the Missouri–Arkansas border next to the Ozark National Forest and go camping, but rather than camp in the traditional camp grounds, they were going to try to make it an authentic outdoor camping experience and go off the trail, avoiding the ranger station. They didn't take any notice, or not enough notice, of the warning signs to keep out, and it was only many years later in 2017 that Terry found out they were so off-road that they were technically no longer in Devil's Den State Park, but on land owned by the Bureau of Land Management. It's an odd piece of land, which to this day has nothing growing on it (the US government pays for someone to keep the small piece of land clear). The entire surrounding area for miles is covered in trees. In 1977, the scenic views were fantastic, and the beautiful landscape seemed ideal for camping. Terry and Toby built a bonfire, got their food out for the night and inflated their air mattresses to go inside their $10 tent. The conversation was good, the weather was pleasant, it was a nice warm June day. What more could the inexperienced but enthusiastic campers ask for?

At around 9 p.m., Terry noticed something peculiar: the ambient sound of the forest – birds, coyotes, foxes and the like – had gone. It was like someone had turned the sound off, there was now an eerie stillness; even the breeze had gone. This unnerved Terry, and he

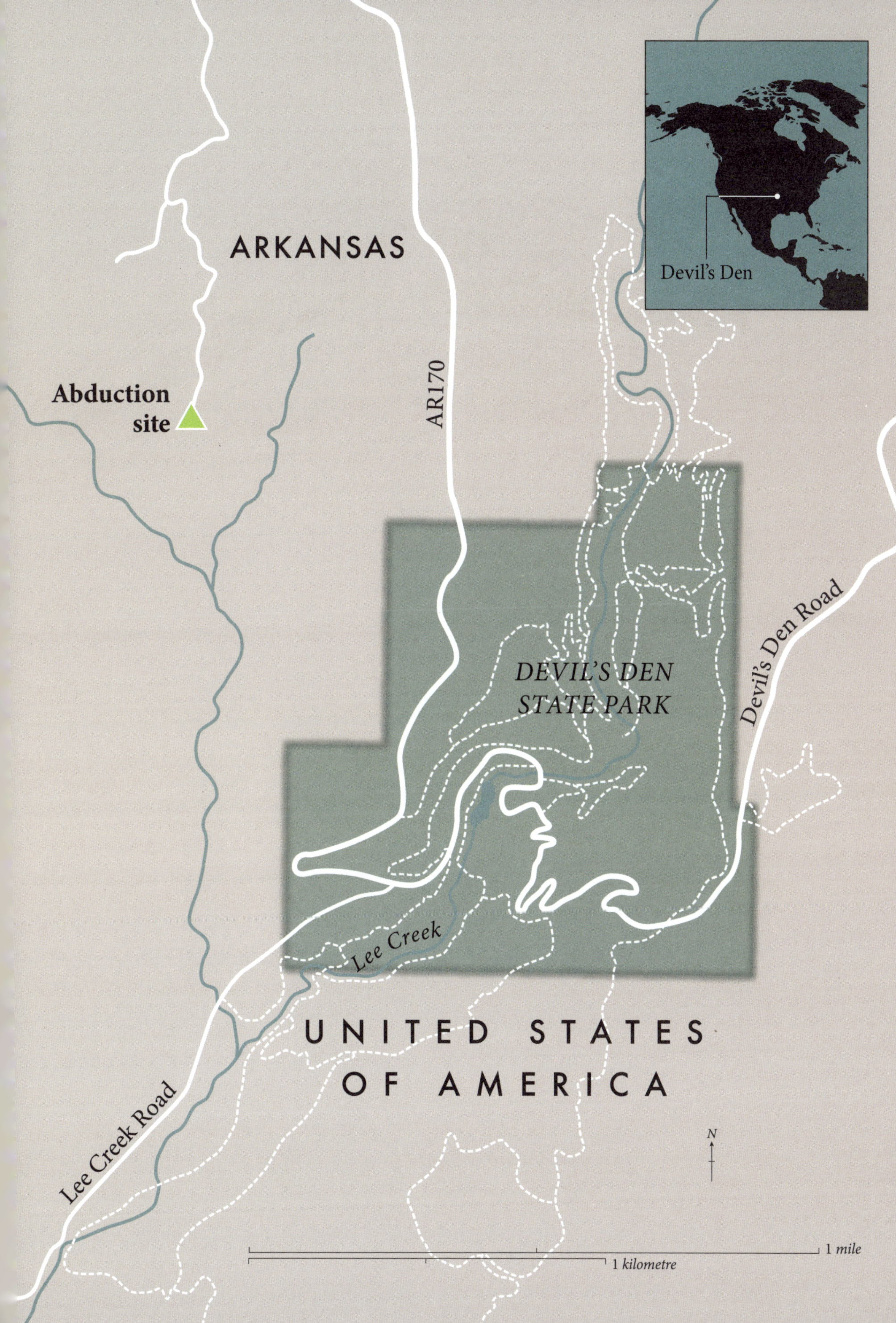

ARKANSAS
Abduction site
AR170
Devil's Den
DEVIL'S DEN STATE PARK
Devil's Den Road
Lee Creek
UNITED STATES OF AMERICA
Lee Creek Road
N
1 mile
1 kilometre

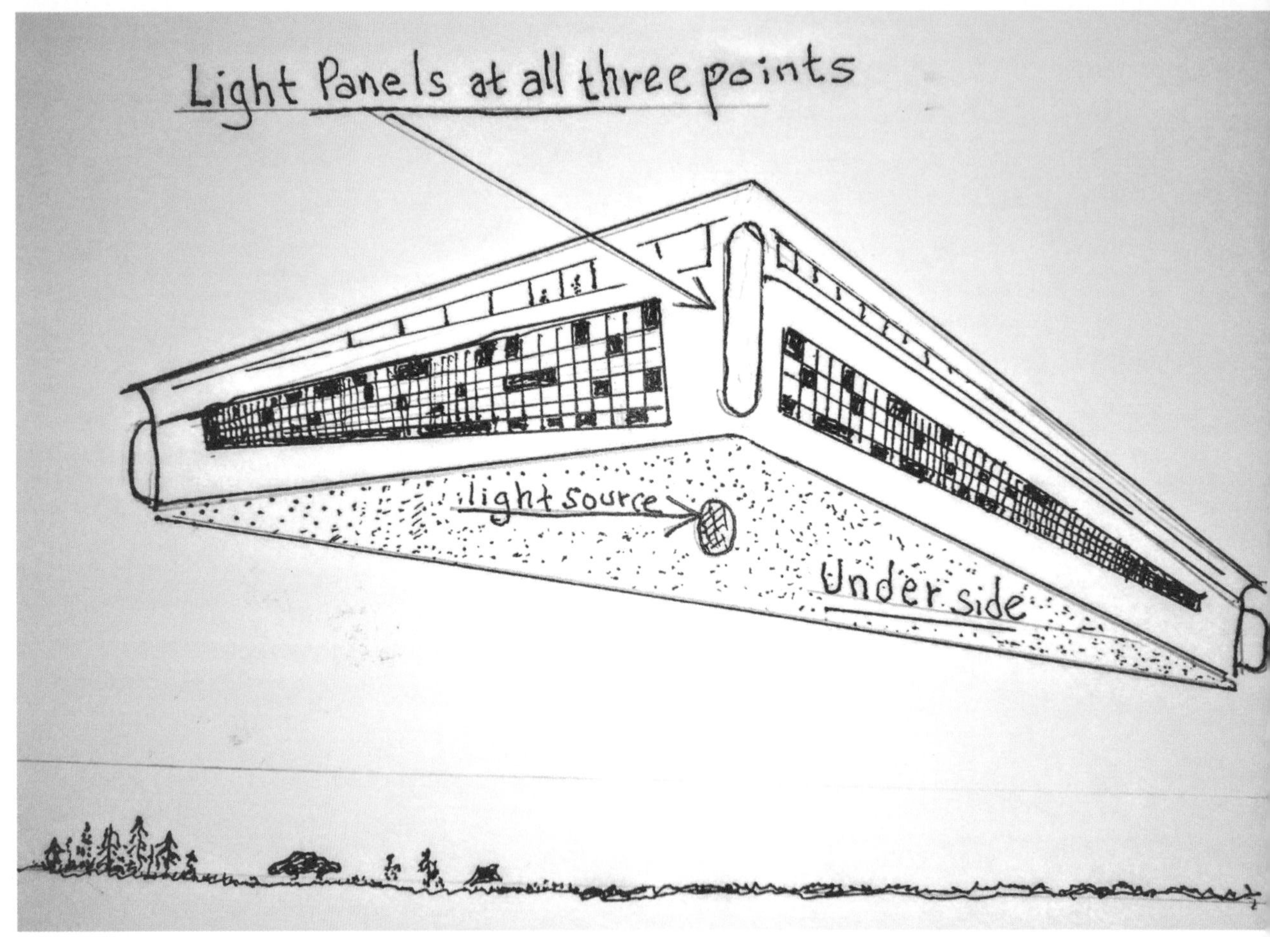


turned to Toby to ask if he noticed the quietness. He hadn't but did notice something else in the distance to the west and asked: 'Terry, were those lights there before?'

There, above the western horizon, were three equally bright, equally sized stars, in a triangular formation. They hadn't noticed them before; they really stood out. As the two campers observed the triangle, it rotated. These weren't stars! All they could do was watch, in the moment, unable to speak even to each other. As they saw the triangle rotate and now point upwards it moved off higher into the sky. Terry explained to me when speaking on *That UFO Podcast*;

*As soon as that happened, I felt a wave of calm wash over me, almost like sedation. All that feeling of nervousness, anxiety that I had experienced earlier was gone. It was an odd experience. It was a sensation that I was more of an observer . . . that I wasn't a participant . . . I had no control over anything . . . that I was just along for the ride.*

The two stunned observers watched the 'three stars' climb into the sky against the black of the night. It then stopped moving, again rotating with the head of the triangle now appearing to point towards them. This new angle showed an object that was now aimed at

ABOVE: Terry Lovelace's drawing of the enormous craft seen in Devil's Den State Park.

RIGHT: A diagram of the interior of the large craft.

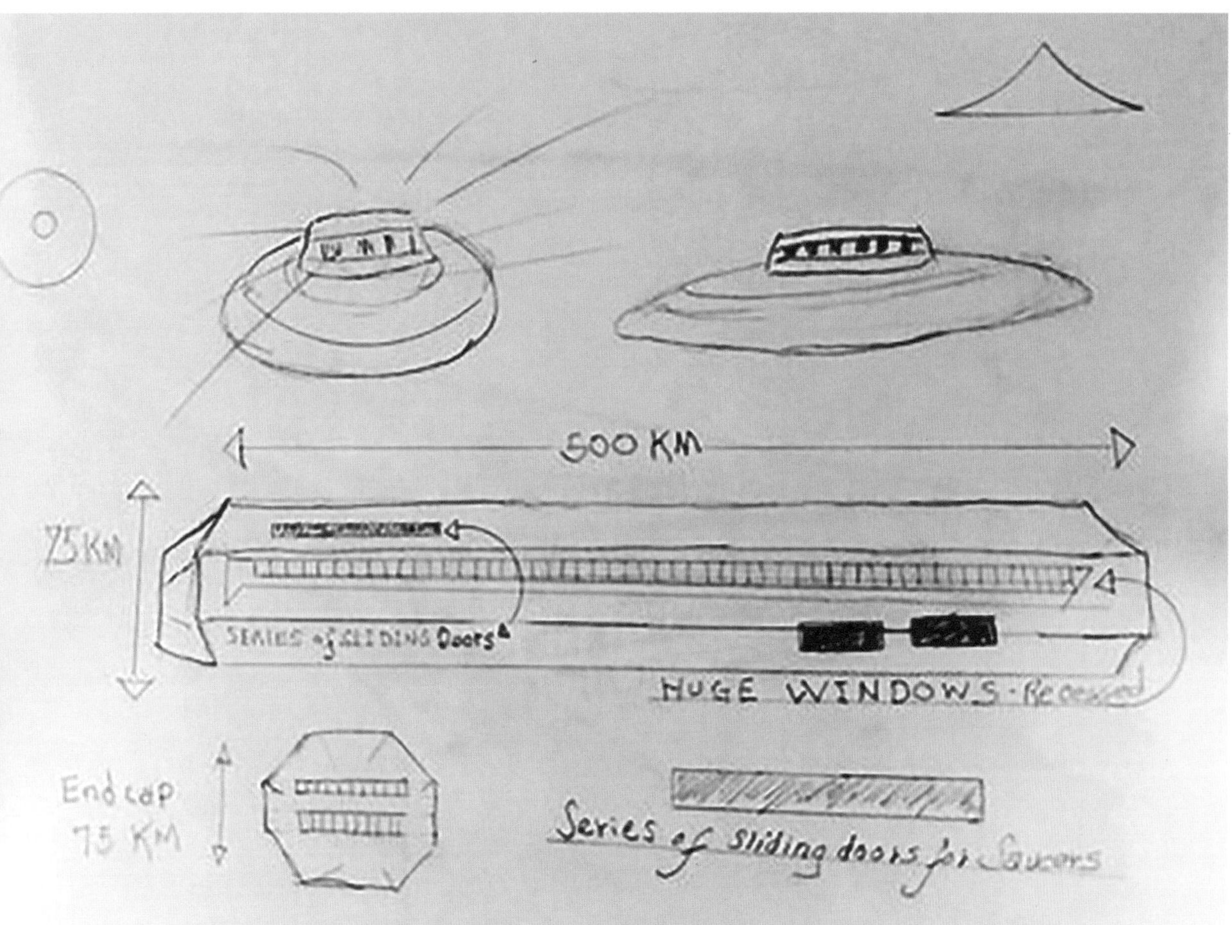


them and gliding, slowly descending towards them, taking several minutes to get closer to them. Terry recalled the object appearing to perform several flips or tumbles, which he feels was to indicate the object was there for their benefit, it was under control. It came to a stop over their campsite; Terry and Toby were off to the side of the campsite. They could now see an enormous craft, they likened it to size of a large shopping mall: it had height, depth, it was massive. This huge object, however, was silent above them, hovering still. The two were still unable to speak. A white light appeared from the object emanating from the centre of the triangle, around 15cm (6in) in diameter and hitting the centre of their camp fire. The light then shut off and was replaced by a laser beam, much slimmer than the light, and described by Terry as reddish-purple in colour, seeming to scan objects on the campsite for a split second, then moving to 'scan' something else, including Toby, then Terry himself in the chest. He said he felt nothing when this happened.

How much time had passed at this point is unclear, but it seemed only a minute or two at most, and the two haven't managed to speak to each other, only watching. The feeling Terry had had of calmness was now being replaced by drowsiness, and Toby felt the same. At this point, Toby turned to Terry and said, 'Show's over,' and made his way to the tent, lay down and went to sleep. Terry did the same, but remembers thinking to himself as he went to sleep that the ambient noise of the forest still hasn't returned. Was the show over?

An indeterminate amount of time passed, and Terry woke up to yellowish bright lights shining through the fabric of the cheap tent. Confused and disorientated, Terry wondered if one of the local rangers had found them trespassing where they shouldn't and they were about to be evicted. It wasn't a park ranger. Terry noticed that the boots he had on had been unlaced; this wasn't how he remembered them when he went to sleep. He pulled his boots off and noticed his socks were on awkwardly; he fixed these and laced his boots up. Something wasn't right; it was like he had been un-dressed then dressed again. Terry noticed Toby looking out of a small flap in the tent, and asked if there were park rangers out there. Toby had tears running down the side of his face, so Terry knew something wasn't right. He looked out for himself and he saw that the same object that had been roughly 1,000m (3,000ft) overhead when they went to bed, was now merely 10m (30ft) above their heads. It had not gone, it wasn't over. With the lights flashing in his eyes, Terry could make out what he thought were children walking around the area of the campsite, ten to fifteen of them, just wandering around, they appeared to be 1m (3 ft) tall. Toby told Terry that he didn't think they are kids, not even human beings, and urged Terry to take a closer look. Terry was horrified to notice his friend was right, these looked like the typical grey beings made famous over the decades in Hollywood films. The beings didn't seem bothered with the two terrified men in the tent. Just then, another light turned on from the craft, and the small beings made their way to the light and it seemed to 'beam' them up, like we have seen on shows like *Star Trek* over the years. They stood in the light and then 'pixelated out' as Terry describes it. Once all the beings had been collected, the light turned off, the points of the triangle lights now changed in intensity and to a solid bright white. The triangle rose up, slowly, silently into the blackness of the night sky.

But this wasn't the end of the incident . . .

Terry had some memories, difficult to understand, but he knew that they had not simply gone to bed and that was it. Largely with the help of hypnotic regression undertaken many years later, Terry recalled being stuck, paralysed, with only his eyes being able to move left and right, being on board the craft prior to seeing the lights in the tent and the little beings disappearing. The small greys were scuttling around; they seemed like worker bees, they had a purpose and were always on the move. At this point, he knew that Toby was by his side, they had both been stripped and there was a tall being next to him. The being was wearing some sort of plain uniform with no markings or distinguishing features. It didn't seem human but was bald with no ears, two slits for nostrils and its eyes were bigger than those of humans, but smaller than those of the greys. He got the feeling this being was in charge, that he was a figure of authority. In common with other abduction experiences, Terry recalls that this being locked eyes with him and they were connected, that this being knew all his emotions, secrets, dreams and memories. Fear was taking over Terry at this point, he couldn't move, he had no idea what the plan was. Would they be released? Could they be released? Were they even still on the planet? While some abductees report almost pleasant or euphoric experiences, there are many who report the opposite, that even when beings are allegedly reassuring them that they aren't there to hurt humans, the experiences, the trauma and the pain all very real.

Other details of the incident that Terry remembers is that there was a hangar containing saucers parked up next to each other, perhaps to be used for various missions not involving the larger ship. Also, he remembered that the ship was even larger on the inside than it was on the outside. There were also rows of other humans: men, women and children, who appeared to be in distress. It was hard to discern a lot. Details were hard to keep up with, as he couldn't move any more than his eyeballs.

Terry remembers Toby being taken by the greys, hearing his screams as it sounded as though they were doing something to him, clearly against his will. He knew it would likely be him next and so it was, as the greys came back in to take Terry. He wasn't walking or being wheeled, but felt as if he was being levitated, or that he was on something that wasn't touching the floor. In another bright white room with a domed ceiling, he was placed onto an examination table and strangely, while he was afraid, he felt it wasn't to be a torture session as he was in a very clean medical setting. He screamed as they did something to his back. He could feel the pain but couldn't move as 2.5m (8–9ft) tall 'Praying Mantis-like' beings were performing the operations. One of these entities communicated telepathically, asking Terry why he was screaming, communicating that there was no need to scream and that he would be returned. They placed a long digit onto his head, and he passed out.

Upon waking up back in the tent and seeing the beings leave in the craft, the two friends noted their watches had stopped at exactly 2.40 a.m. The actual time was uncertain. They decided to leave immediately, and scrambling only for car keys, wallets and essentials, they got into Terry's car, abandoning all the equipment they had taken with them. The conversation in the car was minimal, both Terry and Toby navigating in the dark through the trees, desperate to get closer to home, safety and other human beings. The sun rose, and with that sense of comfort that with the night giving way to day, it was over. They agreed that they wouldn't discuss what had happened, that their story would be that they had to return home due to illness. When they returned to the base, they had to receive medical attention for injuries including sickness, fatigue and burns. On the last day of their hospital stay, Terry recalls the Official of Special Investigation (OSI) paying him a visit, saying that they had found the pair's campsite and wondered what they were doing in such an odd location. Terry told them nothing, saying only that they had left after falling ill, but this didn't sit well with the official from OSI, who accused them of potentially running a marijuana operation from the plot, which would have had serious repercussions, including dishonourable discharge and some jail time. They did ask if they had seen anything unusual at the time. 'No, Sir,' was their reply.

Six to eight weeks later, the OSI again interrogated Terry. He was drugged and they attempted to hypnotise him but Terry resisted by mentally distracting himself. While the hypnosis failed, the drugging or truth serum, as some may call it, was more successful at getting information about the incident from him. It seemed they knew that something had happened. Why were they so insistent to get information out of individuals that they knew had experienced something? Terry was an amateur photographer, this was well known among his colleagues, and he believes that they were worried he would have taken photographs with his camera. He didn't, neither of them had any evidence of the event.

Some sceptical about the event have come forward with various theories, from suggesting it was a secret operation by the US government or there was some shadow entity on a patch of land that those two shouldn't have been on. Had they been drugged and led to believe that the incident had happened? Or on that night, did two friends take the wrong path and end up on a piece of land that was kept strictly private because it was known to be an extraterrestrial landing spot. This is what Terry Lovelace believes.

ABOVE: Lee Creek runs through Devil's Den State Park. Terry Lovelace and Toby accidentally strayed onto territory owned by the Bureau of Land Management, which borders the park.

| *New Hampshire, USA* | 44.5784° N, 71.4129° W |
| --- | --- |

# LANCASTER

Betty and Barney Hill's far from routine journey home

Lancaster is a small, rural town in Coos County, in northern New Hampshire, with a population a little over 3,000. US Route 3 runs through it, a major north-south highway where those driving along can take in stunning views of the White Mountains and sprawling forest. This particular route is famous for more than its landscape, as in 1961, it played host to one of the most incredible abduction stories in history. The background to the story is equally as fascinating and relevant in the context of why this is such a powerful testimony, because its two protagonists, Betty and Barney Hill, were a mixed-race couple. Betty a White woman, Barney a Black man. These days, there is nothing noteworthy about that, but in 1961, such couples were faced with social and political threats just for wanting to be together. Mixed-race couples found it difficult to get married without fear of fines or jail time, there were difficulties in being seen in public without fear of suffering physical and verbal abuse, and it could prove difficult to just get a job. The reason this context is relevant is because it is unlikely that a couple like this would wish to draw attention to themselves in such a hostile climate by making up the story.

On 19 September 1961,the Hills were travelling home from a holiday in Canada. Reports of impending hurricanes worried them so they decided to make the drive back to Portsmouth, New Hampshire early. At around 10.05 p.m. they stopped to eat, then got back on Route 3, expecting to get home sometime around 3 a.m. However, at 10.30 p.m., the Hills both noticed a bright light in the sky. At first Betty thought it was some sort of shooting star, but dismissed this quickly as it was travelling upwards, not the normal behaviour of a shooting star. Barney thought it could have been some sort of satellite in trouble or just off its course. They carried on their journey, keeping a watchful eye on the object as it grew brighter, larger, causing the couple to make several impromptu stops along their drive for a closer look through some binoculars they had in the car. It was difficult to get a good grasp of what they were looking at as it was too bright, but they thought it likely to be some sort of aircraft. After about an hour, the object passed directly alongside them, travelling in the opposite direction as they motored by Cannon Mountain. Was it over, they wondered? No, the object then turned back and began to follow them. Overtaking the couple's car, it was illuminated by the bright moon, so Betty could

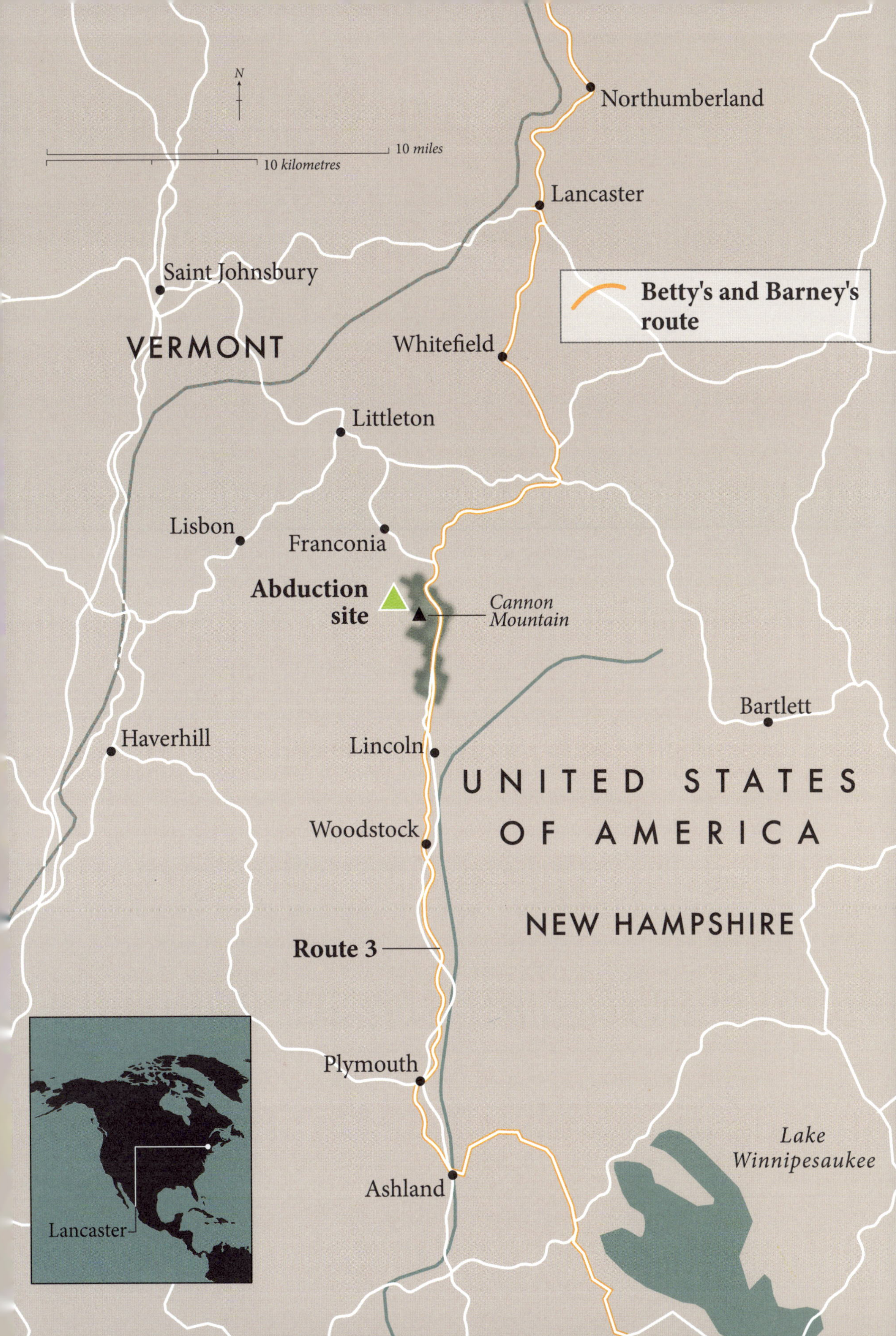

N
10 miles
10 kilometres
Northumberland
Lancaster
Betty's and Barney's route
Saint Johnsbury
VERMONT
Whitefield
Littleton
Lisbon
Franconia
Abduction site
Cannon Mountain
Bartlett
Haverhill
Lincoln
UNITED STATES OF AMERICA
Woodstock
NEW HAMPSHIRE
Route 3
Plymouth
Lake Winnipesaukee
Ashland
Lancaster

make out more detail, and could see that it was a wingless, cigar-shaped craft, with lights underneath flashing red, green, blue and amber. This was a flying saucer, thought Betty. Barney was driving, and dismissive of the idea that this was anything other than an aircraft. However, he reached for a firearm in the car as he was beginning to feel an unease come over him. Something wasn't right.

A little further along the road, there was a motel; stopping and alerting someone to their plight may have been a good idea – safety in numbers, other witnesses – but they decided it was best just to keep moving along the road. The potential safety of the neon motel lights faded as they drove past, back into the darkness of the long road, still at least three hours from home. The object stalking their vehicle sped in front of them, and now was only about 50m (165ft) away, and as Barney could see, just above the tree tops. More details were now apparent on the cigar-like craft: two rows of windows were visible along the side of the object. Betty suggested to Barney that he stop the car, to again use the binoculars to check they were truly seeing what they thought they were: the most unimaginable thing possible. They stopped the car, and the craft settled in a field off to the side. Barney got out of the car and made a motion to get closer to the craft, Betty shouted to her husband to stop, but Barney either couldn't hear or wasn't listening. He raised the binoculars to his eyes and through those windows, he could make out what looked like ten beings, not quite human looking, their large eyes staring back at him. They moved away from the windows, all bar one which remained staring at him, unwavering. This was enough for Barney: he sensed danger as he noticed a ladder-like device extending from the bottom of the craft and he turned and ran back to the car. 'They are going to try and capture us,' he gasped to his wife as he started the car and began to drive off at speed.

As they travelled along the road, attempting to get away from the craft and the beings as fast as possible, a series of strange 'beeps' could be heard, as if they were sonar hail stones

LEFT: A plaque commemorating the site where Betty and Barney Hill were pursued by the object.

RIGHT: Betty and Barney Hill describe the craft that they encountered.

OVERLEAF: An artist's impression of the beings who abducted the Hills, based on descriptions given whilst they were hyponotised.

reflecting off of the car bonnet. With each contact, the car vibrated, sending a sensation through the bodies of the stricken couple and with this, they felt their consciousness slipping and a haze descending over them.

It seemed only a few moments had passed as they opened their eyes again, consciousness coming back. They were a little confused but still driving and the sounds had gone. All was not well though, and it hadn't been seconds, as they noticed they had driven 50km (35 miles) since they had blacked out, and were now in the town of Ashland. They had no idea how they could have driven that far without noticing. They would recall this later, but in that moment they were fighting exhaustion and nausea and, still processing what they had just witnessed, just wanted to get home. Which they did, arriving home around 5 a.m., two hours later than planned, which didn't make sense, as they had not stopped for two hours on the drive. Upon arriving home, the couple noticed that Betty's new dress was stained and torn and Barney's shoes were scuffed, and their watches had also both stopped. It was difficult to recall what had happened after the beeps and before they had ended up in Ashland. Betty recalled making a sharp turn, Barney could faintly remember a road block, but details were sparse. They agreed that they shouldn't talk about what had happened to them as what good would it do, and the best thing would be to get to bed and get some sleep.

However, when they woke later they were still understandably disturbed and Betty couldn't keep it to herself, so she rang her sister and shared the story of what had happened to them less than twenty-four hours earlier. Barney didn't want to discuss the incident; he chose to put it out of mind and try to move on. Betty noticed that on inspection, the boot of the car had 'half-dollar-sized marks' all over it, likely caused by whatever made the beeps that struck the car. She ran a compass over the area and noted that it reacted near those marks, but not anywhere else on the vehicle.

Barney had no interest in taking things further, but Betty couldn't let it go and reported the incident to officials at Pease Air Force Base (AFB); they were interviewed by Major Paul W. Henderson over the phone (taking care to leave out some of the more incredible details as to not appear mentally unstable). The report was passed on to officials involved with Project Blue Book.

In the days that followed, Betty had intense, hyper-realistic dreams, and her friends suggested she write down what was happening in them in case they were repressed memories. The dreams consisted of her and Barney being taken aboard a spacecraft and being examined by alien beings, with them communicating telepathically. Betty now had a real interest in the UFO topic, and was keen to learn more, to try and make sense of what had happened in their encounter. Barney remained uncomfortable. She heard about the National Investigations Committee on Aerial Phenomena (NICAP) in early 1962 and contacted them to dig further and they, of course, were fascinated by her story. Investigator Walter N. Webb served as a science advisor for NICAP, outside of his day job with the Hayden Planetarium where he was an astronomer and lecturer. Webb was intrigued by the story and drove to the couple's home that October to interview them. He structured the interview to try and get them to make a mistake and expose themselves as liars, but their account remained 'iron clad' according to Webb after more than a six-hour interview.

Through 1962 and into 1963, the Hills shared the story among some close friends, but they never went public with it. Barney had become a little more open to talking about the event, but the story wasn't national news. The couple were still looking for answers, though, and in December of that year, met renowned psychiatrist and neurologist, Dr Benjamin

Simon, to begin hypnotic regression therapy, used to dive deep into the subconscious of a patient and help them bring back memories that are either lost, forgotten or repressed. Initially the meetings were consultations and preliminary interviews to help Dr Simon assess their mental wellbeing and decide whether or not the therapy was right for them. After several months of sessions and planning, in February 1964 the sessions began, with incredible, yet terrifying results. Under hypnosis, over eleven hours of tape, a lot of scary details came back to the surface.

**Barney under hypnosis could recall:**

- The beings visible through the windows seemed to be wearing black uniforms.
- The figure who remained at the window seemed to be wearing a shiny black jacket.
- After hearing the beeps, Barney had turned off the highway and into a heavily forested area. This is where they saw an orange glow, and many 'men' in the middle of the road approached the car. But given they were sleepy, they couldn't run. The beings escorted the pair down to the craft.
- Barney believes his feet were dragged while being escorted, resulting in his scuffed shoes.
- He recalled being in a pie-shaped room, clean, like a surgeon's room, with an examining table in the middle.
- He reçalls a physical examination of his body, a stick-like device scratching his arm, a cup being placed around his groin.

**Betty could recall more detail than Barney, including:**

- The beings initially trying to reassure them.
- The bodies of the beings were disproportionate, with large heads not fitting slimmer bodies.
- They were taken up a ramp into the craft, and Betty tried to resist, kicking out, but she was told not to waste her time.
- They were taken along a long hallway to separate rooms.
- She recalled more equipment in the room she was taken to than Barney recalled in his room.
- Multiple beings were present, and they took multiple samples, including skin and ear wax.
- They told Betty they wanted to examine her nervous system, laid her on the table and used a device that looked like it was a cluster of needles.
- She said a large 12cm (5in) needle was inserted into her naval, it was agonisingly painful until the examiner placed a hand over her eyes and the pain disappeared.
- She recalled communicating with the leader and that she wanted some sort of proof to take back. She took a book from a shelf and the leader agreed she could.
- Betty saw a star map which is alleged to be where the beings came from; this was later re-drawn by Betty from memory.
- She was shown Barney's dentures from beings who came into the room; they apparently couldn't understand why his teeth were removable, and Betty's were not
- She was asked a range of simple questions, about food, colours and so on.

Betty remembers that she was then reunited with Barney. The beings took them back towards their car however, the one they called the leader, took the book from her that she'd earlier been given permission to take. Betty was unhappy with this, but she was informed that the others did not want them having any proof of the incident. This whole time, their dog, Delsey, had been in the car with them and they found her under the seat curled up, afraid. They watched the craft leave; it had turned into a large glowing orange ball, a vague memory of which they already had. Dr Simon found their stories remarkably consistent, despite some small details here and there not matching up. He suggested that Betty's dreams might have been discussed between the pair after their ordeal, and that these could have manifested into false memories that the pair now shared in the hypnosis. But he couldn't conclude either way and would only say he found the case interesting.

The case eventually leaked a few years later, in 1965. When the couple shared the story with friends back in 1961, it was recorded without them knowing and this tape made its way to a journalist, John Luttrell at the *Boston Traveler*, who then published several articles

ABOVE: Coos County, New Hampshire is notable for its sprawling forest and mountains which the Hills were travelling through when the incident occurred.

detailing the experience of Betty and Barney. These caught the public's imagination, and the tale made its way into the wider news media too. The Hills decided to take control of their own story, working with author John G. Fuller to publish their own book *The Interrupted Journey* in 1966. The Hills retained their interest in the UFO topic through the decades, until Barney passed away in 1969, having had many health issues following his abduction experience, with stress and anxiety taking its toll on his physical wellbeing. Betty lived a longer life, continuing their legacy by speaking about their abduction and becoming a popular figure in UFOlogy, before she died in 2004.

Many are sceptical of the Hills story. Some cite inconsistencies in their accounts and recollections, and argue that hypnosis should not be held as a true account of something that has happened. Others have claimed a mixture of sleep deprivation and false memories account for what happened to the Hills that night. Given this couple were married in the most difficult of times to be an interracial pair, many struggle to find a reason why they would have gone out of their way to fabricate a story that could only bring the sort of attention that they had sought to avoid in their time together. For many, this story is the atypical abduction experience, one that has lasted the test of time and is firmly cemented in the history books. An unsuspecting couple, on their way home from holiday, had the most incredible of experiences.

| New York State, USA | 41.5423° N, 74.0002° W |
|---|---|

# NEAR KINGSTON

Renowned author Whitley Strieber encounters with otherworldly beings

Whitley Strieber, his wife Ann and their seven-year-old son were spending time in their Upstate New York cabin, a place typically reserved for summer vacations. The cabin was relatively isolated, and at this time of year surrounded by a light dusting of snow, adding to the beauty of the idyllic scenery; it was perfect for a Christmas getaway, isolated, but not completely removed from society. Whitley was at this stage in his career quite famous author, with two early horror works, *The Wolfen* and *The Hunger*, successful books that had been adapted into movies, so he and his family appreciated the quiet away from the hustle and bustle of the city. This setting, perfect for a Christmas movie, was about to become one more suited to the horror genre Whitley was known for.

After a peaceful week at the cabin, and a successful Christmas Day, the Strieber family had finished a meal of Christmas leftovers, then after a nice walk went to bed around 10 p.m. Strieber was suddenly awakened by sounds and movements. To his shock, he found himself no longer in his bed but in a strange, tent-like place. In an interview with me on *That UFO Podcast*, he vividly recalled: 'I was in a strange place, that looked like a tent, there were these strange creatures that looked like insects staring at me.'

Initially, Whitley thought he was having a nightmare and tried to wake himself up. However, it soon became clear that this was not a dream; the more he tried to wake himself, the more real things became. He was fully awake. He heard a mechanical female voice asking what they could do to stop his screaming, a phrase often reported by other abduction victims. He described struggling to escape, that he encountered a machine that he says raped and violated his body, and that a needle was inserted into the side of his head, after which everything went blank.

He woke up the next day feeling unwell and disoriented, his memory foggy. He had bruising and other marks on his body, and asked his wife if someone had been in the house during the night. He experienced traumatic amnesia, not recalling what had just happened hours before, but had some vague memories, particularly of a figure with large black eyes, which he thought must have been an owl he had seen, but that didn't make sense. Over the following days, Strieber struggled with the reality of what had happened. A week later, after many days of feeling off, that something wasn't right, Whitley went for a physical

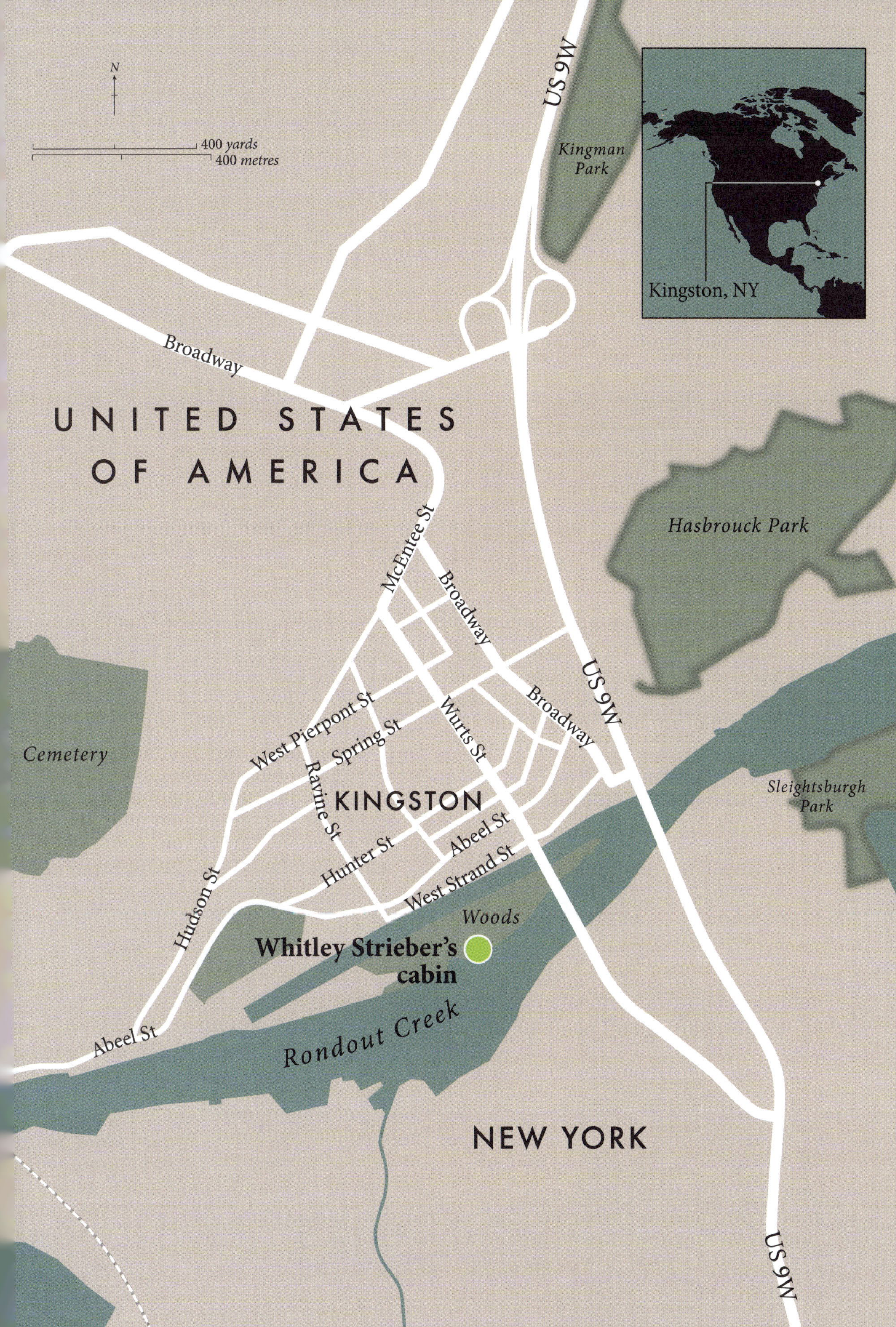
N
400 yards
400 metres
Kingston, NY
US 9W
Kingman Park
Broadway
UNITED STATES
OF AMERICA
Hasbrouck Park
McEntee St
Broadway
US 9W
Broadway
Wurts St
West Pierpont St
Spring St
Ravine St
Cemetery
KINGSTON
Sleightsburgh Park
Hunter St
Abeel St
West Strand St
Hudson St
Woods
Whitley Strieber's cabin
Abeel St
Rondout Creek
NEW YORK
US 9W

examination by his doctor, and it revealed a horrific truth: he had internal damage consistent with having been raped. As the weeks passed, his memories of the incident began to return. Strieber then informed his doctor that he believed he had been taken on board a flying saucer. This was not an easy thing to admit at any time, and his doctor tested him for any brain damage and questioned if he could have been the victim of a crime.

In the new year, Strieber sought the help of Dr Donald F. Klein, a psychiatrist and expert in forensic hypnosis, known for solving criminal cases by helping victims recall difficult memories. Klein's sessions helped Strieber piece together more details of his experience. Far more emerged from Whitley's subconscious. He recalled the inside of the craft: it was lit dimly, it appeared clinical, sterile, clean with various items of technology and medical equipment. He recalled more details of beings, some short, with wrinkled skin. Others appeared slim and taller, with large eyes, like the owl he thought he remembered, and of course colours were the classic greys that are seen in so many of these cases. In the regression tapes, Whitley can be heard screaming, a terrifying noise that sounds almost inhuman, and not unexpected given he had to relive the almost tortuous medical procedures undertaken by these beings.

Over the ensuing months, he and his wife Ann concluded that the experience was real. Strieber even attempted to re-engage with the beings and reported success in doing so. Reflecting on his life, Strieber considered the possibility that these experiences might have been occurring since his childhood. He speculated that his memory might have played tricks on him, but he couldn't shake the feeling that these encounters had happened before. With his natural gift for storytelling, he decided that to help him understand and share his story with others, he would write it down. His resulting book, *Communion*, was a bestseller, and resonated with people around the globe, not least those who came forward to claim they had had similar experiences to Whitley. Other abductees, in reading his story, realised that they were not alone.

Adding another layer to his story, Strieber mentioned that his father's brother, who was in the air force in 1947 when the Roswell incident (see page 14) occurred, reached out after the publication of *Communion*. He revealed to Strieber that his team had taken delivery of the craft debris from the Roswell crash and believed that the materials were not of this world. This revelation was further corroborated by retired Commander General Arthur Exon of Wright-Patterson Air Force Base, who confirmed that within twenty-four hours of the Roswell crash, the team knew the objects were not terrestrial, and informed the President of the United States.

Whitley's life of contact with entities not of this world did not end there. Further events have continued through the years since then. He has seen other beings, different to those he initially encountered, he has been removed from his home and examined in other settings. Famously, he has an implant behind his ear which he believes serves various purposes including tracking and communication with these beings. The contact has even taken on

LEFT: An illustration of the slim, tall creatures with large eyes that abducted Whitley Strieber.

a spiritual aspect. His dear wife Anne passed away, but he has had contact from her many times since. In a recent podcast interview with me, however, he confirmed these 'contacts' have stopped, at least for the time being.

Whitley's abduction case seemed to come at a time that the general public was ready to read about and then see such an incredible story, and it has been made into a Hollywood feature starring Christopher Walken. Strieber's continued encounters and his way with words has allowed him to communicate them to a public with a keen interest in the UFO topic, particularly the abduction phenomena within the experiencer community. It has helped give a voice to a section of UFOlogy that at times can be ignored or appear

LEFT: The Strieber's cabin was located in an isolated part of Upstate New York, close to Kingston.

to be kept quiet as some argue that the conversation isn't one that is ready to be had on the global stage.

It may be the ultimate fear for this truth to e exposed, as not only are we as a species not alone, but we are being taken by more advanced species who treat us like we treat animals on this planet we see as worthy of experiment.

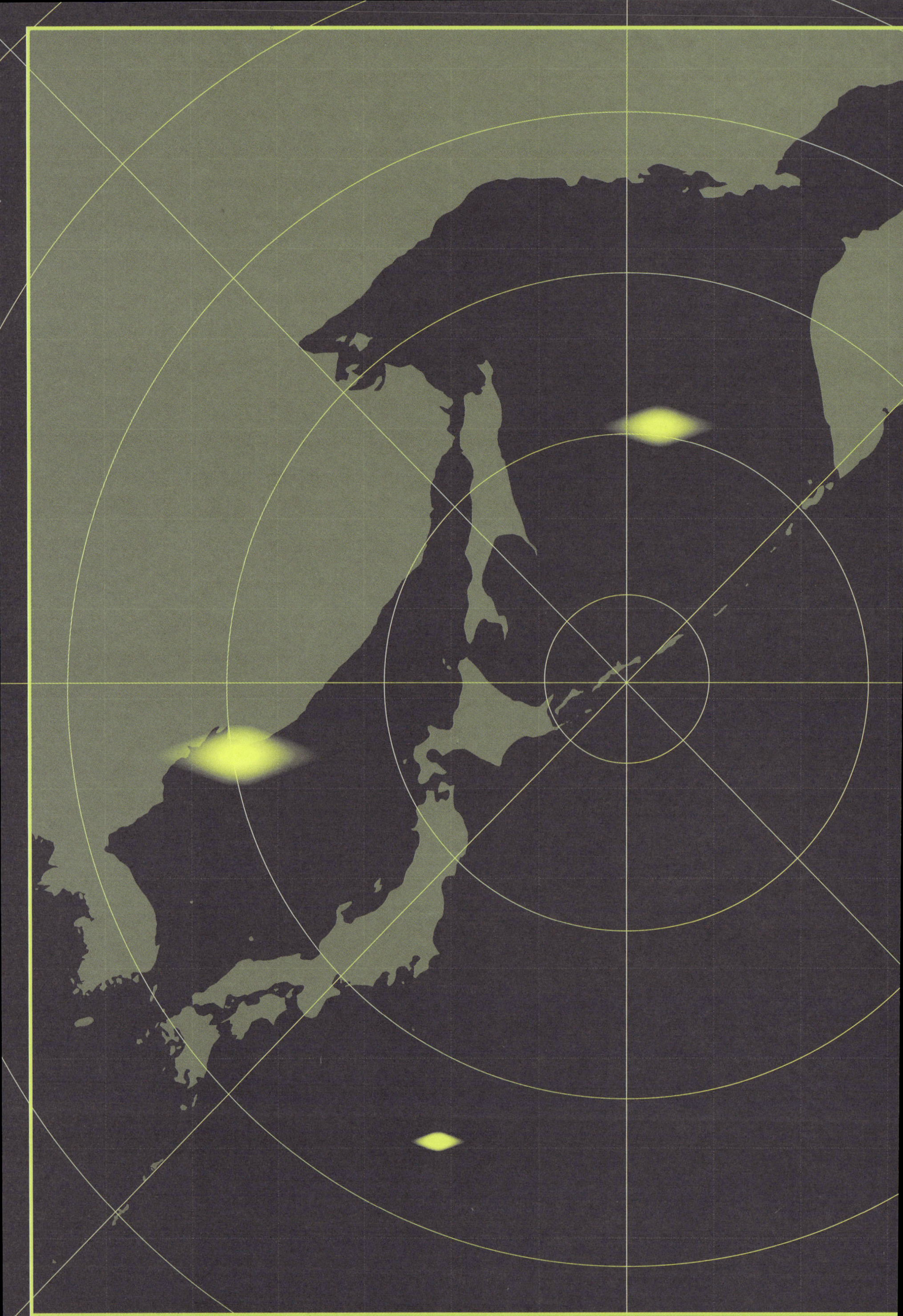

Chapter 3

# MILITARY

| *California, USA* | 31.3358° N, 116.5254° W |
|---|---|

# NEAR SAN DIEGO

Multiple Tic Tac-like objects hover over the ocean observing US military vessels

For many in the UFO community, modern UFOlogy was given somewhat of a rebirth in 2017, as the *New York Times*, one of the most read and respected newspapers on the planet, ran a rather remarkable story. Known for its editorial excellence and boasting more than a hundred Pulitzer prizes, for many it is a beacon of rational, sensible reporting. On 16 December 2017, it surprised much of its readership when it ran the incredible headline 'Glowing Auras and "Black Money": The Pentagon's mysterious U.F.O. Program'. Here the *New York Times*, through prestigious reporters Leslie Kean, Ralph Blumenthal and Helene Cooper, told the incredible story that the US government, who had long denied any interest in UFOs, not only indeed had an interest, but had spent millions of dollars investigating the phenomenon. Within the article it named individuals such as Senator Harry Reid, a longtime supporter of the programme, Luis Elizondo, a decorated military intelligence official who has since become a huge Disclosure advocate in the world of UFOs or UAP (Unidentified Anomalous Phenomena), and many more high-profile names in the world of politics, science and beyond.

During this time, one of the most modern and incredible UFO reports of all time was brought to the public domain. Anything military had seemed to be a thing of the past, going back decades, with little to no footage available, only black and white pictures, old de-classified files and no data for the public to digest. Things were about to change.

Let me take you to November 2004, a large-scale Navy training exercise involving nuclear-powered vessels off the coast of Southern California. Not only was this a sighting, it was picked up by multiple personnel, multiple sensor systems and there was accompanying footage.

F18 Squadron Commander, David Fravor is a 'Top Gun' pilot who graduated top of his flight school, the *crème de la crème* of pilots. He, alongside fellow pilot Lieutenant Alex Dietrich, would come close, almost too close, to something described as potentially 'not of this world'.

The USS *Nimitz* and its carrier strike group was around 160km (100 miles) off the coast of California and for around one week before this incident, the nearby USS *Princeton* had detected multiple objects on the horizon. Hovering for sometimes twelve

UFO flight path

San
Diego

NEVADA
CALIFORNIA
UNITED STATES
OF AMERICA
ARIZONA
Catalina
Island
NAS
Port
San Diego
North
Island
The
Princeton
USS
Nimitz
PACIFIC
OCEAN
MEXICO
N
100 miles
200 kilometres
Guadaloupe Island

hours at a time at a distance, coming in from a ceiling of just over 18,000m down to 15m (approximately 60,000ft to 50ft) above the sea level in a matter of seconds. That sort of speed is unimaginable for any potential technology we have now or could even dream of in decades to come. If there was something of human origin travelling at that speed, anyone on board, made of flesh and bone, would be squished with the G-Forces.

On one particular day, Commander Fravor and Lieutenant Dietrich were sent to investigate these objects. Fravor and his fellow pilots saw an area of white water on a blue sea, as if something was frothing under the water, potentially just submerged. It was described as being about the size of a commercial airliner like a 737, and a cross shape could be made out under the water. Now, was this a solid object, multiple objects, some whales? This wasn't clear; however, just above the water was a small white object, around the same size as their own F18 jets around 12m (40ft) long, like a small Tic Tac mint. This is where the now famous 'Tic Tac' name for UFOs has come from.

The object appeared to notice them, just as they noticed it, and from its position above the frothing water, it began to climb towards the perplexed pilots. Fravor began to descend to get a closer look at the craft, as Dietrich maintained position. The object continued to climb to meet Fravour and his Weapons Systems Officer (WSO) in the back of the aircraft

LEFT: An MH-60R Sea Hawk helicopter performs manoeuvres above USS *Nimitz*.

RIGHT TOP AND BOTTOM: The Tic Tacs were picked up on the military's radar system.

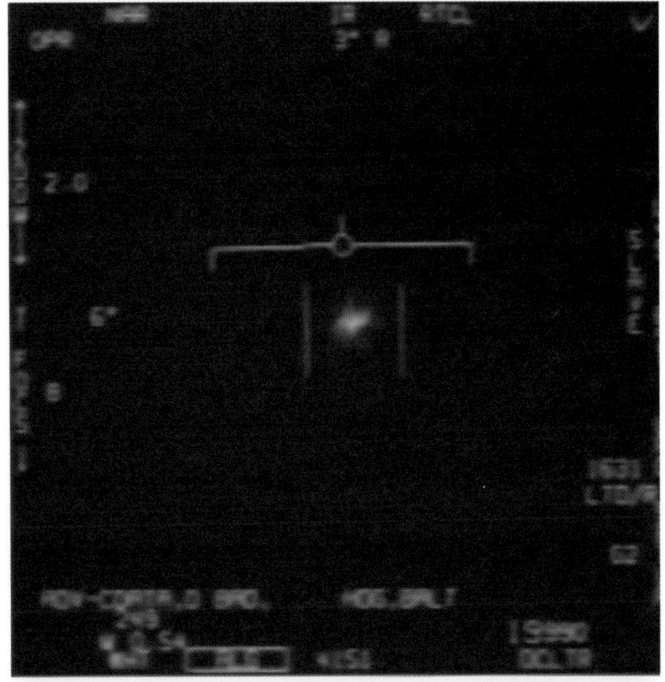

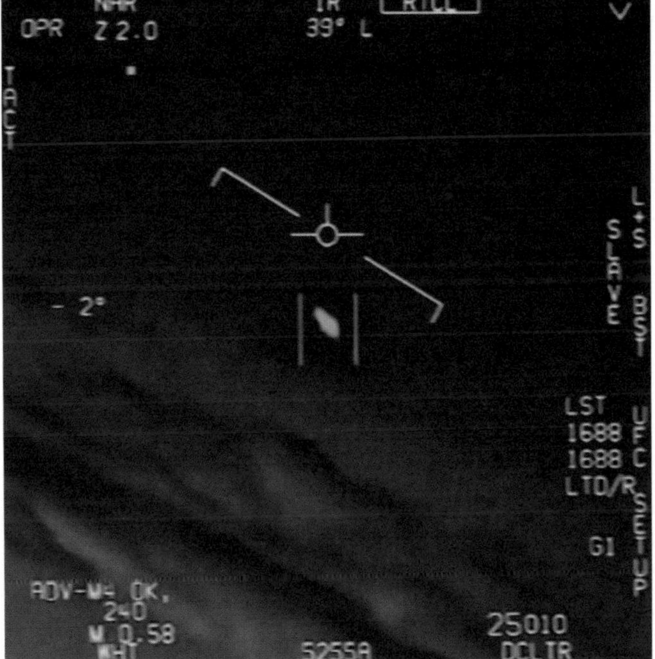


and as it met him, just as quickly as it arrived, it sped off at an incredible rate, almost as if it completely disappeared.

After only a few more seconds, the USS *Princeton* crew managed to lock back on to the Tic Tac object, which had turned up at a rendezvous location known as a 'cap point' (Combat Air Patrol) nearly 100km (60 miles) away, a distance it had travelled in less than one minute. This confused, amazed and bewildered the crew, all experienced and yet unsure exactly what was being encountered.

By the time the two jets arrived at the cap point, the Tic Tac object was gone. There is, however, no famous footage of the alleged ET vehicle. After Fravor's encounter, US Navy

Pilot Chad Underwood was sent out in his F/A-18 Super Hornet and managed to film the object streaking across the water. The video was later declassified and has since been shown thousands of times on news clips and on YouTube across the globe.

Upon returning to the ship, Commander Fravor and his fellow pilots found that many on board the vessels who had become aware of the incident were making fun of it. For many decades before this sighting, there had been a stigma around the topic of UFOs which hindered clear reporting and progress in the topic at military and political levels. From there, the story disappeared, and the pilots got on with their own careers and lives.

The story never made its way into the public domain until the *New York Times* article and the formation of rockstar Tom DeLonge's To The Stars Academy brought these into the public's radar, pardon the pun. It caught the imagination of hardened UFOlogists and researchers who had championed the subject over decades as the days of newsletters and magazines were replaced by social media, blogs and podcasts. The pilots have since come forward to share their version of events on platforms such as *60 minutes* in the US and the popular *Joe Rogan Experience Podcast.* This has started, or some would say kickstarted, a new march towards military and political transparency of a topic shrouded in more than eighty years of official secrecy, mis-information and deception.

Other notable names who were involved on the day have also come forward to talk about the incident, giving their unique insight into this incredible event. Radar operator Gary Voorhis, who was my very first guest on *That UFO Podcast*, was working aboard the USS *Princeton*, expecting a normal day at work. He describes how the vessel had been picking up the contacts on its sensor systems for days before Fravor's and Dietrich's actual encounter. Both he and fellow radar operator Kevin Day have described the Tic Tacs as raining down on the screen in front of them at times. Gary was even told by one of his superiors at the time to take his system down, clean it (that is, to reset it) to see if that would get rid of the tracks they were picking up. It only made them clearer. Gary also reported that the objects appeared to be jamming their radar systems, which is something reported in many UFO cases involving sensor systems like radar. Whether this is a consequence of their propulsion methods or a technique they are deploying is up for debate. It would make sense given the nature of many of these sightings that the objects do not want to be tracked or seen for any length of time. After the event, Gary and others have told how unknown individuals arrived by helicopter onto his ship and confiscated the data relating to the event, leaving no official record of the event on the ship other than the testimony of the individuals who were witnesses, whether with their own eyes or the systems they were in charge of monitoring. Further witnesses from the event have commented that other sites along the US coast picked up and tracked these objects, which would explain how the helicopter with the unknown 'agents' managed to arrive so quickly. Many have speculated these were advanced missile tracking facilities, which could pick up the smallest objects entering or leaving our atmosphere.

Multiple objects for days, hovering in mid-air; what were they doing? Watching, observing the vessels, performing their own tasks at a distance. That still remains unclear and we can only speculate.

Almost all of the individuals involved in the event have commented that this was a life-changing experience. With their combined decades of experience and their decorated careers at the time and since, they haven't been able to come to a satisfactory conclusion as to what the object or objects encountered off the coast of California were.

Given how recenct the event was, the early 2000s, it involved a lot of high-end technological ships, state-of-the-art sensor systems and highly trained personnel. It is fair to suggest that what was encountered that day *could* have been an extremely advanced cutting-edge prototype drone, maybe Chinese, maybe Russian, or even some top secret US craft. However, given the physics-defying nature of the craft's movement, the lack of discernible propulsion and the highly sensitive nature of the area they were operating in, I believe that during those weeks of November 2004, something truly otherworldly was encountered by the US military.

Encounters that, according to multiple witnesses who have come forward, are still happening almost every day.

ABOVE: Commander David Fravor testifies before a House Oversight and Accountability Committee hearing about UFOs in Washington DC, 2023.

| *District of Columbia, USA* | 38.5356° N, 77.0206° W |
|---|---|

# WASHINGTON DC

Multiple people witness the lights of mysterious objects over the capital

When the debate arises around how Disclosure – that's capital 'D' Disclosure – may look, people will often mention 'Aliens landing on the White House lawn'. That would no doubt be undeniable proof, the world would be watching, it's an iconic scene. As yet, we haven't had that landing. But, in July 1952, did this scenario come closer than we think? The area around Washington is far from quiet. Even in the early 1950s, it was a multicultural hub of around 800,000 citizens, in a time when social change and early suburban migration would begin to influence and change the area now known to so many worldwide and made iconic through many movies, TV shows and documentaries. The White House itself is a symbol for many of Western democracy.

Late in the evening on Saturday 19 July 1952, as the clock approached midnight, air traffic controllers working the night shift at Washington National Airport noticed some odd contacts on their radar. The man on duty was Edward Nugent and, alarmed at these pick-ups as they weren't following any expected flight path, he put in a call to notify his boss, Harry Barnes. There were eight reports in total, which ruled out a single aircraft approaching on the wrong path. Minutes after this was reported to Barnes, another ATC worker called Howard Cocklin, who was working above the radar room in the visual control tower, confirmed the same objects, this time seen with his own eyes. He described them as bright lights, moving erratically. The objects were worryingly close to the White House and Capitol Buildings. Later, in a statement to the National Investigations Committee on Aerial Phenomena (NICAP), Barnes was quoted as saying, 'We knew immediately that a very strange situation existed. Their movements were completely radical compared to those of ordinary craft.'

Washington National Airport wasn't the only location that had detected the objects. Andrews Air Force base, roughly 16km (10 miles) away had also registered the strange objects on their radar. This would help rule out equipment malfunction as a possible cause; would all their systems be having the same issue? Around midnight, witnesses there had seen the objects, describing them as 'orange, fiery objects with a trail of sparks'. It's one thing to pick up objects of an unknown origin, but the observations that followed shortly after midnight from various radar technicians were that the speed of the contacts was

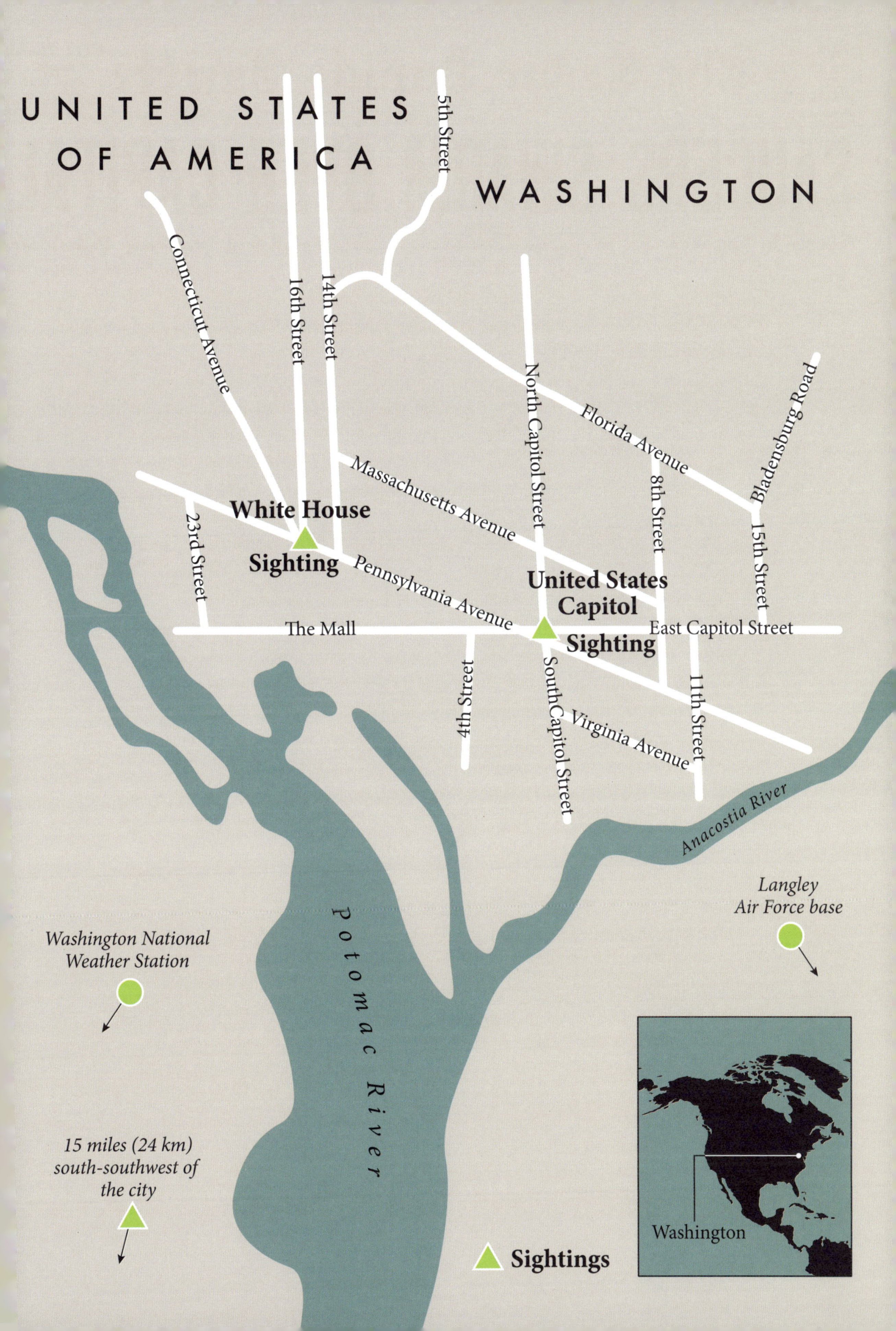

UNITED STATES OF AMERICA

WASHINGTON

Connecticut Avenue
16th Street
14th Street
5th Street
North Capitol Street
Florida Avenue
Bladensburg Road
Massachusetts Avenue
8th Street
15th Street
23rd Street

**White House Sighting**

Pennsylvania Avenue

**United States Capitol Sighting**

The Mall
East Capitol Street
4th Street
SouthCapitol Street
Virginia Avenue
11th Street
*Anacostia River*
Potomac River

*Langley Air Force base*

*Washington National Weather Station*

*15 miles (24 km) south-southwest of the city*

**Sightings**

Washington

Weather---
Partly cloudy tonight with occasional light showers. Low 58-62. Partly cloudy Wednesday with high 80-85. C. R. 2:30 temperatures: NW 82; NE 81; SW 82; SE 80.

The Cedar Rapids Gazette

CITY FINAL
5 CENTS
KCRG NEWS
1600 ON YOUR DIAL

VOLUME 70—NUMBER 202 CEDAR RAPIDS, IOWA, TUESDAY, JULY 29, 1952. ASSOCIATED PRESS, UNITED PRESS, INTERNATIONAL NEWS

# SAUCERS SWARM OVER CAPITAL

C.R. Sewer | Call Voiced | Three Quake | Radar Picks

around 160km/h (100mph), in itself perhaps unspectacular, but they were also observed stopping suddenly, hovering in place, then changing direction, something that wasn't a common movement.

It makes sense that given the proximity to the airports that pilots would also come into range of the objects. Captain Harold W. Casey was at the controls of a National Airlines flight around 3 a.m. now the 20 July. He (soon after) told *The Washington Post* newspaper that he had been able to make out lights, white in colour to him, coming from what seemed to be a much larger craft. He said that they 'twisted and turned in the air, unlike any aircraft I have ever seen'.

By 4 a.m., the situation was becoming increasingly concerning, and potentially a national security issue. Two F-94 jet fighters from Newcastle Air Force Base, located in Delaware, some 150km (93 miles) from Washington DC were scrambled to attempt an intercept of the objects. They were unsuccessful, however, since they were not able to find the objects despite them continuing to be tracked on radar. The jets had to turn back to base as their fuel began to run out. As the night sky gave way to the day, the objects disappeared.

Multiple news outlets had picked up on the story and reported on it the following day. *The Washington Post* had interviews with eyewitnesses, the failed attempt by the Air Force to locate the objects and went into detail about the radar signals picked up. *The Cedar Rapids Gazette* also gave this a front-page coverage, with the spectacular headline 'Saucers Swarm Over Capital'. Interestingly, the head of Project Blue Book at the time, Captain Edward J. Ruppelt was left furious on reading the headlines; not because the event was being reported, but because he hadn't been alerted, and only found out about it after reading the newspaper, giving cause for frustration that he wasn't shy in showing.

Early sceptics of the event put it down to being a case of 'temperature inversion', which is a meteorological phenomenon. Instead of temperature decreasing as you go higher into the atmosphere, it increases, and this can cause radar waves to bend or refract in unusual ways. While this is a fair explanation for what may have been seen on radar, this doesn't explain the strange movements seen by pilots and ATC crew, the fast movements, sudden stops and hovering capabilities. It didn't add up as an official explanation, and Captain Ruppelt himself later stated on the record that it wasn't a satisfactory explanation, given the wealth of data and evidence available.

ABOVE: The flyover made national news: here the *Cedar Rapids Gazette* from Iowa reports on the incident.

RIGHT: This 1952 comic shows how the local population sensationalized the blips spotted.

End of story? Not quite, as one week later on 26 July, the objects were back. Reports started coming in of odd radar contacts as early as 2.30 p.m. that day from Langley AFB. Harry Barnes, back on his usual shift, was first to spot the group on radar, and having had the experience just seven days earlier, he was much quicker to contact Andrews Air Force Base and alert them of the return. They confirmed to that Barnes they too could see the objects on their screens. Multiple airline pilots, passengers and crew also had visual of the objects, with a Captain William B. Patterson, flying for Capital Airlines, even attempting to get closer to four of the objects. He had no luck as they took off at an incredible speed as he came within distance. Another pilot, with a strikingly similar name, this time a Lieutenant William Patterson, was scrambled in an F-94 fighter jet to try intercept the objects, but even in his far speedier craft than that of the airline, his attempts were in vain. While jets did attempt to intercept these objects, it was noted that whatever they were had a sentience or intelligence to them, as they seemed to be playing a game of 'cat and mouse', almost teasing the pursuing jets. Once again, the mysterious lights disappeared with the dawn.

Speaking after the frustrating chase, Lieutenant Patterson is quoted as saying, 'I saw several bright lights. I was at maximum speed, but . . . I ceased chasing them because I saw no chance of overtaking them.' The big flap, as it had been affectionately labelled by the media of the time, had again tightened its grip on a curious public's imagination. A press conference was called to address concerns, and even the president at the time, Harry Truman, was looking for answers. What was going on in the skies directly over the nation's capital? Allegedly, some of President Truman's aides reached out to head of Project Blue Book, Captain Edward J. Ruppelt, to try and get answers. Truman, however, remained dissatisfied, instructing the Air Force to stay on alert, be vigilant in the midst of unknown intrusions and to keep fighter jets on standby in case further incidents occurred. The military prowess of the most powerful nation on earth was being called into question.

A few days after the sightings, with no answers being put forward, a press conference was held by the Director of Intelligence for the US Air Force, Major General John A. Samford. Wanting to re-assure an anxious public, he addressed the crowd filled with eager journalists already doing their own digging, or at least as much as they could. Echoing the initial speculation, Samford put the sightings down to a case of temperature inversion stating that there was no threat to US soil posed by these phantom lights. He went as far as to say that the testimony put forward by military personnel, pilots and civilians still pointed to signs of atmospheric phenomena being the most likely explanation, even though he himself had never spoken to any witnesses to get a better idea of the story. Clips from the press conference are used to this day in almost all UFO documentaries or news reports of note; it's the sort of clip people won't even realise they have seen, until they see it. It was a rare acknowledgment by the US government that there was something there. While maybe at this point not admitting it as something potentially exotic or non-human, at least it showed there was *something* to address.

As would become the norm, the media and the public, while far from accepting of the official explanation, lacked the will or interest to take it further. The story faded, almost as quickly as the objects had as dawn broke, and the event is perhaps best viewed as a moment that the public finally got to see members of the US Government acknowledge a phenomenon growing in popularity. In his comprehensive work, *The UFO Encyclopedia: The Phenomenon from the Beginning*, researcher Jerome Clark says; 'The Washington National Airport sightings of July 1952 were notable not only for the multiplicity of witnesses but also for the serious attention they received from the U.S. Air Force. The events over two weekends raised public awareness and concern, leading to a more systematic approach to UFO investigations by the military.'

RIGHT: The bright lights were spotted worryingly close to the White House and Capitol buildings.

ONLY
ONLY
ONLY

*Suffolk, England* | 52.0520° N, 1.2657° E

# RENDLESHAM FOREST

Strange lights seen near US Airforce bases with possible nuclear links

In the UK, there are few UFO events known as well as the Rendlesham Forest incident. Multiple witnesses, multiple nights and a landed craft have over the years earned it the moniker of 'UK's Roswell'.

The twin Royal Air Force bases of RAF Bentwaters and RAF Woodbridge, both of which closed in 1993, are located in Suffolk, England. The forest of Rendlesham covers an area of around 15.5 square km (6 square miles), and is where one of the most incredible UFO encounters of all time occurred over a few wild nights during Christmas 1980. What's even more interesting is that it was American servicemen and women who observed the event.

It was 3 a.m. on 26 December. The usual soundtrack of the forest at night was about to be disturbed, as strange lights were observed by US Air Force security patrolmen, one of whom was Airman First Class John Burroughs. Initially, he thought that it could be an aircraft downed in the forest, so called it in to the base, which noted that something had appeared on radar in that area but had since disappeared. For this reason, Burroughs got permission to go off base to check it out. He was accompanied by Airman First Class Edward Cabansag and Staff Sergeant Jim Penniston, who all headed towards the lights to investigate. As they approached the area where the lights were seen, it soon became apparent that this wasn't a simple case of a downed aircraft or, as some have suggested over the years, lights from a nearby lighthouse; this was something far more exotic.

It's worth noting that what happens next, well, that depends on who you speak to. Burroughs says the light grew brighter, the servicemen ducked down out of the way and whatever it was took off into the night and that was all the excitement for night one. However, Jim Penniston's story is far more remarkable: he claims that rather than the craft shooting off into the night, there was time for him to get up and approach a clear, metallic craft with some hieroglyphic-like writing and markings on it. Penniston went as far as touching it and receiving an 'information download'. He believed that the craft had given him messages, potentially information or co-ordinates. This isn't something that Burroughs or Cabansag have corroborated, but in UFO reports with multiple witnesses it is common for witnesses to describe and experience very different things while being a part of the same event. Penniston even says he took multiple photographs of the craft, describing it as

N
2 miles
2 kilometres
UNITED
KINGDOM
RAF Bentwaters
RENDLESHAM
FOREST
Landing
Site
The East Gate
Lighthouse
New
Trees
RAF
Woodbridge
Capel
Green

Rendlesham
Forest

around 1m by 1m (3ft by 3ft), sitting on the ground on small landing gears. In the days that followed, investigations in the area showed that the trees around where the craft was reported were burned, and the ground showed small indentations exactly where Penniston reported the landing gears were situated.

The following evening, on 27 December around 9.30 p.m., some lights returned, less spectacular than those reported on the first and what would be seen on the third night. Whether these belonged to the same object or not is unclear. The lights on this second night were observed by staff at the East Gate of RAF Woodbridge, and described as being multicoloured, though no craft like the one Jim Penniston encountered was seen.

The next morning, in the early hours of 28 December, Lieutenant Colonel Charles Halt received reports of the events of the previous nights, and as the deputy base commander, he decided to investigate personally. He led a team, which included John Burroughs, into the forest equipped with a tape recorder to document the investigation. Taking readings as they tracked the previous nights' movements and where the object had been seen, Halt recorded high radiation readings in the area, an often-reported sign that some strange phenomena have been present. As they progressed, the meter continuing to pick up radiation, they noticed a strange red-yellow light up ahead, moving towards them. The audio recording reveals the tension in the voice of Halt and the others with him. They turned off their torches, trying to observe the light as it moved through and above the trees 200 to 300 meters/yards away. They also reported beams of light being shot down into the forest.

There has been a lot of speculation about the beams of light and their purpose, however, in the years since and with the bases' closure, it's been a poorly kept secret that it was very

LEFT: The East Gate of RAF Woodbridge where the lights were observed on the second night.

ABOVE: A sculpture of the UFO observed in Rendlesham Forest.

likely the bases of RAF Woodbridge and RAF Bentwaters were hosting multiple nuclear weapons. After questions were asked in the House of Lords following allegations in *Left At East Gate*, an account by Larry Warren, one of those involved in the incident, the Ministry of Defence refused to comment about whether nuclear weapons had or had not been based there. But over the decades their presence has been implied by staff members, and various declassified documents mention the presence of weapons in that vicinity for strategic reasons.

So were UFOs monitoring the base for its nuclear capabilities? It's a common theory that many UFO sightings in or around military installations are there to check out what we have in terms of weaponry, with some installations even reporting weapons being turned on and off, perhaps in a show of technological dominance, or as some kind of warning? We don't know for sure.

In the weeks, months and years after the events of Christmas 1980 in Rendlesham, the legend has only grown. Most details have remained consistent, and some new parties have come forward to add to the story; some would say to potentially muddy the waters. Reports were filed after the investigations at the base, including those involved going under hypnotic regression to try and bring out their memories of what happened on those nights. Charles Halt's memorandum received by the British Ministry of Defence, known as the 'Halt Memo', was released and is a key piece of evidence as to what happened over the three nights.

British UFO researcher and author Jenny Randles has written multiple books on the subject and says: 'The Rendlesham Forest incident is an enigma. It is a case that has stood the test of time, with credible military witnesses and intriguing physical evidence. It remains one of the most perplexing and compelling UFO cases in history.'

ABOVE: There were sightings in Rendlesham Forest over three consecutive nights.

| *Nova Scotia, Canada* | 43.2960° N, 65.4160° W |
| --- | --- |

# SHAG HARBOUR

UFO or an enemy submarine?

The United States is known globally as the epicentre for all things UFO-related, whether it's the potential for Disclosure, the modern-day mix of UFOs and politics or just some of the most well-known events in UFOlogical history. However, just slightly north of the US is its neighbour Canada, which quietly plays host to its own UFO history, including an incredible event that happened in 1967, in a little fishing village. Shag Harbour can be found on the southwestern point of Nova Scotia, Canada. Facing out into the Atlantic Ocean, it boasts some stunning coastline, growing more popular with tourists as the years pass. As you move along its rugged coast, you'll find small islands, sheltered harbours and many boats out fishing for lobster, shellfish and other prized catches. The Cape Sable Lighthouse nearby is a staple attraction, offering breathtaking views of the blue waters and the ocean expanse out to the horizon. If you venture into Shag Harbour, you can expect to be greeted by a small, close community which appreciates the beauty of the land it lives on but knows that the visiting tourists are a big part of its economy too. Given it is a maritime village, there are tales going back decades of all sorts of myth and legend: stories of mermaids, ghost ships and sea serpents are told among the fishermen. There isn't a single local, though, who won't be able to tell you about the incredible events of 1967 and the alleged UFO that may have crashed into its waters.

It was a dark, cold night on 4 October 1967, and the blue waters of daylight had been replaced by a chilling black sea, only broken up by patches of moonlight, and the odd fishing vessel still out trying to get its final catch of the day. Around 10 p.m., reports were made of lights in the sky from along the coast, near Halifax. By 11 p.m., several more reports had come in, with most detailing the same four orange lights in the night sky, unclear on any shape or detail other than the eerie glow. A group of five teenagers had also observed the lights floating over the harbour, watching them flash in sequence and then at a 45-degree angle, head-down towards the water. The object then seemed to float on the surface about nearly a kilometre (half a mile) from the shore. One of these teenagers was Laurie Wickens, who believed that an aircraft had crashed into the water and, panicking that life could be lost, called this into the Royal Canadian Mounted Police (RCMP) based locally in Barrington Passage. Already on patrol was RCMP Constable Ron Pound, who

New Brunswick
Saint John
Halifax Stanfield International Airport
Windsor
CANADA
Nova Scotia
Digby
Halifax
Mahone Bay
Liverpool
Yarmouth
Shelburne
Government Point
Barrington Passage
Shag Harbour
Sightings
Royal Canadian Mounted Police (RCMP)
Cape Sable Lighthouse
Nova Scotia
N
30 miles
50 kilometres

had a visual of the object in the sky before it lost altitude; he observed the lights being part of a larger craft, approximately 18m (60ft) long. He followed it in the direction of the shore, noticing a yellow-looking light in the water, with a sort of yellow foam in its wake. He was eventually joined by local observers and colleagues from the RCMP, Police Corporal Victor Werbieki and Constable Ron O'Brien, and they too locked eyes on the strange light moving in the water, the glowing foam trailing it. All three then saw the light dim as it descended further down into the water, unsure whether this was a manoeuvre or if it was something that has sunk. They immediately coordinated with local fishermen and the Coast Guard, and a rescue or recovery mission was launched to help the stricken craft, many still under the assumption that some sort of aircraft could have gone down. The lights in the water were seen by at least eleven witnesses.

The search continued in the early hours of the morning, and by 3 a.m. there was still no sign of any wreckage or debris, and the decision was made to call off the search. The

ABOVE: The Shag Harbour UFO Incident Interpretive Centre chronicles the sighting of the UFO in 1967.

object had been picked up by local fishermen on their radar systems earlier, so there was definitely a solid object that had gone into the waters, it just wasn't anywhere to be found. The following day, as the sun rose, a report was filed by the Rescue Coordination Centre in Halifax with the Canadian Forces Headquarters in Ottawa. With little to go on other than the testimony and little sensory data, they had to classify the object as being of 'unknown origin'. By this time, the close-knit community was abuzz with the story and it made its way to local newspaper, *The Halifax Chronical Herald*, which ran the following front-page headline: 'Could be something concrete in Shag Harbour UFO – RCAF'. The article details the events of 4 October into the early hours of the morning of the 5th, witness testimony, the strange lights being reported and that the Royal Canadian Air Force was now involved. Forty-eight hours after the object had entered the water, the Navy sent divers into the water to try and search the seabed, but they came up empty-handed. Reporting that nothing was there, the crew from the Fleet Diving Unit Atlantic said there was no sign of anything having been there. Extensive checks were carried out of multiple radar systems and flight logs which showed no aircraft were missing or had been reported missing.

There are rumours that the authorities could have found something and decided to keep it from public knowledge, which would fit with a common narrative around any potential crash recoveries. However, many years later, one of the foremost researchers of this particular case, Chris Styles, believes he unearthed additional information. In his book *Dark Object*, Styles says that he managed to contact former military insiders who, along with members of the diving unit that attended the location, confirmed that an orange orb had submerged on its own, it didn't sink and that it travelled to a spot, 40km (25 miles) away, on the seabed just off the Shelburne coast near Government Point. This area would later be confirmed as the location for a secret US military base, which had been disguised as an oceanographic institute. It was using special underwater microphones and acoustic equipment to detect and track enemy submarines. Remember, this event occurred at the height of the Cold War, so there is some small possibility that this could have been Soviet submarines testing something, perhaps a missile or surveillance equipment. There is no evidence, though, to corroborate that theory.

To this day, Shag Harbour commemorates the event in a variety of ways, including a small museum dedicated to the event, with various articles from newspapers around the globe, photographs and witness stories on display. There is also an annual UFO festival, which while boosting tourism, keeps the story alive for the locals and future generations. This remains one of the only UFO events in history to have such public government involvement, investigation and follow up. It was classed as case #34 in the Condon Report, a scientific study of the UFO phenomenon conducted in the mid 1960s, being classified as 'Unsolved'.

ABOVE: On 4 October 1967, there were multiple observations of orange lights floating over Shag Harbour.

| *Multiple sites, Belgium* | *Multiple* |
| --- | --- |

# BELGIUM

A six-month wave of similar sightings across the country

Belgium is a small country, with a modest population of eleven million packed into small landmass, surrounded by France, the Netherlands, Germany, Luxembourg and the North Sea. Interestingly, it has not one, not two, but three main languages across its three main regions: Dutch, which is spoken by those who reside in Flanders (the north); French, spoken by those in Wallonia (the south); and German, the native tongue of a smaller population in the east of the country. Its capital city, Brussels, is also famous for being the capital city of the European Union, which is home to the European Parliament, Council of the European Union and the European Commission.

In the late 1980s, when the account of this sighting begins, the country was known for its success in sports, boasting a successful cycling team and its football side going through what is considered by many to be its first 'golden age'. Belgium has long been noted as a bastion of culinary excellence, especially famed for chocolate production and beer. It's fitting that as, a country made up of multiple working parts that come together as a whole, it is best known in UFOlogy for not one sighting, but a wave of sightings that happened over several months, not hours or days.

It all began then on a cold night in 1989. On 29 November, two police officers on duty near the border of Germany in an area called Eupen were about to have the most incredible encounter. Eupen itself is a small city, located in the province of Liege, in eastern Belgium. It's a popular destination for hikers, cyclists and other tourists looking to soak in some of its picturesque surroundings and rich heritage. On this night, however, Officers Hubert Von Montigny and Heinrich Nicoll were about to spot something quite exceptional. It was around 5.30 p.m., and the officers driving down the highway some 3km (1.8 miles) outside of Eupen, surrounded by fields shrouded in the darkness of a winter's night, were startled by a sudden light illuminating a patch of the field. There, hovering in the sky above, was a triangular-shaped craft, unlike anything they had ever seen before, or perhaps ever would again, its eerie quietness very much apparent. It was reportedly 30m (100ft) long on all sides, hanging in place, or if moving at all, doing so quietly, beams of light shining down in columns from each corner and with a light in the centre, red in colour, flashing.

Roermond
Herentals
Mol
Bree
Beringen
Genk
Aarschot
Hasselt
Heerlen
Maastricht
Sint-
Truiden
BELGIUM
3rd sighting,
February 1990
4th sighting,
30–31 March 1990
Ramillies
Eupen
Liège
Verviers
2nd sighting,
11 December 1989
Eghezée
1st sighting,
19 November 1989
Lake
Gileppe
Namur
Durbuy
Liège
N
Ciney
March-en-
Famenne
15 miles
15 kilometres

Speaking after the event, Heinrich was quoted as saying: 'We saw a large triangular platform, and underneath it three powerful lights, and in the middle, there was a flashing red light. The object made no noise.'

The trained observers were stunned: the object's movements just didn't quite work in the same way those of a conventional aircraft would. A helicopter can hover, but with incredible noise and disturbance to anything in the path of its blades; an aircraft like a plane would be in constant motion, accompanied by the familiar whirr of its engines. The difference in this craft was unmistakable, even in the dark of the night, its incredible shape amplified by the bright lights. The craft eventually moved off silently away in the direction of Lake Gileppe and the Gileppe Dam. Many civilians also spotted it, and it reportedly stayed hovering over that area for an hour. Reports varied. Some said the object stopped and hovered over their homes, others felt it followed their cars, and a group of friends out walking together spotted the object, and reported the same thing that the two police officers had shortly before. Some investigators believe that the spread of sightings, the number of witnesses and some of the testimony could indicate that there was more than one craft. This has never been verified and is still just speculation.

This was not the end of the incident. Multiple further events would take place between then and April 1990. Some reports of similar objects lacking sufficient details were made of triangular craft on 1 December. Days later, on 11 December 1989, the Gilmard family were in their car driving between Eghezee and Ramillies, when an object, similar to that seen in Eupen, appeared overhead. A large, triangular-shaped craft cruised silently, stopping in a hover above their heads. The father of the family, Pierre Gilmard, was interviewed about the sighting and he said: 'We were driving home when we saw a huge, triangular craft hovering above us. It had three white lights at each corner and a red light in the centre. It followed us for several kilometres, completely silent. We were all terrified.'

What I love about this event is not the testimony of the family, but that their young son, Frederic, was able to add to their story by including some drawings of what they saw. Not only did his drawing depict the triangular object, but he drew three separate views of the craft, which corroborated other witness statements about the various shapes in reports of the exotic objects moving around overhead. Overall, more than twenty witnesses would report sightings of similar objects on 11 December.

The sightings continued into the new year, as more triangular UFOs were reported from February 1990 and into March, including witnesses seeing silent objects floating over Liege.

The most spectacular of the later sightings occured in late March, overnight on 30 March and into the early hours of 31 March. It was around 5.45 p.m., and Lieutenant Colonel André Amond and his wife were enjoying a drive near the village of Ramillies when they noticed from their car windows a peculiar looking object in the sky. There, against the spring sky, was a large, triangular craft with the same three bright lights in each corner, similar to the objects that had been appearing over Belgium for six months now. Until then, it had been civilians and police officers reporting sightings, now a high-ranking military official reported seeing the remarkable craft. The Belgian UFO reporting network, SOBEPS, quoted Lieutenant Colonel Amond as saying;

RIGHT: Triangular crafts were spotted in various locations from November 1989 until March 1990.

*The object was of a triangular shape with rounded angles. At each angle, there was a very strong white light which did not dazzle. In the middle of the lower surface, there was a blinking, slightly orange-red light, more intense than the others. The object moved very slowly, without the slightest noise.*

This sighting was reported along with those of many other civilians at the same time. It was the beginning of the most well-documented of all the nights in the wave of sightings. Around 11 p.m. that evening, the military was about to get involved; after picking up multiple objects on their radar, they had no other choice. Not just one radar operator, but multiple stations had now picked up objects, displaying unusual aircraft characteristics, including rapid acceleration, deceleration and changes in altitude.

The matter escalated from mere sightings and testimony from the public to a potential security threat, and two F-16s were scrambled by the Belgian Air Force to attempt an intercept. In common with many other attempts by pilots around the globe over the decades, as they approached the targets, the experienced pilots had trouble locking on to the objects. There were around nine confirmed radar lock-ons, with one unnamed pilot saying: 'We could lock on the target for just a few seconds. Our radar systems were reacting very strangely, and the object seemed to move in a way that defied the laws of physics.'

Immediately after, analysis of radar data and other sensor systems showed objects performing manoeuvres that our earthbound aircraft just could not possibly manage. Going from around 250km/h (150 mph) to more than 1,600km/h (1,000 mph) in seconds, would result in forces that would likely cause catastrophic failures in any craft that we know of, not to mention in any potential occupants .

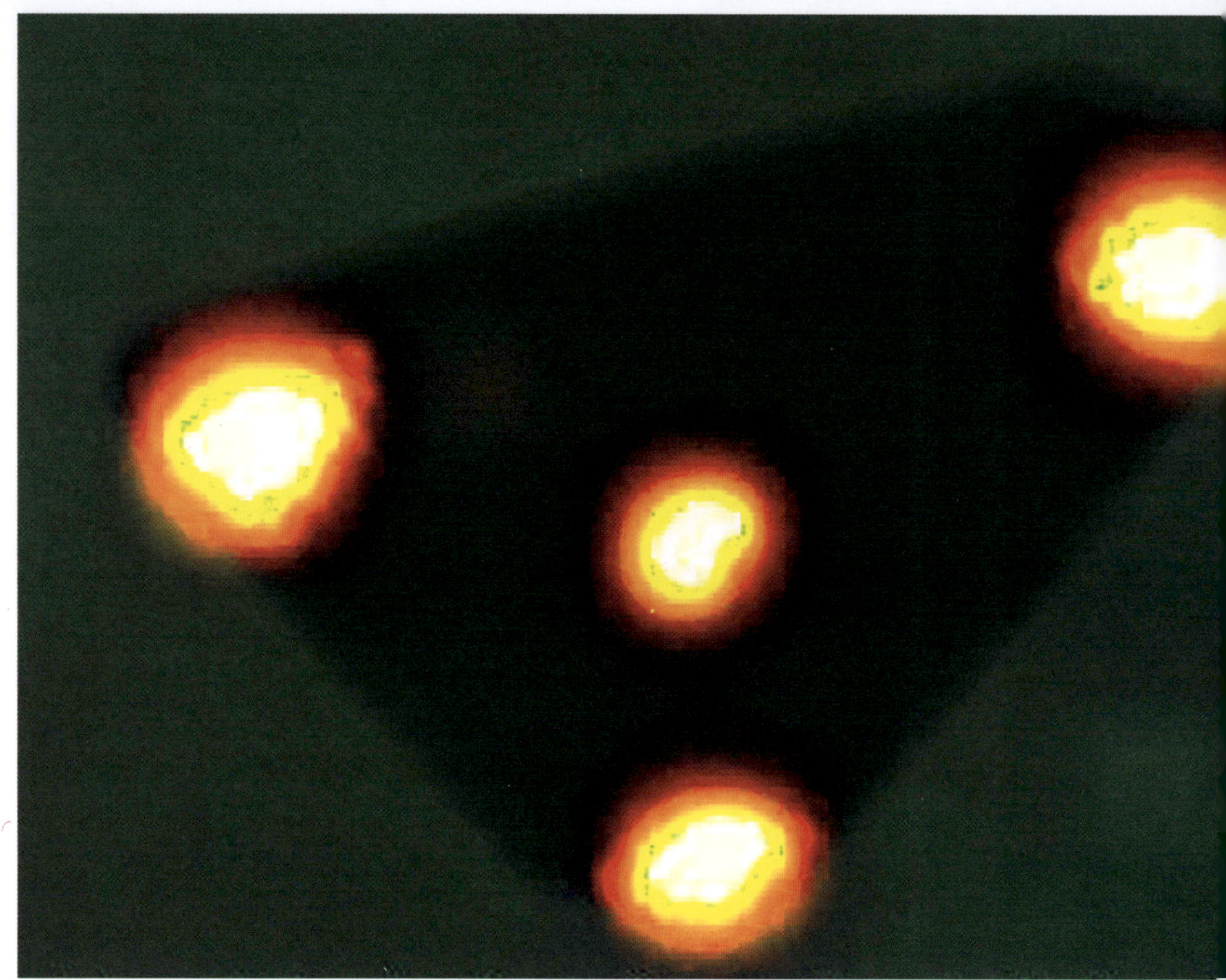

With the wave of sightings having been consistently in the public mind since late November (so now in its sixth month), along now with the military witnesses and response, the media finally became interested. A picture emerged by a photographer known as Patrick M., which became famously attached to this Belgian 'wave'. It gained a lot of notoriety in the UFO world and with the media, as it showed one of the alleged triangles from underneath in spectacularly close fashion. For years it was given pride of place in many a documentary, article or report, but in 2011 the photographer came forward to admit the photograph was a hoax, made with simple polystyrene and lamps at the time to see who could be fooled. While this is disappointing, it should not take away from the many genuine reports made of the event, not least the attempted failed intercepts by the Belgian Air Force of the unknown objects.

The events continued, though no night was quite as spectacular as that of late March 1990, and by the end of 1991, reports from the public had tailed off altogether. In one of several press conferences about the event, Major General Wilfried De Brouwer, who was the Chief of Operations for the Belgian Air Force during the time of the sightings commented:

*The UFOs were able to outmanoeuvre our F-16s, disappearing from radar and reappearing instantly elsewhere . . . We have systematically attempted to identify the phenomena reported by our pilots, radar operators, and civilians. The results are inconclusive and puzzling.*

LEFT: The infamous UFO photographed by Patrick M. was revealed to be a fake.

BELOW: A number of sightings took place over or near the village of Ramillies.

This event has so much data, so many sets of eyes from the ordinary public to trained observers like police officers and military personnel. Could so many people be wrong, be misidentifying something more prosaic, not once, but over and over again? Some sceptics of the event suggest it was some sort of mass hysteria, with one misidentification of a possible downed Soviet satellite beginning a chain reaction of people wanting to see something that just wasn't there. Others have suggested that maybe this was a kind of test aircraft, military or private, even belonging to the United States. That wouldn't make a lot of sense in this circumstance; to bring out multiple craft more than once over such a prolonged period would be downright reckless and irresponsible. At its heart, there are so many testimonies of the same type of craft, the same lights, radar data tracking incredible speeds, and the same movements, that it's hard to believe that hundreds of witnesses (with perhaps thousands more going unreported) could all be so wrong. The Belgian UFO wave will retain a special place in UFOlogy. Maybe the mystery of another wave, with today's social media, mobile phones and instant news, could be cracked open in a big way.

LEFT: The first UFO sighting was observed over Eupen, in east Belgium.

| *Tehran Province, Iran* | 35.4524° N, 51.2911° E |
| --- | --- |

# TEHRAN

Close encounters in the skies of Iran

In 1976, the city of Tehran, the capital of Iran, was home to around 4.5 million people. Western influence had touched the land, with modernization, rapid urban growth and the shoots of industrialization shaping a new future. This delicate balance of the traditional and the modern made for a rich environment with art galleries, theatres, shops and more adorning the landscape as its populous made its way around the busy streets. While the 1979 Iranian Revolution was still three years away, Tehran was a city under the strain of political change. However, late on 18 September 1976, the city would feel a different unease set in, as an incredible event was about to unfold over it.

It was shortly before midnight on a cool desert night, with a clear sky showcasing the Milky Way above, that citizens of Tehran were witness to an astonishing site. A bright light, too bright or close to be a star, was moving in the space above them. It was at a low altitude, circling the city, as if looking for something. It startled people so much that they started making calls to the local police station; there were several calls in the space of forty-five minutes, some even finding their way to Air Traffic Control (ATC) at the nearby Mehrabad International Airport. One worker at ATC, Houssain Pirouzi, received multiple calls from concerned civilians, so he decided to move it further up the chain. He even had a visual himself of the strange object, describing it as changing colours and shape. His own radar was down for maintenance at the time, so he had no radar sight of his own, just his eyes. Noting at first that it appeared to be rectangular, he corrected this to likely be cylindrical. Pirouzi had a job to do before he could call anything in, dealing with four commercial airliners over Tehran. After an hour, realising that this was something not only strange but potentially hazardous to air traffic, Pirouzi contacted the Imperial Iranian Air Force who then scrambled an F-4 Phantom II jet to take a closer look.

This first jet was piloted by Lieutenant Yadi Nazeri who, along with his backseat weapons officer, took to the sky at 1.30 a.m., streaking towards to the large object, which by now had been seen more than a 100km (70 miles) away. As Lieutenant Nazeri and his fellow officer approached the object, before they could even attempt to engage in any way with the glowing light in front of them, their systems began to malfunction at a distance of 25 nautical miles. Radio communications stopped working and became garbled

First F-4 flight path
Second F-4 flight path
UFO flight path
Caspian Sea
Rasht
Zanjan
Qazvin
Sighting
Sighting
Karaj
Mehrabad International Airport
Tehran
Rey
Second UFO
UFO Landing site
Varamin
IRAN
Shahrokhi air base
Hamadan
Saveh
Qom
Malayer
Arak
Kashan
Tehran
N
50 miles
50 kilometres

and they could no longer speak to their counterparts on the ground. Other instruments important for staying in the air safely began to glitch. They decided to get away from the object, and, having gained some distance from it, their systems returned to normal. Was the object itself jamming their systems in a display of superiority? Was there some sort of field around the object that as a consequence of the distance between them was stopping their instrumentation from operating correctly? One could only guess.

A short time later in those still early hours of 19 September, at around 1.40 a.m., the Imperial Iranian Air Force sent another jet out, led this time by Squadron Commander Parviz Jafari, accompanied by his backseat systems operator Jalal Damirian. They took another F-4 Phantom II out towards the still circling object. As he approached, Jafari, could make out some detail, later describing the craft as:

*. . . flashing with intense red, green, orange and blue lights. So bright that I was not able to see its body. The lights formed a diamond shape. Just brilliant lights. No solid structure could be seen through or around them. The sequence of flashes was extremely fast, like a strobe light. Maybe the lights were only one part of a bigger object which we couldn't see. There was no way to know.*

Much like the first failed attempt to engage the object, Jafari's aircraft suffered similar issues, with its systems starting to malfunction as they grew closer to the strange glowing object. The object made incredible manoeuvres at seemingly impossible speeds as they approached, appearing to move so fast as to almost vanish and reappear at another place. The object also stopped, hovering in place and defying the laws of gravity, at least as we know them. By this time, radar had managed to lock onto the object, confirming that there was indeed some sort of solid object there, so it couldn't have just been some form of energy, ball lighting or the sort.

Things, however, took a sudden turn, as on approach to the object, Jafar noticed that the glowing craft had released a smaller, bright object from underneath it, which was heading straight for them at speed. A missile? A drone of some kind? With the time to investigate rapidly running out, the pilot thought about using a heat-seeking missile to intercept whatever this was approaching his aircraft, but his systems were not working. There was no defence. As quickly as it was heading for him, this smaller object stopped and began to retreat back to the larger object it had come from. The two pilots in the F-4 Phantom were amazed, equal parts in awe and in fear of what they were encountering. Another bright object then left the main craft, descending closer to the ground, illuminating the surrounding area for as far as an estimated 3 square km (1.8 square miles). It appeared to land on the desert below; however, the pilots could not investigate further, as on approach their systems malfunctioned. (It is interesting to note that the area was investigated the following day but nothing was found on the ground.)The large glowing object then ascended up into the night sky and sped off, leaving a trail of light, it moved so fast. As all this happened, Jafari and his fellow officer again experienced a failure in their

LEFT: Iran's capital city Tehran sits in the foothills of the Alborz Mountains.

LEFT: Major Parviz Jafaris aircraft seemed to malfunction as it got closer to the craft.

RIGHT: An artist's rendering of the events.

communications; at the same time a commercial airliner in the area also reported a communications failure, but did not report seeing the UFO.

With the craft seemingly gone, Parviz Jafari turned his craft back towards home base, a confusing return trip as Damirian and he tried to process everything that had just happened. No amount of training or knowledge of combat situations could help the two pilots understand what had just happened. The following morning, as is protocol, the pilots debriefed the Air Force on what had gone on just hours before. Interestingly, as well as the Iranian officials present, two Americans, Colonel Olin Mooy and Colonel Frank McKenzie of the US Air Force, who were stationed in the area at the time, listened in. They were a part of the US Military Assistance and Advisory group (MAAG). Colonel Mooy prepared a teletype message of the incident to report back to his own superiors and the message made its way to multiple government offices, including the CIA, NSA and the Pentagon.

Speaking to Leslie Kean for her book *UFOs – Generals, Pilots, and Government Officials Go on the Record*, Jafari said 'To this day, I don't know what I saw. But for sure,

it was not an aircraft. It was not a flying object that human beings on earth can make. It moved way too fast. Imagine, I was looking at it about 70 miles [around 100km] out, and it jumped all of a sudden to 10 [degrees] to my right. This 10 [degrees] represented about 6.7 miles [10km] per moment, and I don't say per second, because it was much less than a second.'

Some sceptics have surmised that on that strange night in 1976, the pilots, civilians and military personnel combined multiple misidentifications to come up with the incredible event. These include the bright star being the planet Jupiter and the equipment failures being down to pilot error. Surely not! What about all those civilians, the radar data, the close proximity event? The debunking conclusions seem more of a stretch than anything more exotic?

To this day, the event remains one of the most incredible close encounters documented by any military personnel worldwide.

| *Pará, Brazil* | *Multiple* |
|---|---|

# COLARES

Mass sightings in lead to a military report

In the North Region of Brazil, there is a tranquil island called Colares, located in the largest river delta in the world, the Amazon River Delta. It has a population now of roughly 30,000 people, which can go up or down throughout the year depending on the local conditions and migration. As with many parts of Brazil, it is visited by tourists who want to explore its vast rainforests and stunning beaches. However, it is for the infamous and somewhat terrifying UFO flap of 1977 that it is mostly known.

While UFO events often happen over a short period of time, frequently mere minutes or hours, in the history of monitoring UFOs the event at Colares and the surrounding region is one that is unique, in that the UFO encounters happened to many people over not days or weeks, but months. In early August 1977, things started off with locals seeing lights in the sky. As the nights went on, more people across the island managed to catch a glimpse of these bright objects in the sky. At times, the objects would stay hovering, still against the blackness; other witnesses reported in the early days that the objects would move erratically, unlike any conventional aircraft that could be seen in the skies above. Some reports suggested that the craft emitted strong beams of light. By late August these beams of light were becoming a concern, not only appearing to scan the ground as if mapping or looking for something, but as revealed in a trickle of shocking reports to the Brazilian authorities, people were being struck by the lights and they were causing injury. Doctors were treating a variety of burns, lesions and bruises, and many of the victims were found to have extremely low levels of iron in their blood. Victims reported that the beams of light penetrated the roofs of their homes, coming through solid materials and striking them as they sat in their living rooms.

Rather than fade away or fizzle out, the sightings not only increased in number but intensified, becoming more of a danger to human life as time passed. It got so bad that come late October, the Brazilian military had to step in as reports poured in from alarmed locals. *Operação Prato*, 'Operation Plate/Saucer' began: so many reports had been received that the air force had to do something. Led by Captain Uyrange Hollanda, at the time a non-believer in UFOs, they made their way to the island to begin collecting data on this incredible situation.

Baía do Gurupi
Benevides
PARÁ
Marajo Bay
Sighting
Município of Vigia
Colares
Sighting
Santo Antônio
do Ubintub
Sighting
Baía do
Sol-Mosqueiro
Sighting
Sighting
Chapéu
Virado-Mosqueiro
Campo
Cerrado
Sighting
Sighting
Santo Antônio
do Tauá
BRAZIL
Sighting
Castanhal
Sighting
Benevides
Belem Air Base
PARÁ
Belém
Rio Guamá
Colares
N
20 miles
20 kilometres

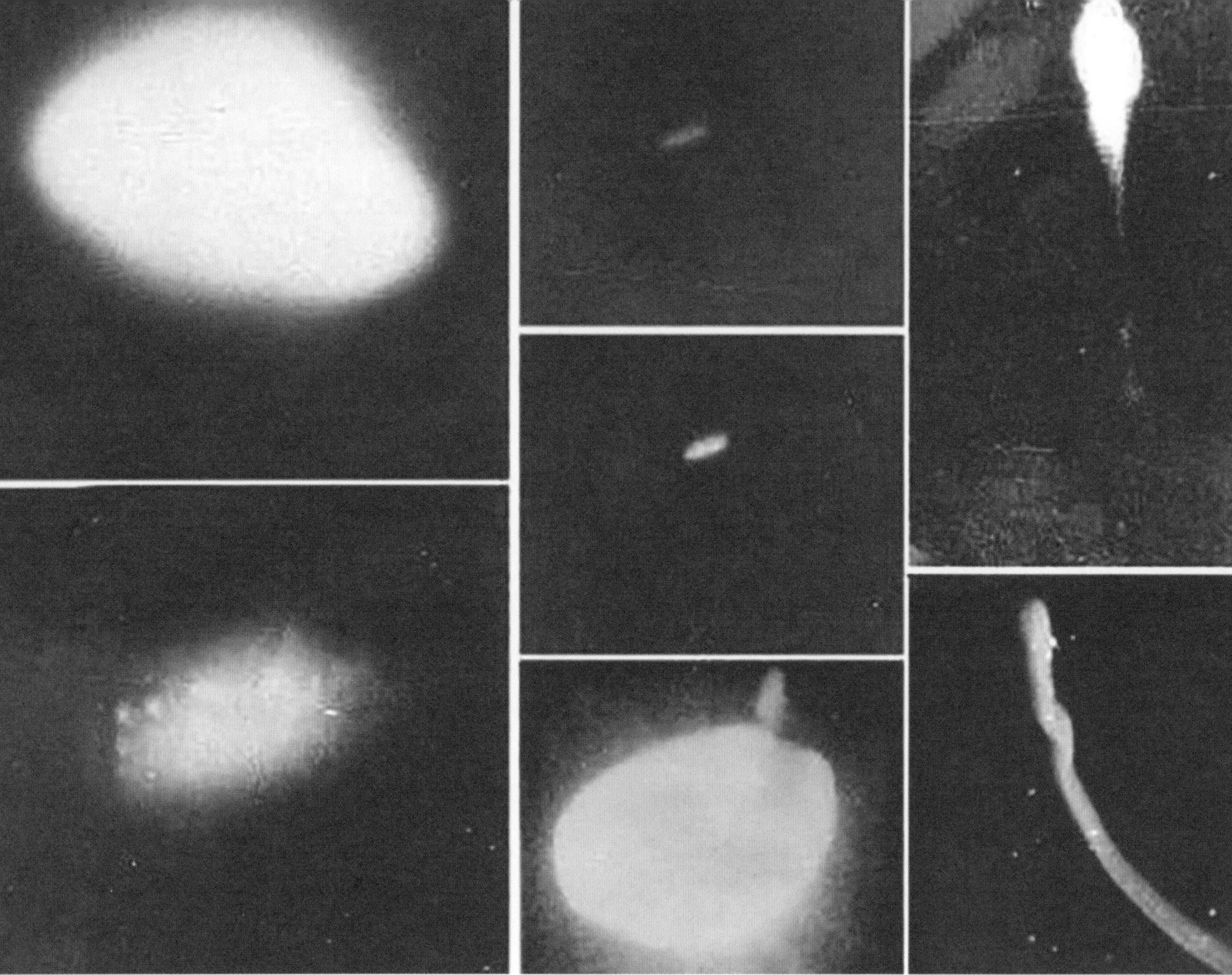

November arrived on Colares and the objects were still present, taking the events into a fourth month, now with the military there to observe and report on it. During the month, the military spoke to witnesses on the ground, hearing their testimonies. They were also gathering data using their own equipment, including radar which gave them a new perspective on the objects that the eye witnesses couldn't. Whether they believed the witnesses or not mattered little, especially as they had to report that their own aircraft were being followed and normally reliable instruments had been failing and malfunctioning. On 16 November, Captain Hollanda, along with other witnesses, saw one of the objects for himself. The official report stated it was 'a large, cigar-shaped object, with lights flashing in rapid succession'. Many years later, in an interview released on video, Hollanda described seeing 'a large black disc' directly overhead with other military, no more than 500m (about 1640 ft) above them. It had a solid yellow/amber light in the middle and every now and then made a noise 'like a bike being pedalled backwards'. The object then shone an intense beam of light onto the ground that illuminated the surroundings. The light turned off, then back on every few seconds before the object finished its task and left. Hollanda would say later that at the time he knew he couldn't inform the public about the events; it had to remain classified.

By December, Operation Plate was over, and while the sightings hadn't stopped completely, they had reduced considerably from their peak in October/November. Of course, there was and continues to be a lasting impact on the people of Colares who were physically

LEFT: Photos of the various UFOs spotted over the Colares region in 1977.

RIGHT: An illustration of the triangle UFOs observed from the Operation Prato documents.

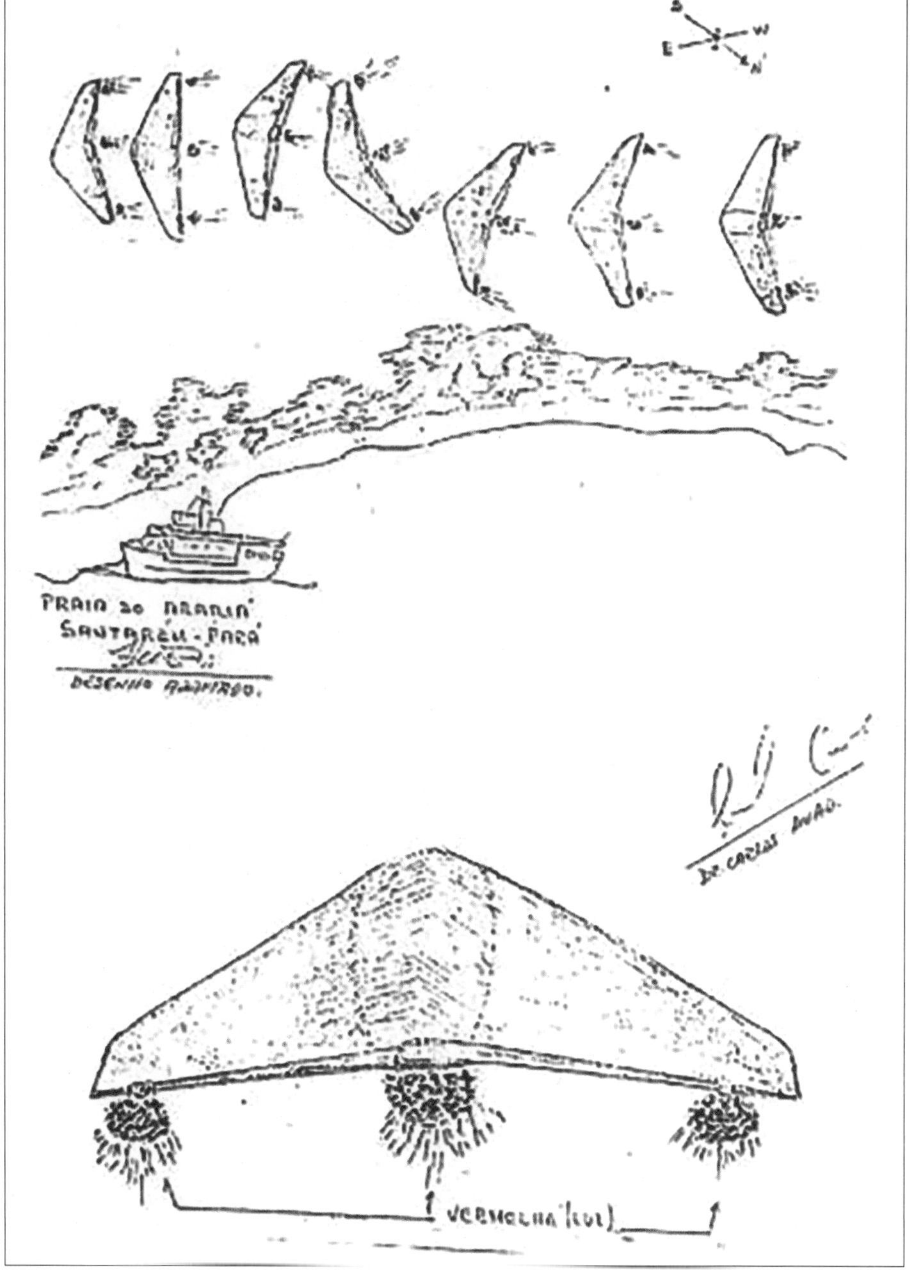

and emotionally scarred by months of uncertainty, attacks and the military presence. Leader of the military operation, Captain Hollanda, resigned from the Brazilian air force in 1978, due to the strain this event had taken on him emotionally, physically and mentally.

The case was kept classified and out of the public domain until 2004, when many years of pressure and persistence from UFO researchers paid off and some of the documents were declassified by the Brazilian air force. The reports, which although contained some of the data collected, pictures, witness statements and conclusions drawn at the time, are not complete, with many redactions still in place to hide details that could harm national security. They have nevertheless been pored over many times since their public reveal.

So what happened to the unsuspecting people of Colares over those months in the second half of 1977? Many theories have been put forward:

RIGHT: Colares is a small island situated in the Amazon River Delta, in the north of Brazil.

- Mass hysteria? This is doubtful given the sheer volume of reports, medical records and data collected.
- Was this some sort of secret government project to scare its own people?
- Was it a foreign government carrying out these 'raids' with top secret tech? It's probably not a surprise to many to learn that rumours have long persisted that the US military were involved at the time in an operation to collect data, and these rumours suggest that important video and other evidence has to this day been kept locked away on US soil. This was confirmed by legendary reporter George Knapp on his own podcast in 2024, in which he says he has seen files and documents on the Colares case.
- Or indeed, was this a genuine case of a non-human intelligence carrying out some sort of attack and surveillance on a human population?

It doesn't seem to line-up with your typical low key abduction scenarios reported throughout history.

What we know for certain is that hundreds of people were terrorized by unknown objects over many months. Some were injured or became ill due to the strange lights that appeared to target them. The case stands as one of the most well-documented instances of widespread health damage linked to UFO encounters. But, as with so many other unexplained phenomena, the full truth may remain locked away, buried in the vaults of some 'three-letter agency', and only time will reveal whether the answers will ever come to light.

| *Río Negro, Argentina* | 41.0335° S, 71.0733° W |
|---|---|

# SAN CARLOS DE BARILOCHE

A pilot's unusual encounter as he lands his plane

On 31 July 1995, Aeorlinas Argentinas (Argentine Airlines) Flight 674 was making its final approach to land at Teniente Luis Candelaria International Airport, in San Carlos de Bariloche, Argentina. It had been a pretty standard domestic flight, having left Buenos Aires around two hours earlier. The bright daylight of take-off was now replaced by a clear night sky as Captain Jorge Polanco and his flight crew made final preparations to land the aircraft. It's worth noting that at this time the only two objects in the sky on the Air Traffic Control's (ATC) radar were Flight 674 and a military jet several miles away.

The aircraft, a Boeing 727, was on approach at around 8.15 p.m., when Captain Jorge Polanco (along with others on board) noticed a bright light. Concerned that there should have been no traffic and with nothing registering on his systems, he radioed to ATC on the ground to ask if they had noted this other aircraft on their radar. While nothing other than Flight 674 and the military jet that wasn't close by was visible, something could still show up on ATC sensors. Captain Polanco proceeded in his descent with caution, unsure what this other object in the vicinity was, his already heightened state of awareness that comes with any pilot, especially during take-offs and landing, raised even more.

By now, the passengers on board had noticed the bright light outside; against the dark of the night sky they couldn't help but notice it. Melina Mazzolina, a passenger on board, was interviewed after the event and said that through her window she could see the object and from her perspective it had blue and orange lights, 'People were very nervous, they didn't know what was happening. Everyone chatted inside and talked…'

The strange object was now dangerously close to the aircraft, its brilliant lights making it difficult to tell just how close it was; it's proximity made it difficult to see anything other than the light. Captain Polanco described how it appeared to him to have an orange light on top, with green lights around the outside. It was too difficult to make out any more details, so the shape of the craft remained elusive, but there were no signs of wings or a means of propulsion. Despite the proximity of the object to the aircraft, on the radar system on the ground there was still no sign of the object.

Things then took a dangerous turn when on the ground the runway lights went off, and a widespread power cut in the city below meant that everything was in darkness. Captain

Plane's route
UFO flight path
Bariloche
NEUQUÉN
ARGENTINA
Buenos Aires
Lago Nahuel Huapi
Mountain Military School
Bariloche
Squadron 34 National Military Base
Teniente Luis Candelaria International Airport
RÍO NEGRO
N
10 miles
10 kilometres

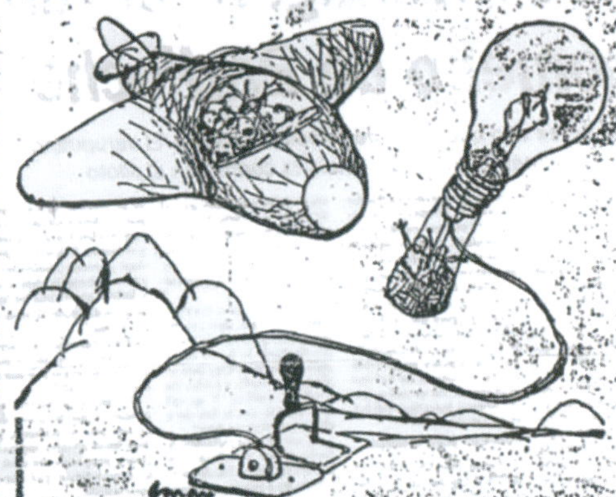

DICEN QUE LO SIGUIO UNA LUZ BLANCA INTENSA

# Un extraño fenómeno complicó el vuelo de un avión en Bariloche

*Fue el lunes a las 20.15. El piloto del vuelo 674 de Aerolíneas Argentinas dijo que la luz "parecía que iba a chocar el aparato, pero se detuvo a unos cien metros de la nave". En ese momento había un apagón en tierra y el personal de la torre del aeropuerto dijo que "los instrumentos de control se enloquecieron".*

Una luz intensa, de procedencia no identificada, siguió durante 15 minutos a un avión de Aerolíneas Argentinas que se aproximaba al Aeropuerto de Bariloche para aterrizar. Durante la aparición del fenómeno –que coincidió con un apagón en toda la ciudad– fallaron los instrumentos de la torre de control. Mucha gente dijo que lo había visto.

El hecho ocurrió el lunes a las 20.15, cuando el vuelo 674 de Aerolíneas, comandado por el piloto Jorge Polanco, iniciaba las maniobras de aproximación. Quince minutos antes de la hora prevista para el aterrizaje, un corte de luz en el aeropuerto obligó al aparato a permanecer en espera durante diez minutos, hasta que se restableció la energía.

En ese momento comenzó a acercarse una luz al avión, por lo que Polanco preguntó a la torre de control si había otro aparato "con rumbo convergente" al aeropuerto. "Le dijimos que no –contó a Clarín el jefe de turno, suboficial principal Daniel García–. Pero al mismo tiempo vimos que se acercaba al avión una luz entre ámbar y blanca, una especie de estrella pero bastante más grande y con una luz de lo más intensa".

Polanco comentó a Clarín que "parecía que la luz iba a chocar con nuestra nave, pero se detuvo a unos 100 metros de nosotros" (ver Tenía forma...). El piloto relató que "la luz hizo un giro extraño acompañando el viraje del avión, y se colocó en forma paralela, a 100 metros". El ingeniero de vuelo Jorge Allende dijo que "el objeto venía a una velocidad de unos 2.000 km/h" y que "tanto esa velocidad como el movimiento del

...tó que posteriormente, "la tripulación de Gendarmería nos dijo que creían que esa luz nos iba a chocar". El mayor Jorge Oviedo, máxima autoridad del aeropuerto, dijo que "el personal de meteorología, de la torre de control, el piloto y la tripulación del avión avistaron un ovni".

Durante el avistaje, el suboficial ayudante Blanco y el cabo principal informaron a García que "se había enloquecido" el instrumental de control. A bordo del avión, según el piloto, los aparatos funcionaban bien. Pero en la torre "algunos instrumentos empezaron a moverse para un lado y para el otro sin ningún sentido", indicó García.

Otro apagón y nervios

Nahuel Huapi, y entonces vimos que la luz se le acercaba mucho más". El aparato se mantuvo sobrevolando la zona a 3.000 metros hasta que se autorizó el aterrizaje. Polanco señaló: "Al vernos descender se perdió a toda velocidad hacia el sudeste".

Carlos Angueira, presidente de la Asociación Amigos de la Astronomía, "descartó que haya sido un meteorito, porque no se detienen en el aire y siguen una trayectoria de parábola. Tampoco puede ser un fenómeno de refracción, de reflejos en nubes con cristales de hielo".

Con los mismos datos pero con la experiencia vivida todavía fresca, el piloto del avión se animó a describir cómo se sentía cuando detuvo la máquina: "Al aterrizar tuve que esperar cinco minutos en la cabina, porque tenía el corazón en la boca".

*Mariano Cordero (desde Bariloche) y Sibila Camps*

ABOVE: Captain Jorge Polanco's experience was reported in the national press.

RIGHT: San Carlos de Bariloche in situated in Patagonia, surrounded by the Andes mountains.

Polanco had to think quickly, as he could now no longer see where to land. Below on the runway, the ground crew, which included one Ruben Breza, tried to restore power but couldn't get the emergency lights to stay on without malfunctioning, so they informed the ATC that the pilot should be instructed to abort his landing.

When the object moved away from his aircraft and shot off into the distance, Captain Polanco was relieved to see the city of Bariloche suddenly light up below him, with the power restored. During the power cut, many witnesses on the ground below had caught sight of the strange light in the sky, including a police officer who later corroborated Jorge Polanco's story.

By the night after the encounter, Jorge Polanco had written his report on the encounter and returned to Buenos Aires on the same plane. When asked about the event many years later in an interview for *La Nación*, he said that the following day 'I felt like I had had all the

energy taken from me. Do you know when you have a liver attack or when you get punched a lot? My whole body hurt. That night I told my wife at the time and she didn't believe me, she told me to ease up on the wine.'

There is little evidence from this event, other than the testimony of those who were caught up in a rather terrifying encounter. In the same interview with *La Nación*, Captain Polanco put forward this theory: 'About thirty nuclear physicists were on my plane going to an event in Barlioche. I think that without realizing it, there is another world that is controlling and supervising us so that we do not kill each other.'

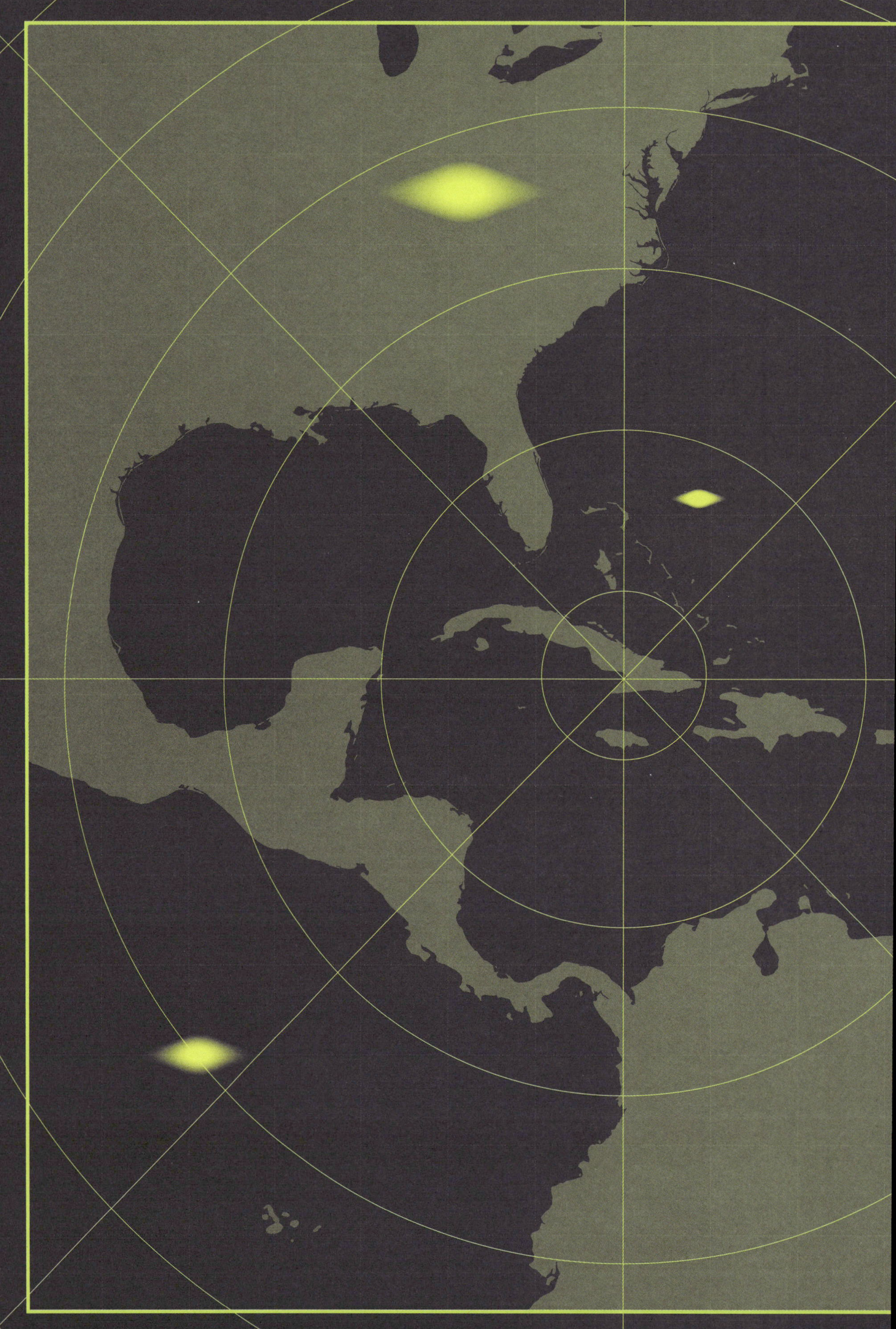

# Chapter 4

# CIVILIAN

| Provence, France | 43.3123° N, 6.2848° E |
|---|---|

# TRANS-EN-PROVENCE

A flying saucer pays a brief visit to a Provençale farm

The small village of Trans-en-Provence is located in the Var department (an administrative division) in southeastern France. The wider area is known for its beautiful Mediterranean coastline with popular holiday destinations such as Saint-Tropez, as well as many vineyards and historical villages. While those who travel to the area from afar may be there to enjoy its weather and amenities, those more local, when asked about the subject of UFOs, tell of an incident some would compare to being their own 'Roswell'.

The date was 8 January 1981, and though cold on this winter's day, the skies were mostly clear, ideal for a UFO sighting you would think. But, on this occasion, the witness's eyes were not drawn to an object hovering in the sky or performing incredible manoeuvres some distance away. No, this was something on the ground, right in front and only metres away from our witness, fifty-five-year-old local farmer, Renato Nicolai.

Renato told police in his report that he had heard a noise, a strange noise, a faint whistling to the east, which drew his attention away from the concrete water pump shelter he was building. As he turned to look behind him, there in his garden on this wintery late afternoon, was a flying saucer, descending from the height of a nearby pine tree to land. It sat there for around thirty seconds before it raised up off the ground, and disappeared off into the distance at speed, tilting as it left (a commonly observed trait of saucers' position of travel).

Speaking in an official report to the French government agency for UFO studies at the time, GEPAN (Groupe d'Études des Phénomènes Aérospatiaux Non-identifiés), Renato said: 'The object had the shape of two saucers, one inverted on top of the other. It must have measured about 1.5m (5ft) in height and had a diameter of about 2.5m (8ft). The object, which was grey in colour, stood near the edge of my field about 50m (165ft) from my house. It made a slight whistling sound and then took off.'

As it rose, he noted what seemed to be small feet or reactors underneath; he couldn't be sure what they were but guessed they were around 20cm (8in) at most in length. The craft had few other distinguishing features. In awe of what he had just seen, he had to wait until his wife returned home to tell someone. She was bemused as he recounted this unlikely encounter and initially thought he was joking. As much as he assured her of the validity of the story, she thought it more likely he had been working too hard, and was suffering from exhaustion or heat stroke.

Wooded hills

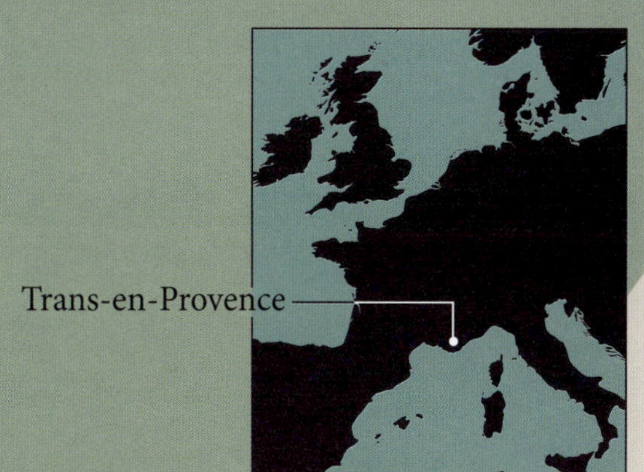
Trans-en-Provence

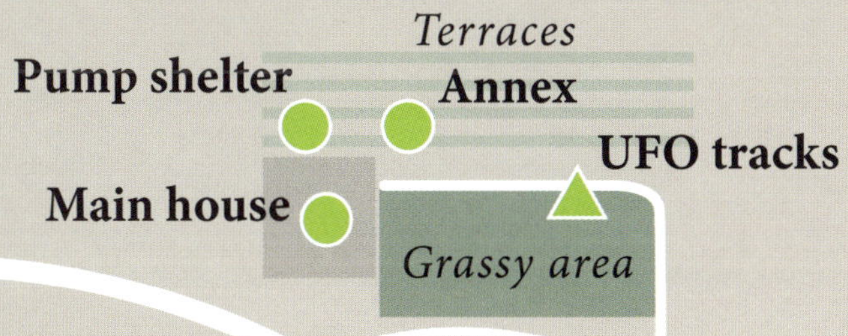
Terraces
Pump shelter
Annex
UFO tracks
Main house
Grassy area

FRANCE
Vallée de la Rise

The following morning in the light of day, they went out to study the exact spot the craft had landed and settled the previous evening and found definite signs that something had been there, so Renato and his wife reported it to the police who, along with some scientists, came out to collect samples and statements.

Investigation results from the craft landing site showed compression of soil indicating an object of 3.5–4.5 tonnes (4–5 tons) had landed there. Police noted also that there seemed to be a circular impression on the ground, around 2m (6ft) in diameter, roughly consistent with Renato's observations..

GEPAN was notified on the 10 January 1981 and began its own investigation. It also collected soil and plant samples from the immediate area. Over the months that followed, results came back to add weight to the notion that something strange had almost certainly happened in the garden of Renato's farmhouse. Soil analysis carried out at various facilities showed that there were signs of thermal and mechanical pressure, the soil itself appearing 'baked' and altered. Plants at the site had been damaged due to heating, perhaps because

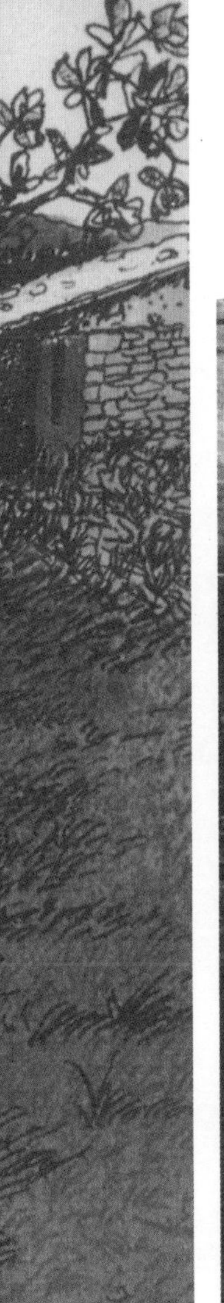

LEFT: The cover illustration of *Lumieres dans la Nuit*, August/September 1981 issue, depicting the UFO in Renato Niccolai's garden.

BELOW: The landing site. The letters indicate the indentations from the craft in the soil.

of microwave energy, surmised researcher Dr Peter Sturrock, a Professor of Astrophysics at Stanford University. The plants analysed by Dr Michel Bounias, at INRA (National Institute of Agronomy Research) came back to show, incredibly, that they had undergone significant bio-chemical changes, with levels of chlorophyll reduced by 30–50 per cent, which would indicate exposure to an electromagnetic field. Describing the young leaves to a journalist from *France-Soir* magazine in 1983, Bounias said: 'From an anatomical and physiological point, the (leaves) had all the characteristics of their age, but they presented the biochemical characteristics of leaves of an advanced age: old leaves! And that doesn't resemble anything that we know on our planet.'

In the months that followed, a report was released from GEPAN, highlighting the unusual nature of the changes, both physical and biochemical, that the soil and plants had undergone.

UFO researcher Jean-Jacques Velasco cites this as one of the best-documented and researched UFO cases of modern times , as the nature of evidence collected indicates that the craft had had a clear effect on its immediate surroundings. Speaking in 2004, Mr Velasco

is quoted as saying, 'The Trans-en-Provence case is unique due to the rigorous scientific methodology applied to the investigation. The physical and biological evidence collected supports the credibility of the witness's testimony and indicates that a highly unusual event took place.'

With this case having only one witness to it, there isn't much evidence to prove either way what truly happened to Renato Nicolai in early January 1981. Locals, upon hearing of his report, called him a 'crazy UFO guy' but he was adamant at the time that he wasn't saying he had seen aliens, or UFOs, just that he had seen something that he couldn't explain. Something potentially remarkable. He had sketched it out himself, a crude drawing showing that classic saucer shape, while other artists chipped in with more crafted examples.

Renato himself at first thought that maybe it was some sort of experimental aircraft from the Cannet-des-maures air base, which was located around 15km (9 miles) away. If indeed this was some sort of advanced human technology, it confused and perplexed our farmer. Could it be technology we had reversed-engineered ourselves from something more exotic? Or did Mr Nicolai come in close contact, only for less than a minute, with something non-human.

ABOVE: Trans-en-Provence is known as the 'Roswell of France' after the 1981 incident.

| *Zhejiang Province, China* | 30.1612° N, 120.2638° E |
|---|---|

# XIAOSHAN

## Trouble at the airport

Hangzhou is the capital city of Zhejiang Province in Eastern China and is home to Xiaoshan International Airport. Every year, millions of passengers pass through its doors on flights to many domestic and major destinations all around the globe. In 2010, more than fifteen million travellers boarded aircraft here, making it one of the busiest airports in the nation. In July they will have been happy to be jetting off, as the weather then is a real mixed bag, with intense heat, hurricanes and it is largely cloudy. Humidity is normally high, making the mid-thirty degrees Celsius (mid-nineties Fahrenheit) temperatures feel even warmer. However, this is balanced with heavy rainfalls and thunderstorms.

It was after 8.30 p.m. on 7 July 2010, a particularly cloudy, muggy day with rain breaking out intermittently, and spray flying off of the tarmac on both runways of the airport. While the weather was to be expected, what was far less expected was the radar contact picked up by staff on duty. On-duty manager at airport, Luo Miao-Xing, is quoted as saying: 'There was a suspected unidentified flying object in the airspace above the airport. All the other flights were redirected to nearby airports to ensure their safety.' When something that shouldn't be there appears on its screens, action has to be taken, swiftly. Eighteen flights were quickly diverted to neighbouring airports in Ningbo and Wuxi. The crew of a flight who were already on descent to the airport noticed the hovering red light in its path; a worrying sight for any pilot and crew. Hundreds of passengers were about to be inconvenienced too, as notifications rang around the terminals to let travellers know the airport was temporarily being shut down.

A little earlier that very afternoon, residents of Hangzhou had spotted an object in the sky, with some claiming to have taken pictures of a golden light, seemingly with a tail like you would see on a comet. Researchers believe it was likely to be unrelated and suspect it was an aircraft reflecting sunlight. However, some witnesses to the event beyond the airport did come forward. One local, Ma Shijun, was on an evening walk with his wife when they saw the object. He told local media:

*I felt a beam of light over my head. Looking up, I saw a streak of bright, white light flying across the sky, so I picked up the camera and took the photo. The time was 8:26 p.m. However, whether the object was a plane, or whether it was Xiaoshan Airport's UFO, I don't have a clear answer.*

Linping
CHINA
Qiantang River
Hangzhou
Hangzhou Xiaoshan
International Airport
Sighting
Xiaoshan
Qianqing
Hangzhou
N
5 miles
5 kilometres

Back on the tarmac, pilots preparing for take-off aborted their procedures, as confused passengers were asked to remain in their seats and await further news. According to reports, up to two thousand passengers were affected in some way by the unwelcome intrusion. China is a notoriously strict regime, so any news getting out of China is sparse, let alone witness statements from an alleged UFO event which has shut down an entire airport and caused a bit of a media frenzy. Various statements that did make it out revealing details such as the object was a round, a glowing orb and it moved erratically in the sky above the airport.

Unsurprisingly, the news spread quickly around local, regional and national news outlets. Theories ran wild, with speculation ranging from a US or Russian missile, an experimental aircraft or just some sort of atmospheric phenomenon (where have we heard that before?). There were some murmurings of it being a non-human explanation; the UFO topic is popular in China, with UFO clubs memberships running into the millions in the secretive society, albeit that these clubs are heavily monitored by the Chinese authorities.

The following day, the Civil Aviation Administration of China (CAAC) released a statement, under pressure given the nationwide coverage. It acknowledged that an unidentified object had indeed caused some disruption at the airport but remained light on any further details. It is likely they did not know much more than that themselves. On 9 July, only 48 hours on from the incident, an unnamed Chinese official commented that the unknown object had a 'military connection', but was not willing to give any more detail than that, saying that in future there would be more information released pending a further investigation, inferring that this was a military aircraft prototype of some description. This further

LEFT: This photo is claimed to have been taken by a resident in Xiaoshan at 9pm although some experts question it's authenticity.

ABOVE: Xiaoshan International Airport where the UFO was first spotted.

information as of today, has yet to come to light. Perhaps this was some sort of military exercise, maybe even one that had gone wrong, causing a test aircraft to veer wildly off its path and end up near the airport. A member of the Shanghai Observatory, Zhu Dayi, told the state-run newspaper *China Daily*, 'If the speed of the twinkling object is extremely high, it could be a military craft. But no conclusion can be drawn now, as the information is limited.'

It would not be uncommon for a state-run paper to publish quotes from officials wanting to play down any exotic explanations for this event. Even if it had been adversarial technology coming from a neighbouring super power, such as Russia or the United States, China wouldn't want to look weak in the eyes of its people. In the days, months and years that followed, multiple photos and videos of the alleged object have surfaced, with many being disproven as misidentifications or CGI hoaxes. What is for certain, is that an unidentified object, still to this day of unknown origin, stopped the operations of a major airport. For many this should be a wake-up call that aviation safety is at risk, whether unintentionally or not, from Unidentified Flying Objects and is worthy of further study.

Shortly after this event, there were further reports of Unidentified Objects in the region. On 15 July 2010, in Chongqing Municipality, multiple witnesses reported seeing four 'lanternlike objects' in formation, like a diamond, hovering in place above Shaping Park for around an hour. Reportedly, they eventually ascended to the sky and out of sight. Again, these were labelled as likely to be some sort of weather-related phenomena or misidentified rockets being launched. Many believe these sightings have kickstarted a more serious interest in the UFO phenomenon for the Chinese Government.

| *Washington State, USA* | 46.4827° N, 122.0801° W |
| --- | --- |

# MOUNT RAINIER

A term is born: 'flying saucer' enters the vocabulary

If there were many roots to the origins of the UFO story, then one of those would certainly begin with the Kenneth Arnold sighting from 24 June 1947. The world at this time was still reeling from the effects of the Second World War, millions of deaths were being mourned, and many countries were trying to get back on their feet, but the early signs of recovery were there. Financial aid packages were being put in place to help European countries rebuild, agricultural sectors were restoring their capabilities to produce crops for distribution and new governments were being put into place, in the wake of so much destruction, of so many weapons having been developed, deployed and used, none more so than the atomic bombs dropped on Hiroshima and Nagasaki less than two years prior in 1945. It was a fragile new age for the planet.

With this in mind, perhaps it shouldn't be a complete surprise to many that with the nuclear age dawning and incomprehensible destruction happening across the planet, this may have drawn the attention of some other civilisation(s) out there who were already keeping a close eye on a relatively new species in the universal scale of things. Only a few weeks before the events at Roswell, New Mexico (see page 14), a businessman, Kenneth Arnold was about to thrust himself into the UFO conversation for decades to come.

Kenneth was flying from the Washington city of Chehalis to a business meeting in Yakima in a small aircraft, a CallAir Model A-3. He wanted to stop on the way to help in the search for a missing United States Marine Corps (USMC) transport aircraft in the Mount Rainier area. While at an altitude just below 3,000m (10,000ft), a bright flash of light caught his eye, and not thinking anything other than it perhaps being the sun reflecting off another aircraft, it didn't bother him. That was until his vision settled, and he noticed that it wasn't another aircraft, at least not one he was familiar with. It was a chain of nine objects, travelling at phenomenal speed across the sky.

Safely back on the ground, this incredible sight prompted him to contact the local newspaper, the *Eastern Oregonian* in Pendleton, Oregon. The story was soon picking up attention of the media across the country. This story is where the term 'flying saucer' came from, although not directly from Kenneth Arnold himself. It's important to remember that this was really one of the first ever reported sightings of objects such as these, so there wasn't

CANADA
British
olumbia
Washington State
Mt.
Baker
Kenneth Arnold flight path
UFO flight path
UNITED
STATES OF
AMERICA
Seattle
Location of missing United
States Marine Corps
transport aircraft
Mt.
Rainier
Chehalis
Yakima
Approximate path
of the objects
WASHINGTON
Mt.
Adams
OREGON
Portland
N
30 miles
30 kilometres

the vocabulary and Mr Arnold had to come up with his own description of what he was seeing, what could he compare these objects too. He told journalists the following;

*They flew like a saucer would if you skipped it across the water . . . I thought it was a new type of jet. I was amazed at how they flew. . . They were half-moon shaped, oval in front and convex in the rear. I was in a beautiful position to watch them, and I did for three minutes. . . I clocked them by my watch at about 1,200 miles per hour [nearly 2,000km/hour] . . . They were not round; they were like a pie plate that was cut in half with a convex triangle in the rear.*

That initial statement about saucers skipping across the water is what journalists used to coin the term, 'flying saucer', which of course lights up the imagination with all sorts of imagery. While the sighting itself is perhaps less extraordinary than many that would follow, this set the benchmark. It gave people a picture to associate with unidentified flying objects in their minds: the classic saucer, which would become a hallmark of many sightings over the years, even though it was not what Kenneth Arnold saw himself. The phrase would embed itself across the science fiction world, as a term, in popular culture, books, comics, TV shows, movies and more. It still evokes many different emotions in people to this day; maybe for

Page 9

I have received lots of requests from people who told me to make a lot of wild guesses. I have based what I have written here in this article on positive facts and as far as guessing what it was I observed, it is just as much a mystery to me as it is to the rest of the world.

My pilot's license is 333487. I fly a Callair airplane; it is a three-place single engine land ship that is designed and manufactured at Afton, Wyoming as an extremely high performance, high altitude airplane that was made for mountain work. The national certificate of my plane is 33355.

Kenneth Arnold
Box 587
Boise, Idaho.

traveling this way

TOP

they seemed longer than wide their thickness was about $\frac{1}{20}$ of their width

traveling this way

Mirror Bright

They did not appear to me to whirl or spin but seemed in fixed position traveling as I have made drawing.

Kenneth Arnold.

17

UNCLAS

some there is still a stigma attached to the language, but there is no doubting its significant cultural impact.

UFO historian and author Jerome Clark, in his work *The UFO Encyclopedia*, suggested that Arnold's credibility and standing as a businessman made it difficult to dismiss the sighting as a simple misidentification or hoax. That hasn't stopped sceptics over the years suggesting, somewhat fairly, that it could have been something more prosaic, such as ice crystals in the atmosphere reflecting the sun, which could explain some of the unusual shapes and movements.

Regardless of the lack of additional data for this particular sighting, it's a launch pad for UFOlogy, a case that in any discussion of the beginnings of the subject has to be mentioned. What did Kenneth Arnold see that day? It's just as relevant in modern day, as pilots across the world in various militaries have reported seeing similar formations of multiple craft flying across our skies, performing similarly incredible manoeuvres at impossible speeds. Kenneth Arnold's sighting was perhaps best summed up by famous UFO historian, initially a sceptic turned believer, the late Dr J. Allen Hynek, as 'significant but inconclusive', emphasising the need for scientific study.

LEFT: When flying close to Mount Rainier, Kenneth Arnold spotted nine objects flying at incredible speed.

TOP LEFT: Kenneth Arnold stands beside his private aircraft which he was flying on 24 June 1947.

TOP RIGHT: Kenneth Arnold's report to the Army Air Forces.

| *Texas, USA* | 32.1301° N, 98°1214° W |
|---|---|

# STEPHENVILLE

UFOs seen in cowboy country

The small town of Stephenville, is located in the heart of Texas not too far from the Fort Worth-Dallas area. With a humble population of around 17,000, it is nevertheless known as the 'cowboy capital of the world'. The town's popular rodeo events and competitions attract riders and spectators from across the region and further afield.. Like many US towns, it takes great pride in its high school football team.

On a clear, cool night on 8 January 2008, Stephenville was about to be put on the map for another reason, this time not involving Stetsons or saddles. That evening, multiple residents from the area started seeing strange lights in the sky. As the evening wore on, concerned citizens gazing skyward could see some unusual lights, and noted that they were white in colour, but changing to red, then back to white, moving at 'high speeds and making rapid manoeuvres'. Now, at first sight, it might be fair to presume that relatively nearby military installations could be the cause of these craft. There are a number of withing a 160-km (100-mile) radius of Stephenville, including:

- Fort Hood, which is one of the biggest military bases on the planet and a major training hub for the US Army.
- Naval Air Station Fort Worth Joint Reserve Base, a dual-defence facility which covers training and support for multiple facets of the US Army, including the marines, Navy and more.
- Dyess Air Force Base, another major base which is home to the 7th Bomb Wing and 317th Airlift Wing.
- Fort Worth Meacham International Airport. This is now a civilian airport but, significantly, it was previously Carswell Air Force Base, a strategic command base home to B-52 bombers.

With so many bases surrounding the town, could it be that on this particular evening there were just some craft in the air being misidentified? It would be easy for any untrained observer or civilian to mistake a new aircraft or prototype being tested out for something mysterious. But over civilian airspace? That's definitely not to be expected, given the huge expanses of

UFO flight path

UNITED STATES OF AMERICA

Denton

Fort Worth Meacham International Airport

Naval Air Station Joint Reserve Base Fort Worth

Fort Worth

Abilene

Dyess Air Force Base

Sighting

Cleburne

Sighting

Stephenville

Sighting

Sighting

Sighting

Sighting

Brownwood

Military Training Centre

Waco

Fort Cavazos military training base (Fort Hood)

TEXAS

Killeen

Temple

N

30 *miles*

30 *kilometres*

Austin

training range available to the US military, or indeed any private contractors developing cutting-edge technologies.

One of the foremost researchers of the Stephenville case is Robert Powell, who after spending time investigating the event said exclusively for this book: 'Over twenty-five witnesses made reports of UFO sightings in the Stephenville, Texas, area on January 8, 2008. Radar data obtained from the Federal Aviation Administration confirms what the witnesses saw. At three different times, radar showed an object in the same direction as seen by witnesses. Two objects were detected at 6:15 p.m. and 7:26 p.m. that appear to be traveling at about 2000 mph [3,200km/h].'

While such speeds in modern times are very much achievable by man-made craft, physics as we currently understand it suggests that turning at sharp angles or making hard stops at those speeds would rip machinery and indeed the human body to pieces. According to reports by witnesses, the lights were seen travelling in formation, first as a single horizontal arc, and later as a vertical formation. Others in the area observing this amazing sight, including local business man Steve Allen, reported to various news outlets that the lights were intensely bright and stretched over 1.6km (1 mile) long. Whether this was one long object or multiple objects, no one knows for sure. But there certainly were objects, given the corroborating radar data from the Federal Aviation Authority.

Almost as quickly as they had come, the lights vanished without a trace. By this time, news outlets, not only regionally but nationwide, were to the story.

In the aftermath of the event the town residents were still reeling over what had occurred and were not inclined to let it go and move on. They wanted answers. They held forum meetings to try and get to the bottom of things. Initially, the Mutual UFO Network, (MUFON) held a public hearing a few weeks later, with hundreds of confused residents in

LEFT AND RIGHT: The Air Force claimed that F-16 training exercises had been taking place at the time of the sightings.

attendance. The hearing consisted of many locals giving their version of events, describing what they witnessed from their own vantage points. MUFON shared with them the radar data confirming that indeed an object was picked up, moving at varying speeds, which included signs of both rapid acceleration and deceleration. Among the witnesses were local police officers sharing their own sightings, one talking about how they had seen a large, stationary object with not only lights but features too.

Also worth noting is that some two weeks before the mass sighting was reported, another 300 individuals also saw something, including one civilian in the area who reported that, while hunting, he saw a metallic object in the sky. Through his rifle scope he could see enough detail to tell it was seamless and hovered silently before shooting off at unfathomable speed. His

RIGHT: A reconstruction of one of the sightings Stephenville area on 8 January 2008 that appeared in Glen Schulze's and Robert Powell's 2010 report 'Stephenville Lights: A Comprehensive Radar and Witness Report Study'.

name was Ricky Sorrells, and he reported his sighting afterwards to local law enforcement, Constable Lee Roy Gaitan. He suddenly stopped talking about it, though, after several strange events like finding a military grade bullet on his car dashboard and his cattle being rattled by helicopters. Was Ricky visited by a 'men in black' type organisation? Whatever it was, it certainly put him off discussing the event further.

Around the time of the public hearing, the air force had waded into the conversation, stating there had been F-16 training exercises going on at that very time, which would account for the witnesses' sightings, since they dropped flares used as decoys for anti-aircraft missiles, so case closed?

Not quite. The locals couldn't believe that the objects they had seen performing those incredible manoeuvres could be F-16 jets; they knew hows conventional aircraft moved, looked and sounded like. MUFON released its final report on the investigation around July 2008, and they concluded that the sightings were of a genuine Unidentified Object or Objects, with the eye witness statements being given additional weight and strength not only by the volume and consistency of reporting, but the radar data available.

| *Pembrokeshire, Wales* | 51.4643° N, 5.0600° W |
| --- | --- |

# BROAD HAVEN

Could nearly five hundred people be wrong?

Situated on the west coast of Pembrokeshire in Wales, is the small quiet village of Broad Haven. It's known for its sandy beaches and stunning coastline, making it popular with those interested in aquatic sports, like swimming, surfing, kayaking and more. Its slower pace and modest population make it idyllic for anyone looking for a quiet getaway, away from the hustle and bustle of a busy city lifestyle. Modern-day Broad Haven is a vibrant destination for tourists, who give a welcome boost to the economy. Local seafood a popular delicacy, with fresh fish being delivered from nearby fishing operations in Milford Haven, one of the UK's largest fishing ports. Wildlife enthusiasts from all around flock to the sea to catch a glimpse of, and photograph, seals, dolphins and a plethora of sea birds.

In 1977, where this set of incidents took place, the village of Broad Haven was even quieter, a rural community base with farming and agriculture the staples of employment. One of the best documented, researched and written-about sightings in UK history took place here, on 4 February. It was around 1 p.m., lunchtime for the children of Broad Haven Community Primary School, and a group of friends were together in the playground. In a field next to their school, something was there, an object caught their eye. As the boys clambered for a closer look, they couldn't believe their eyes. Just over the playground was a long, metallic object, cigar-shaped with a domed top. Some of the children also reported portholes or windows along the top of it, with a length of anywhere from 12–15m (40–50ft). This sighting did not last long; seconds later the object rose from the ground and took off.

One of the witnesses, David Davies, was only nine years old at the time, and has spoken many times of the incident. He hadn't seen anything of the original incident, as he had spent his break time in the class, not generally playing with the other children. When they returned from their break, talking about spaceships, spacemen and the like, he had to go and see for himself. He got up and wandered out into the playground and over towards the field. There, he would also see what he described as 'a silver cigar-shaped craft with a dome covering the middle third'. Speaking to BBC Wales on the fortieth anniversary of the event, he said: 'My sighting lasted only seconds.' It popped up and then went back behind a tree . . .'

RAF Brawdy
Newgale
WALES
Broad Haven Community Primary School, sighting on 4 and 17 February 1977
Simpson Cross
Withybush
Haverfordwest
Haven Fort Hotel, sighting 18 April 1977
Broad Haven
Little Haven
Johnston
Marloes
Milford Haven
Neyland
Pembroke Dock
Pembroke
Castlemartin
Bosherston
Broad Haven
N
4 miles
5 kilometres

Asked at the time on a local TV interview if it could have been something else, maybe a helicopter, Shaun Garrison, another pupil, said; 'Well a helicopter could land there but that's private property and they could be prosecuted. And the only thing you could get in there is a Harrier.'

Ralph Llewellyn was the school headmaster, and upon hearing the commotion and the boys' incredible stories, he rounded them up and got them to sit, quietly as if in an exam, and draw what they had seen, curious to see if the depictions of the crafts would match up. To his surprise, despite some variation that you would expect from young children, there were definite themes to what they were putting down on paper. The shape, the portholes or windows, the colour, a red light flashing on the top. Could it be these children had actually seen something otherworldly? Something else was apparent in the drawings too: some, though not all, of the children drew figures of a spaceman-like figure, in a silvery looking one-piece suit.

News of the event reached Hugh Turnbull, who was a local reporter for the *Western Telegraph*. He had received a call from investigator Randall Jones Pugh to join him at the scene. He had just heard that something inexplicable had been seen, with little other detail. He spoke to the group of children, aged between nine and eleven years old, and also saw the drawings that Mr Llewellyn asked the boys to draw. While sceptical, Hugh was intrigued, surmising it likely that at least something had been seen, though he was unsure as to what. He headed along to the field, close to where the object had been spotted. One theory that the local sewage works had parked a tanker in the field was quickly ruled out as just a case of misidentification when the company confirmed nothing like that had been in the field.

Turnbull decided this story was worth taking to print. It's one thing for some children to report a story like this, but here was a journalist deciding to take it seriously and put it out to a wider audience. Publishing the story was key in propelling it not only into local minds, but garnering international interest in the small town of Broad Haven. Major networks, newspapers, magazines and radio would pick up and run with the story, bringing people from around the globe to the village.

David Davies recalled in various interviews that in the days following the event, it was hard for lessons to go ahead as normal. Teachers would be called constantly on the phone, mail was coming in from all over, people would appear at the school looking for interviews with adults, children, anyone who had maybe seen something. Between the initial sighting on the Friday and the Monday, the story had exploded. Children at the school and some staff reported a further sighting two weeks later on the 17 February. Once again, a similar looking object took off after a few seconds. Through March 1977, residents of the village would file multiple reports of bright lights or shapes moving in the sky. It's plausible, and only fair, to say that maybe a flying-saucer fever gripped the village. With so much attention on the topic, people were looking for anything that could be a UFO; any small light in the sky was being taken as something non-human. It's very hard to tell if any of the sightings were real.

However, a few months after that initial sighting, on the 18 April 1977, a much closer encounter would take place, one that was more than just a bright light in the sky. Not too

4 PAGE PULL-OUT

THE YEAR OF THE UFO

THE SHARP eyes of a group of primary school children looked with astonishment towards a clump of trees 300 yards from their school playing field

What they claim they saw was silvery and metallic, a craft of a kind none had seen before, cigar-shaped with an upturned saucer-shaped back.

Beside it some—not all—saw a figure in a silver suit. The children ran. One fell and became hysterical. Another who saw it twice, cried.

To this day — almost exactly a year later — none of those 14 children at Broad Haven Primary School in Dyfed, West Wales, waver in their assertion of what they say they saw.

The sightings, first during the lunch break at about one o'clock and then when school was over at approximately 1.45 p.m., lasted just a few minutes.

# THE SILVER CIGAR

...AS SEEN BY FOURTEEN WITNESSES

AT lunchtime two boys came dashing in to tell the headmaster, Ralph Llewellyn, that they had seen something strange. "I think they said 'a flying thing,'" he recalls. "Anyway, we were having a staff meeting and I disbelieved them, so I sent them away."

... west corner of the field to look again. Again an object was there. The children ran home to tell their families.

On Monday morning, under pressure from the children involved in the incident, Mr Llewellyn went with them to the spot where they said they had ...

... definite thread running through what they said," he recalls. "So I put them in a classroom and made them independently write down and draw their impressions of what they saw.

"This was carried out under the supervision of one of the staff, Mrs Lester."

... drawings are shown above. Here are excerpts from what they wrote — slightly tidied up in some cases but, headmaster Llewellyn testifies, unaltered in their text.

David John Davies, 10, said: "Up from the bush popped a cigar-shaped object ...

... go to the toilet with him. Tudor Jones was nearly crying because he was scared that he was going to be disintegrated or something, so we all rushed in."

Tudor Owen Lloyd Jones, 10: "The thing was on the ground behind a bush. I saw a kind of man and ...

FACT

● AFTER a flood of reports of a UFO over Morocco in September 1976, King Hassan himself stepped in and ordered his ...

RIGHT: The 23 February 1978 edition of the *Daily Express* reports on the pupils' encounter.

far from the school was a little hotel in a converted former smugglers' port, run by its owner Rosa Granville. Not long after getting into bed on the property's second floor, she noticed a pulsating light at the window. Getting out of her bed to investigate, she looked down to the garden below and there was a huge glowing light, with two figures coming out of it. She described them as having long arms and long legs but was unable to make out too much detail. The heat from the saucer-shaped craft was so intense it was burning her skin through the window. At this point, the heat became stronger and the object flew up into the night sky at incredible speed. On his return from a trip, Rosa's husband investigated the area outside, and found the grass was burned and clearly affected by something which had been there. Rosa wrote to her local MP, Nicholas Edwards, stressing how disturbed she had been and wanting to make it known this was not something she wanted to experience again. The MP spoke to the local RAF base who sent someone to investigate. Flight Lieutenant Tony Cowan travelled to the site to look for himself but found little evidence to comment on other than testimony. He sent a reply, more humorous perhaps than Mrs Granville would have appreciated, stating: 'Should a UFO arrive at RAF Brawdy, we will charge normal landing fees and inform you immediately.' The dismissal and disinterest in investigating UFO sightings by the UK military or government, then and now, has not particularly changed.

This wasn't the Granville's last eerie encounter, however, as late one night Rosa's daughter Francine remembers hearing a knock at the door. It was around 2 a.m. and no noise had been heard of anyone approaching the hotel. Her mother answered the door, to be greeted by two figures with identical features. She described them as being smooth-skinned, with slick-backed hair. They talked at the same time, as if it was one a voice coming out of two mouths, which Rosa found very odd. People at another farm, who had experienced cows being transported from one field to another, reported speaking to the same men at their door at the same time as Rosa. Whether they were the fabled 'Men in Black' or beings or entities of some other kind is likely to remain a mystery.

All of these sightings over the course of several months, from the school playground to the hotel, and public reports from the surrounding areas, collectively became known as the 'Broad Haven Triangle'. Sceptics say there are multiple potential explanations, more terrestrial and mundane than those of space aliens or flying saucers. Firstly, there are many who claim it was simple misidentification by the children and their imaginations running wild. The 1970s was a time period when there was a popularity boom in sci-fi, and the film *Close Encounters of the Third Kind* would release later in 1977. It was the middle of the Cold War, with relations between the US and the Soviet Union in a frightening place for the world, for surely a nuclear exchange between the two would be catastrophic for the globe? Because of the delicate game of tactical chess, the United States had military stationed in many other nations, not least the UK. Some sceptics believe that perhaps the sightings of more strange lights and 'spacemen' in silver suits were nothing more than the presence of US military personnel and more aircraft in the skies.

But this doesn't account for a lot of what was reported. Let's take the Granville's sighting. It doesn't explain the flying saucer seen up close, the intense heat, the strange beings. There are other reports of it being pranks by local businessmen, and mass hysteria brought on by the combination of the Cold War and just a chain reaction from the original school playground sightings. Much like the UFO reports themselves in this case, there is a lack of evidence to show either way; it is largely testimony, albeit widespread testimony, against theories, and evidence lacking conclusions.

What is for certain, is that over the period of a few months in 1977, in a small village in Wales, some incredible events were seen and reported by more than 450 people. The debate over whether this was the result of some sort of hysteria fuelled by sci-fi and overactive imaginations or if indeed the people of Broad Haven experienced something otherworldly, will rage on in UFOlogical debates.

LEFT TOP: Pupils of Broad Haven Community School pose with their drawings of the craft and figures they saw.

LEFT BOTTOM: One of drawings of the cigar-shaped ship.

ABOVE: Broad Haven is a idyllic village on the Pembrokeshire coast.

| *National Capital Territory (NCT), India* | 28.5835° N, 77.2111° E |
| --- | --- |

# NEW DELHI

Giant airborne cigar in the skies over New Delhi

New Delhi, the capital city of India is a remarkable city, home to more than 32 million people, in 1951 it was a far quieter place, with a more humble 1.75 million people. Long before its rapid urbanisation and population growth, India was only a few years removed from having gained its independence from Britain in 1947, in its formative days as a sovereign nation. New Delhi would play a key role in driving forward economic growth across the wider country. It also marked a year of change: 1951 saw the country's first general election held late in October and running through to the following February. The city had seen a substantial influx of refugees since 1947, adding to the growing population, which was demanding the new government met the needs of its people, and fast. It was the classic melting point of differing cultures, as the rich traditions of what had been were mixing with the new, the modern, changing the face of the city and the entire country. It was a time of great change, opportunity and growth.

India's culture is steeped in tradition. Its ancient texts passed down through the centuries such as the Vedas, Mahabharata and Ramayana contain many references to 'flying machines' known as Vimanas, and there are mentions of celestial beings too. So the notion that something may be visiting us from somewhere else, in the past or now, isn't entirely unusual for this society.

Shortly after 10 a.m. on 15 March 1951, one of the earliest recorded instances of Unidentified Aerial Phenomena post-war was to take place. Staff on duty at the air force station in Delhi observed in the sky an object, describing it as cigar-shaped, metallic and not having any wings or signs of visible propulsion. These were no mere civilians, there were trained personnel who would be expected to be able to identify aircraft of different varieties in the air. It was noticed first by Squadron Leader D.S. Mangat and several of his colleagues. They had observed the object moving rapidly high in the air, far exceeding any speed expected of a conventional jet or plane. Radar systems also picked up the object, corroborating the visual sighting by those on the ground. Air force personnel, radar operators and others all observed the object travelling steadily from north to south over New Delhi. Adding to them, members of New Delhi Flying Club were also witness to the object, with more than twenty-five bearing witness to the strange metallic craft. Pilots and ground crew at the New Delhi Flying Club,

UFO flight path
New Delhi
Urban Extension Road-II
Grand Trunk Road
BHALSWA
Doctor KB Hedgewar Marg
Flyover
LONI
MODEL TOWN
Wazirabad Road
Mangolpuri
PITAMPURA
Rohtak Road
DELHI
Shandara Flyover
CONNAUGHT PLACE
Shivaji Marg
Ring Road
NEW DELHI
Flyover
New Delhi Flying Club
LODHI COUNTY
RAJ NAGAR II
NOIDA
Mahatma Gandhi Marg
Air Force station
Delhi-Gurugram Expressway
Ho Chi Minh Marg
Acharya Shri Tulsi Marg
LIBIZA TOWN
DND-KMP Expressway
Mathura Road
Progression of the UFO
GURUGRAM
FARIDABAD
N
5 miles
5 kilometers

including the Chief Aerial Engineer and his two assistants, were curious when they spotted the cigar shaped tube streaking across the skies they regularly flew in; it was worrying that there could be unaccounted objects above them. One unclassified document on the case contains the following unattributed comment: 'I do not understand why it is called a flying saucer, it is not shaped like a saucer but more like a cigar. Perhaps when this object is viewed from the underside it may have the shape of a saucer.'

This was a sighting now, with multiple witnesses, from multiple disciplines with decades of various experience and flying time between them. There were also civilians who had spotted the craft flying later that morning, while perhaps less reliable in terms of identifying a craft at altitude performing out of character, they at least added more weight of testimony that indeed something was spotted.

Despite air force investigations, a lack of substantial sensor data and no video evidence meant they drew a blank on further identification of the object. Could it have been another nation's craft being tested? Remember this was only a few years removed from the war so tensions were still high in a world that had been broken for so many years. Official statements played it safe, while the public and media allowed imaginations to run wild with speculation about extraterrestrial visitors and more exotic explanations, but the officials in charge declined to speculate. However, they stopped short of drawing a conclusion, admitting there was not enough evidence to do so.

Official documents on the topic have since been declassified and are available to the public. One Air Intelligence Information Report states: 'The object sighted was shaped like a cigar with no outer visible control surfaces. It was about one hundred feet [30m] long and as big as around as a C-47 fuselage, bare metal colour and only one object sighted.'

At the time, it managed to make some limited international news media and it was included in reports in the United States such as Project Blue Book, which was the US Army's investigation into UFOs, now infamous in UFOlogy. The sighting came at a time when sightings would be on the rise, although events such as Roswell (1947, see page 14) happened in a time of limited international communication and were not common knowledge across the minds of the public.

RIGHT TOP: The growing city of New Delhi in 1950.

RIGHT BOTTOM: Safdarjung Airport, the location of the New Delhi Flying Club.

| *Primorsky Krai, Russia* | 44.3412° N, 135.3430° E |
| --- | --- |

# DALNEGORSK

Extraterrestrial orb crashes into Russian hillside

In the remote mining village of Dalnegorsk, in the Primorsky Krai Region of the then Soviet Union, one of the most well-studied UFO crashes of the last fifty years took place in 1986, often dubbed Russia's 'Roswell'. Dalnegorsk is an isolated town, with rugged terrain and a difficult climate with extremely cold winters and summers that are cooler than many would wish. The town was reliant on its mineral resources: large deposits of lead, zinc and boron are extracted from a number of mines in the area. While the wider Soviet Union, under the leadership of Mikhail Gorbachev in 1986, was pushing to kickstart what had become a somewhat stagnant power on the world stage, the people of Dalnegorsk were yet to feel the effects of this, due to their remoteness. They were a small, close community and it would still be some time before the shockwaves of reform would reach them.

It was a typically cold evening on 29 January 1986 when shortly before 8 p.m., the residents of Dalnegorsk noticed a red, spherical object floating through the sky above their small village. It looked similar in colour to burning stainless steel, according to witness reports, and as it moved, silently, across the sky, it rose and fell, its glow changing as it did so. Reportedly around 3m (10ft) wide, it was relatively low to the ground, so those observing could tell it wasn't just a small light or satellite much higher up. A few minutes after it was first sighted, the shocked onlookers gazed on as it crashed into the side of Mount Izvestkovaya, known locally as Height 611. Normally, when an object crashes you would expect a loud noise to echo through the surrounding area, but after the orb hit the side of the mountain, there was nothing but a muted thump. Witnesses claimed there was no loud sound, no flames from a fiery crash, no explosions. Newspaper editor for *Trudovoye Slovo*, V. Korotko, said that following a short, but powerful explosion, he witnessed 'large reddish white flames'. Just stillness and a glow, with some residents believing the object burned for up to an hour.

The following day when the local authorities and scientists had been made aware of the event, made their way to the impact site. This wasn't easy as the area was covered in deep snow, but they did find a scorched area where something had hit the mountain. There was a considerable-sized impact zone where the orb had landed, slid along and damaged the ground and trees round about. The examining scientists also noticed strange metallic debris, which included small balls of lead and mesh all around the zone of impact.

RUSSIA

Mount Izvestkovaya
(Height 611)

1st sighting
29 January 1986

2nd sighting
7 February 1986

3rd sighting
28 November 1987

DALNEGORSK

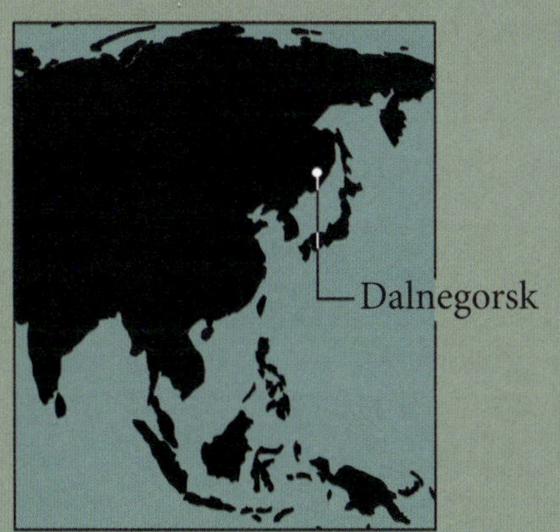


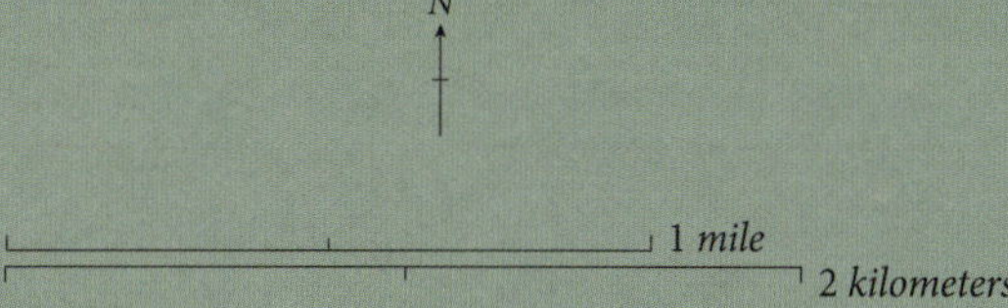

Investigations continued into the afternoon as locals were interviewed about what they had witnessed. All the stories were consistent, telling of a red, glowing ball appearing in the skies above and before crashing into the side of the mountain.

Scientists who had recovered materials continued their investigations into the month of February and beyond, with the help of well-known Soviet UFOlogist and investigator Dr Valery Dvuzhilny. He conducted more thorough analysis of the materials and said they had strange properties. For example, some had a high resistance to intense heat and anomalous magnetic properties. Other rock and soil samples from the site were examined, which revealed they had unexpected isotopic compositions, and did not look as expected for the area. This lends weight to the theory that perhaps these materials were not from this earth, and maybe the glowing ball that hit the mountain was a visiting craft or probe from somewhere else. Even more interestingly, the area remained anomalous for three years after the incident, also affecting some equipment when people would attempt to study the area more thoroughly. Reports even stress that some locals suffered health effects from the area.

This wasn't the end of the story in that area, however. Nine days after the initial incident, residents were astonished to see two yellowish orbs appear in the area, making their way to the red sphere's crash site from the week before. Witnesses noted they spent some time over the site, circling four times and then flying off. Could this have been some sort of recovery mission from wherever the initial orb had come from?

Nearly two years after the original incidents, thirty-two reported objects made their way over the area, just before midnight on Saturday 28 November 1987. Witnesses numbered into the hundreds and included military personnel as well as civilians. The objects broke off into groups, with thirteen of them making their way to the site at Dalnegorsk, some hovering

around and another five heading over to the mountain side, manoeuvring like they were looking for something. There were no signs of propulsion on these craft, no noise, no wings. Witnesses didn't immediately conclude that these were UFOs but surmised they were likely to be falling meteorites or perhaps aircraft that were malfunctioning at first. Some reported that as the objects were overhead, their TVs suffered with interference. Local quarry workers gave detailed reports of an object that was a giant cylinder, around 200–300m (650–1,000ft) in length, moving silently overhead. They could see that the front of the object leading the way seemed to be burning like molten metal. It was so low they were concerned it could be about to crash into their quarry. A local school teacher reported seeing a blindingly bright sphere over the school, perhaps the height of a ten-storey building, not too high in the sky. Again reporting it to move silently, she said that at the front was a dark, elongated object around 10m (30ft) long, which shone a violet/blue light or beam, illuminating the ground below as it swept over it. It seemed to be searching for something, lighting up the objects around it as it shone, but oddly not creating any shadows, as if the light wasn't really there.

This incident, along with the others in the area, were all investigated, and Dr Dvuzhilny concluded that an extraterrestrial probe had crashed in 1986 and that these follow ups were searching for it. CIA documents published in 1989 concerning various Soviet events, include the Dalnegorsk event. An extract says: 'Some of the scientists have concluded that the object that crashed into Hill 611 was an "extraterrestrial" space vehicle constructed by highly intelligent beings. Doctor of Chemical Sciences V. Vysotskiy stated that "without doubt, this is evidence of a high technology, and it is not anything of a natural of terrestrial origin".'

ABOVE: Between January 1986 and November 1987, inhabitants of the village Dalnegorsk observed number of UFOs floating in the sky.

| *Honam, South Korea* | 35.0943° N, 126.5114° E |
| --- | --- |

# GWANGJU

A UFO hovers for hours above a South Korean city

Gwangju is a city located in the southwest of South Korea, historically seen as an important political and cultural centre; it has a strong, proud history of fighting off foreign invasions. In 1976 particularly, it was a time of great tension as it had been under authoritarian rule of President Park Chung-hee since 1961. There was a sense that more and more of its people wanted democratisation. This time in South Korea's history is also known as 'the miracle on the Han River'; a time of great social and economic growth, urbanisation was skyrocketing with industrialisation key to prosperity. The residents of Gwangju were seeing their city change quickly before their eyes, as a more traditional society was being swept away and replaced by a modern way of living. With this change, it still kept many of its cultural roots, its vibrant music and dance scene popular with a thriving creative community, playing host to many different cultural festivals, such as folk song and temple festivals. This society was in a state of flux in so many ways, not knowing yet that huge change was just on the horizon. For a moment, though, everything would stop as a sighting in late 1976 would capture the imaginations of many who lived there.

It was early morning on 23 November and the residents of Gwangju were preparing for their day, with agricultural workers making their way to work, others heading to factories that had sprung up in recent years due to rapid industrialization, or setting up market stalls and such. When, in the breaking daylight above their heads, an unusual object caught their eyes, many witnesses looked up, motioning for those around them to do the same to make sure they were indeed seeing what they were seeing. Against the blue of the sky was a shiny, metal disc-shaped object, hovering silently some witnesses mentioned that there appeared to be some kind of dome on top.

Korean attitudes towards UFOs, particularly in the mid 1970s, was one of scepticism. The public largely believed any sightings were a mix of simple misidentifications and unfamiliar natural phenomena. However, on this day, the sceptics were seeing with their own eyes the very same thing as everyone else was seeing. And the disc-shaped object wasn't there and gone in a few seconds; it stayed there for many hours according to reports. By midday, with word spreading of the strange intruder in their skies, many more people were on alert for any potential sightings, and they certainly weren't disappointed. The reports from the

SOUTH KOREA
Yeongsan
Agricultural area
Sighting
Sighting
Sighting
Factory District
Gwangji
Sightings
Sighting
Gwangju
N
2 miles
2 kilometres

RIGHT: Residents of the city of Gwangju observed a disc-shaped object flying above them early in the morning of 23rd November, 1976.

afternoon tell of the object no longer merely hovering, but making rapid manoeuvres in the sky, executing a mixture of sudden stops, rising and falling; some witnesses also claimed that it changed colours as it moved.

The reports came from a range of people: students, teachers, local police and other authority figures, as well as the agricultural and factory workers, and stall holders. The police noted that when viewed through binoculars, the object definitely displayed strange characteristics as it behaved erratically. Sometime later in the afternoon, the object took off at speed.

With the city abuzz with the widespread sightings and reports, some local papers such as *Kwangju Ilbo* and *Jeonnam Daily* decided to run front page stories. While short-lived, the story was also picked up and run by national media outlets, which led to a new interest in the UFO topic for many Koreans. Memberships for regional UFO clubs increased manyfold and newsletters focusing on the topic saw massive increase too.

So what did the people see that day? With limited technologies available, and no official government investigation or information, there is a real lack of data. It is not perhaps unfair to consider that a type of balloon prototype, high-altitude weather balloon or spy balloon had drifted off course; this would explain the erratic movements at height. Perhaps the hovering was just a trick of the eye, and the colours were the object reflecting the sun at various times. Though, so much testimony reports details like the dome, the changing colours, the sudden movements and turns.

Whether it was something prosaic, or a top-secret aircraft being tested, or indeed perhaps an object of extraterrestrial origin, it remains a mystery. But the impact on the people who saw it remains to this day, with Korean people maintaining an interest in the phenomenon culturally. On 7 April 2021 a UFO was caught on a live news broadcast, which sparked huge interest again in the topic, showing truly this is an international phenomenon.

Chapter 5

# CLOSE ENCOUNTER

| *Texas, USA* | 30.0926° N, 95.1109° W |
|---|---|

# DAYTON

Diamond lights, intense heat and a swarm of helicopters

Just 65km (40 miles) northeast of Houston, Texas is the small city of Dayton. Known for its agriculture and tightknit communities like many similarly remote cities and towns in the US, it boasts beautiful clear skies at night with little light pollution. The stunning countryside is covered by vast fields, and is popular with those who enjoy scenic hiking, fishing and other outdoor activities. All of this provides an incredible setting for one of the most astounding Close Encounters in UFOlogical history, as a late-night drive would change the lives of three individuals forever.

It was a cold evening on 29 December 1980 near Dayton, on a dark road between New Caney and Huffman. Friends Betty Cash and Vickie Landrum, along with Vickie's young grandson Colby, were travelling home from an unsuccessful evening where two bingo games had been cancelled. Instead, they had gone to a local truck stop for food in New Caney. Betty was at the wheel driving southwest towards Dayton on the Farm-to-Market Road 1485; it's a wooded area with trees on either side of the vehicle. The sky was clear at around 9 p.m. when Betty and Vickie noticed a bright light above and behind the trees; as they continued to drive, the light disappeared. There were no houses, shops, factories or anything of note nearby, so this light was odd. While it had caught their attention, it wasn't on their minds for long, dismissed as perhaps a helicopter or low-flying aircraft, not that unusual. Not unusual at all that is, until a few minutes later when the light appeared again. This time, much closer, it was brighter and closer to the woodland floor.

It was now directly over the road in front of them, and not wanting to pass under the incredible light, Betty slammed her brakes to bring the car to a halt, hoping to avoid a potential collision if it dropped further, and wanting to keep a safe distance. With the car's sudden stop, Vickie put her hand out in front of herself to take some of the force out of the quick braking. She noticed something, something peculiar: as she took her hand off the dashboard, her handprint was there in front of her, embedded in the dashboard. It had previously been a solid surface but somehow had softened and retained the shape of her hand. As their wits returned, so did their focus on the object ahead; no longer a bright light now, a solid shape could be clearly seen. The three occupants of the car were awed by a metallic glowing diamond, hovering above the road, only a few feet in front of them.

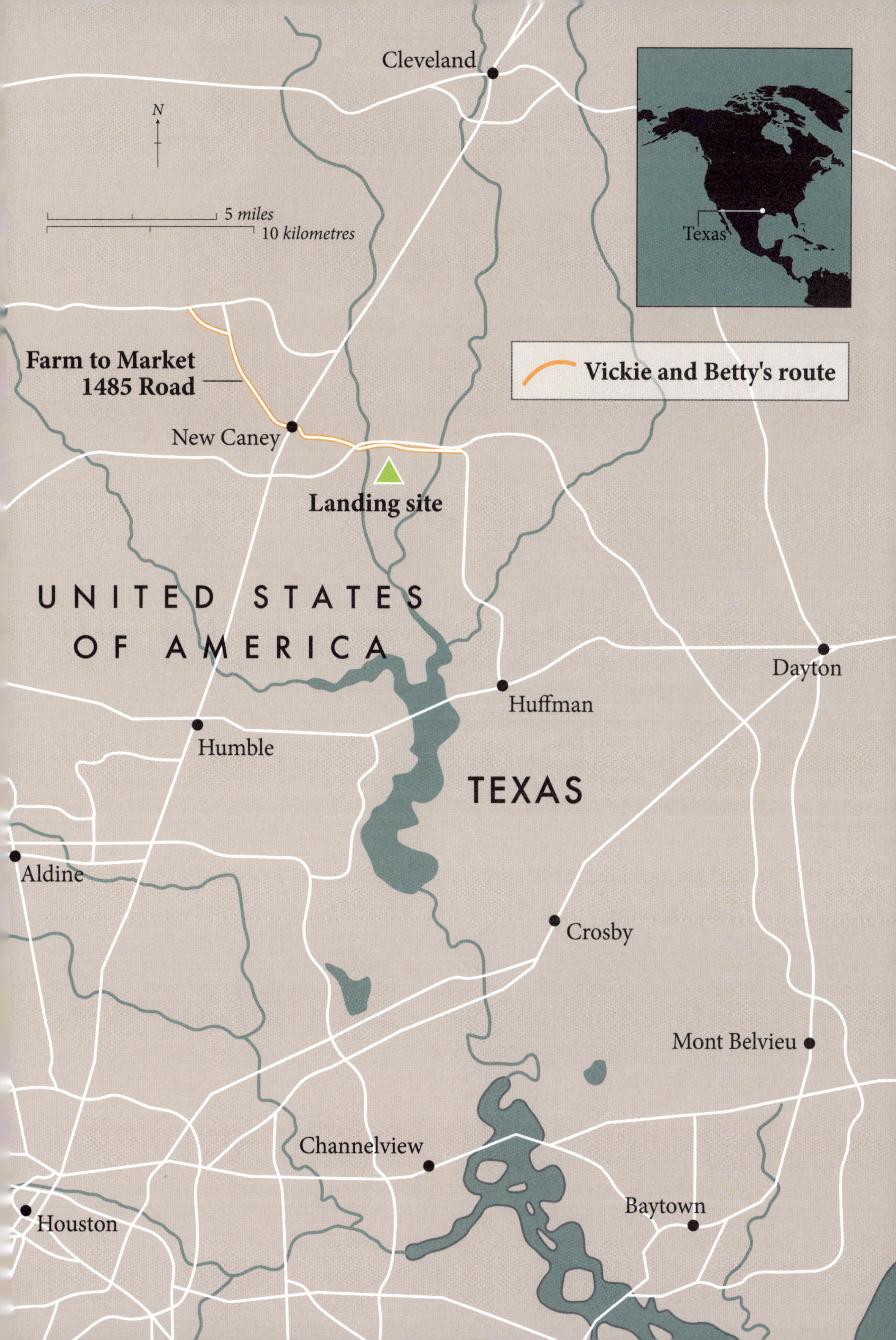
Cleveland
N
5 miles
10 kilometres
Texas
Vickie and Betty's route
Farm to Market
1485 Road
New Caney
Landing site
UNITED STATES
OF AMERICA
Dayton
Huffman
Humble
TEXAS
Aldine
Crosby
Mont Belvieu
Channelview
Baytown
Houston

Not only was there a brightness from the object, it was emitting an intense heat from flames shooting out from beneath the craft, a heat that was engulfing the car, making it difficult to stay inside. Accompanying this light and heat were a series of shrill beeps, which seemed to pierce their ears; perhaps they were deliberately there to disorientate. Vickie and Betty stepped out of the car to get some air, but Colby, only seven years old and absolutely terrified by this point, was desperately trying to pull his grandmother back into the car.

Getting back in, Vickie consoled her grandson, as best she could, unsure of what exactly was going on around them. Both Betty and Vickie were in their late fifties, and were religious folk. They would later say that at the time, in the confusion of it all, they believed this to be some sort of spiritual event, perhaps a sign of the end of time. Out there in the isolation and darkness, they weren't to know if the same sort of thing was happening just to them or perhaps to others further afield, too. It's now widely speculated that many of the mentions in religious texts of angels, demons and other spiritual entities might actually refer to non-human Intelligences. Could they be one and the same? Labels given in a time where there was far less knowledge and understanding of what is out there in the universe suggest this is quite possible.

Vickie stated later that during the incident, she told her grandson that this was Jesus appearing before them, and that he didn't need to be afraid, thinking to herself this was a second coming type scenario. During this exchange, Betty remained outside the vehicle, battling the intense heat, trying to get a closer look at the diamond craft overhead. She was struggling, though, her insides feeling like they were cooking, the rising temperature getting the better of her. She fought her way back inside the vehicle, burning her hand on the door handle as it sizzled.

LEFT: Vickie Landrum and Betty Cash shortly after their encounter.

RIGHT: Betty Cash's hand was badly burnt by the flames coming from the craft.

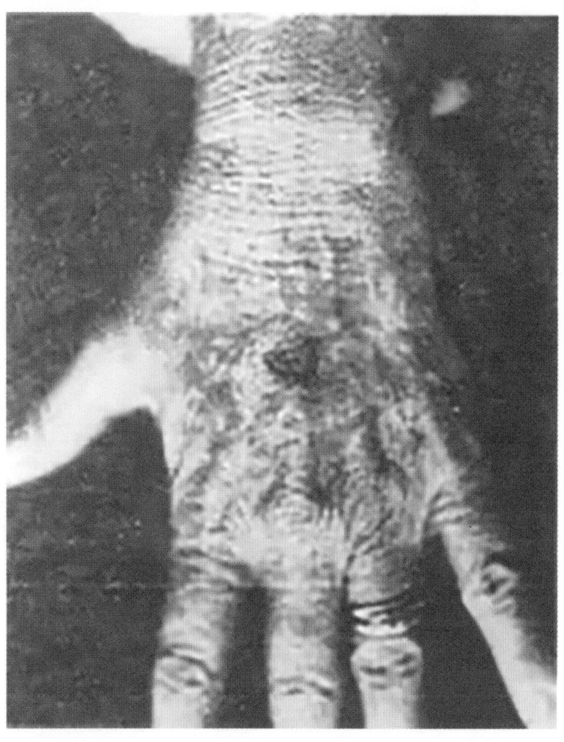

Their ordeal wasn't over. After twenty minutes, which felt like hours, the object was no longer alone, as a swarm of twenty-three helicopters surrounded the object, counted precisely by Colby. This caused the object to tilt on its side, break its hover and slowly glide off. Believing the helicopters to be military in origin, the women after the event managed to identify them as at least twelve Chinooks, a standard military vehicle. Whether they were chasing the object, escorting it or warning it off, potentially trying to force it to land, they stayed with it as it moved off south, towards Galveston Bay. Now, this is an interesting side note in this story, as in the direction the diamond shaped craft was moving were two particular areas that may be of interest. One, NASA's Johnson Space Center, located near the shore of Clear Lake, is the home of the famous Mission Control, which manages human missions into space. The other, Ellington Field Joint Reserve Base, is a military base used not only by NASA but other agencies. Was it coincidence that the object moved off in that direction? It's difficult to say, but certainly worth mentioning.

With the object now in the distance, Betty managed to get the car started and continue the weary drive home, as all three were shaken, disturbed but still capable of the onward journey. As they carried on along the dark, rural road, they could still see the light of the UFO in the distance, being chaperoned by the helicopters that just moments before had either knowingly or unknowingly come to their rescue. They were startled once more, as in the stunned silence in the car, their radio burst into life; it had never been turned off, but seemingly the presence of the unknown craft had interfered with their signal. They hadn't noticed till now, not surprising given the incredible event that had just occurred. Again, radios and car engines being shut off by UFO's during any close encounter are a common feature of these events.

The large diamond-shaped craft, which had got so close to them, terrorising them for what seemed a lot longer than it was, may have been out of sight, but that wasn't the

end of their experience, . Unfortunately, there was lasting damage. All three witnesses in the aftermath reported multiple health issues and the intense heat given off had burned their skin, leaving it blistered, particularly Betty who had spent far longer out of the car exposed to the object's intensity. She had suffered the most severe effects, not surprising given she had been closest to it and for the longest time. Other than the skin problems, she had swelling of the skin, her hair began falling out and ultimately she had to be hospitalised on 3 January 1981. Upon visiting, Betty's daughter didn't recognise her when she walked into her hospital room, her face was so badly affected. The three reported other less-severe symptoms, like an incredible thirst, vomiting, nausea and diarrhoea. Strung together, the symptoms and resulting effects lend credence to some sort of radiation exposure, which is something that continues to be reported by witnesses of crafts experiencing close encounters all around the globe. Hesitant at first to tell the doctors what had happened, Betty finally explained what had what happened on the road only days before: the diamond craft, the heat, all of it. The doctors didn't dismiss her story, given the severity of the injuries. In later years Betty developed breast cancer, perhaps linked to the radiation exposure from the event.

After some enquiries, the women eventually sought compensation for their injuries, looking for a sum in the range of $20m. It was dismissed in 1986, as there was a lack of evidence, not least because the US Government would not admit to any knowledge or part in the event. The claims were centred around the mysterious Chinook helicopters and the possibility it was a craft the US was experimenting with, or at least knew about. This was always going to be difficult, if indeed impossible to prove with no photographs, no video. Just testimony and

ABOVE: Twenty-three Chinook helicopters surrounded the craft as it hovered above.

the aftereffects of exposure to *something*. If the trio on that evening had stumbled across an experimental craft, belonging to a government agency or some private contractor, they were never going to admit to that. It may explain the presence of the helicopters, and it would also make sense, given the close proximity to the military base used by NASA and other three letter agencies. Physical effects, like those suffered by Betty Cash, Vickie Landrum and Colby Landrum are common with close-proximity experiences. Many have come forward over the years with rare illness and disease, potentially linked to an otherworldly vehicle or even entity. Pilots, military personnel and civilians would have the biggest lawsuit in human history on their hands if it was proven that they had been not only exposed to non-human craft or experimental test craft, but that their own government had been complicit in covering this up. All the more reason for those behind the scenes orchestrating the cover-ups to want to keep these phenomena under wraps.

One of the prominent investigators involved in the aftermath of the event was John F. Schuessler who is quoted as saying:

*Based on the evidence, it appears that the Cash-Landrum sighting involved a man-made, highly sophisticated aircraft, possibly a nuclear-powered vehicle, being tested or deployed by a covert section of the U.S. military. The severe health effects experienced by the witnesses suggest exposure to high levels of radiation or other hazardous materials.*

Some other witnesses came forward in the years after the event, and while none had reported seeing the strange object, several mentioned that on that particular date in the vicinity there were at least a dozen black Chinook helicopters out on some sort of patrol. Of course this was denied by government officials. Investigating the incident afterwards, Lieutenant Colonel George Sarran said:

*There is no tangible evidence that the helicopters witnessed by the individuals were associated with any branch of the military or any operations being conducted at the time. The nature of the object observed remains unexplained, and the source of the health effects reported by the witnesses could not be determined by with the information available.*

This was a blanket dismissal of any involvement or knowledge, of a type that is commonplace and the norm, told many times over hundreds of reported UFO events.

What was seen on that night in December 1980 on a dark road near Dayton will likely forever remain a mystery. Betty and Vickie have since passed on, Colby, however, is still very much alive and hoping one day to get answers to what they witnessed that night, and to find out what caused the health problems suffered by his grandmother, her friend and himself.

RIGHT: Dayton is a small, agricultural city surrounded by fields.

| *Victoria, Australia* | 37.5630° S, 145.0810° E |
|---|---|

# MELBOURNE

## Flying saucers over the Westall School playground

Clayton South is a large residential suburb in Melbourne, Australia. After the Second World War, it saw an increase in its population as soldiers returned from the fighting and the baby boom kicked in. The Australian government was actively pushing the development of suburban areas to help house the ever-increasing population and areas like Clayton South came into being. It is a diverse area; its school demographics reflect the years of immigration post-war as many Europeans and Asians made their way to work in the new factories and industrial estates popping up across Australia. In 1966, it was still developing into the commercially vibrant place it is now, filled with retail centres, business parks and the like, but the seeds of growth were very much planted. These days it has a multitude of schools and transport options are plentiful, but in the mid 1960s there were more modest options as basic local grocery stores catered for the needs of school children and their parents. It was these very school children that would be witness to one of the greatest mass sightings in history; one that prominent Westall researcher, Shane Ryan, has described as 'the biggest daylight mass sighting in UFO history'.

6 April 1966 was the second-last day of term for the children of Westall School, in Clayton South. When a commotion was heard, some children were already outside their classrooms in the playground for physical activities like cricket, while others were still inside, waiting to go out for break time. It truly made for a remarkable event because there were so many witnesses, with so many different vantage points.

Terry Pec, one of those many witnesses to the event, said: 'We were out playing sports on the oval, one of the kids yelled out, "Look up in the sky, it's flying saucers!" We all looked up and it was a flying saucer. A round silver disc, it seemed to be very low over the school. Children were screaming and running inside.'

As the bell rang for the children's break, they swarmed outside, desperate to get a look at what was causing the noise. They pushed open the school doors and headed out, scrambling at first, unsure where to look, but there across the cricket ground, was a large disc-shaped object starting to descend slowly behind some trees, an area known as 'the grange' or 'the Grange Reserve', a place known for its cover as children would hide there to play or smoke out of the sight of the adults. It moved down slowly behind the trees, then rose up, shooting off at great

N
1,000 yards
750 meters
Wellington Road
Dandenong Road
CLAYTON
Centre Road
Princes Highway
Centre Road
CLAYTON SOUTH
Springs Road
Clayton Road
Main Road
Westall Road
Whiteside Road
WESTALL
Westall Secondary School
Fairbank Road
Sighting
Bourke Road
CLARINDA
AUSTRALIA
SPRINGVALE
Springvale Road
Clayton Road
The Grange
Westall Road
Landing site
Heatherton Road
Dingley Bypass
Spring Road
Tootal Road
SPRINGVALE SOUTH
Westall Road Extension
Clarke Road
DINGLEY VILLAGE
Spring Road
Clayton South

speed. Many children had already begun to run over in the direction of the saucer, trying to get closer to it for a better look. Several children, the ones quicker on their feet, managed to get pretty close to the object and according to one student, Jacqueline Argent, along with at least one other child, Tanya, had passed out and was later taken away in an ambulance and reportedly never returned back to the school. According to Terry, there was a large yellow scorch mark on the grass where the object would have likely come down, in the same shape as the saucer that they had seen. Other children, one of whom was Victor Zakruzny, reported there were actually two craft that had landed further over, just outside the school perimeter. He described feeling an intense heat coming from the objects as he got to within one metre (a few feet) of them, before they rose off the ground and then took off slowly into the sky. He managed to make sketches of these, describing them as being smooth, seamless with no joins or signs of metal being welded, moving silently. As the saucers left their field of view, teachers attempted to regain control of the children, raucous from having just moments before witnessed such an incredible sight. Headmaster of the school, Frank Samblebe immediately called an all-school assembly, in which he instructed the students to not discuss what they had seen. Telling hundreds of children to remain silent is one thing, enforcing that would be a different matter altogether. Joy Clarke is one of those former students who remembers the assembly, and the police arriving shortly after as the media began to surround the school. Cameras, notepads and pencils were shoved under the noses of the students as teachers tried to keep control and tell the children to not talk to the wanting media. These entreaties proved to be in vain, as several students appeared on TV or the front pages of local newspapers, sharing their stories and versions of events.

One of the chemistry teachers, Barbara Robbins, had grabbed a nearby camera and began to take as many photographs as possible at the time of the incident. Had she taken some of the most incredible photographs of all time? We have no idea, because, as recounted by one

# FLYING SAUCER MYSTERY: SCHOOL SILENT

## What was it?

YOUR DISTRICT NEWSPAPER — EVERY TUESDAY and THURSDAY

THE DANDENONG Journal

ESTABLISHED 1865

More than 19,500 copies of each issue circulate extensively through Dandenong, Springvale, Noble Park, Waverley, Berwick, Oakleigh, Clayton, Cranbourne, Knox and Sherbrooke.

1 Scott St., Dandenong. Ph. Dandenong 2 0251, 2 0365. Price 4 cents

Vol. 105, No. 28 THURSDAY, APRIL 14, 1966 48 Pages

**CLAYTON.— After more than a week of investigation, mystery still surrounds the reported sighting last Wednesday of a flying saucer near the Westall High School, Clayton.**

**Investigations of the report have been hampered by the reluctance of school authorities to permit interviews with eye-witness students and staff members.**

of the older students, school captain Graham Simmonds, he was monitoring the hallways after the event and noticed a scuffle at the end of the hall. There was Ms Robbins, having a disagreement with headteacher Mr Samblebe who was demanding she hand over the camera as a uniformed man stood behind them awaiting it. The camera would never be returned to Barbara Robbins. Who the uniform belonged to is also a mystery, and it wasn't the only strange uniform to be seen that day in the area.

It wasn't only those at the school who witnessed the incredible objects. Paul Smith was working alongside his boss, digging up vegetables to get ready for market on a property adjacent to the school when he looked up and saw the object in the sky. Standing agape, they saw the children running over to them, eventually making their way onto the property to try to get near the object. Paul recalled 'army trucks looking camouflaged' along with soldiers in uniform turning up shortly after the object had left. Given that they arrived within twenty minutes of the objects' sighting, it seems likely that this wasn't a branch of the military that would normally respond to routine callouts, but perhaps an organisation that had been tracking the objects before they even got to the school?

Even though the sighting was witnessed by so many and so much was going on all at once, there wasn't as much attention paid after it as you would expect. The media coverage didn't last long and what coverage there was, was mixed. Some newspapers, like the local *Dandenong Journal*, went for sensational headlines, with 'Flying saucer' adorning the front pages. Other, more highbrow papers in the Melbourne area, such as *The Age*, speculated that this was likely to be some sort of weather balloon. Either way, interest fell away, and the story faded until many decades later when researchers such as Shane Ryan brought the story back to life with fresh research, new witness statements and additional information. A permanent memorial at the site of the grange now stands to inform the public of what happened on that day in 1966. Many of the witnesses, now well into their adult years, are still firm in their testimony, knowing that what they saw in the school playground was something unexplainable. Joy Clarke is one: 'For years and years we were made fun of. You got told: "How crazy were you? What drugs were you on?" For God's sake, I was twelve and a half and at school. I wasn't dropping LSD!'

LEFT: A photo of the UFO taken by teacher Barbara Robbins.

ABOVE: The *Dandenong Journal* headline covering the sighting in Clayton South. © Clarion Ledger – USA TODAY NETWORK via Imagn Images.

| *Mashonaland East Province, Zimbabwe* | 17.5150° S, 31.1728° E |
|---|---|

# RUWA

Strange beings visit Ariel School to deliver an environmental message

Ruwa is a quiet rural area in Zimbabwe situated roughly 22km (14 miles) outside Harare. Its humble setting is characterised by farming and its large open spaces were the site of one of the most well-documented UFO cases of all time.

A few days before the main occurrence, sightings of a UFO in the sky were reported above the capital Harare. The story appeared on the evening news at the time, with many witnesses discussing seeing the objects.

On the morning of 16 September 1994, at Ariel School in Ruwa, the children were on their morning break. Much like they did on any other day, they played in the school grounds, some on their own, some in groups, but unlike any other day many of their lives were about to be shaped and changed by an event like no other. A number of the children spotted in the sky what appeared to be at least one, some said several, metallic, shiny, disc-shaped objects. In short, your classic flying saucers. The children reported that they made erratic movements in the sky, and some said they appeared to be silver, others said they were more grey.

Suddenly, one of the objects landed just on the outskirts of the school grounds. What followed is one of the most widely reported mass sightings in UFO history.

More than sixty of the children would provide their own testimony of what they saw, and the innocence of the children's stories, their fear in retelling what they saw, the uncertainty for many only adds to the credibility. While small details change across the varying stories, this happens with any recounting of a traumatic event, and in this case the consistencies remain.

Details of what the children saw varies: some say that the object landed and appeared to hover, others that it had an almost glitching effect, that it was there, but at times wasn't there. Like there was some sort of field obscuring a clear view of what and where the object was exactly, however, they all consistently claimed to see the arrival of something.

The most incredible details given by the children come not from the description of the craft but of the beings that appear to have emerged from the landed objects.

BBC Reporter Tim Leach was one of the first on the scene just three days after the incident, there to speak to more than sixty of the children about what they had seen. Children reported a being with a large head, large black oval-shaped eyes and wearing an all-black body suit stared back at them. Some said they were as close as 1m (3ft) away.

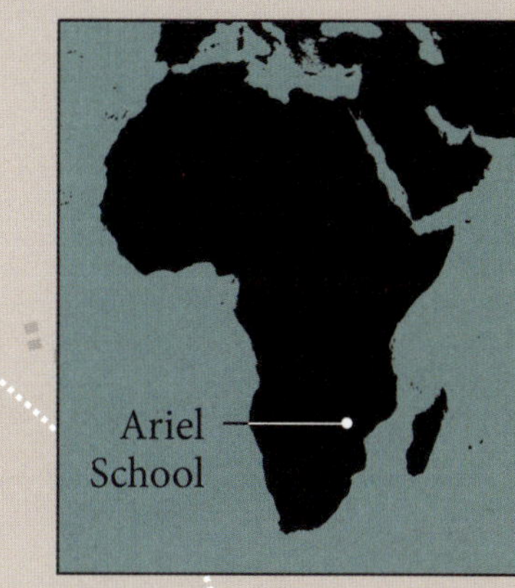


ZIMBABWE

*22km (14 miles) to Harare/*
*11km (6.8km) to Ruwa*

**Ariel School**
**Landing site**

Tarisa Road

*N*

150 *yards*
150 *meters*

Brian Robins

The testimony was put under further scrutiny by noted Harvard University Professor of Psychiatry, Dr John Mack, who upon hearing of the incident, travelled to Ruwa to speak to the children himself. Given his background, he not only questioned the children on what they saw, but dug deeper into how they felt, and how these being made them feel. They mentioned that they felt scared of the intensity of the glare from the beings and their strange appearance. Similar to other reports of UFO sightings from around the world, the children mentioned forms of telepathic communication occurring. Talking about the incident now in adulthood, one of the children, Lisil Field, said that she got the feeling as she made eye contact that she was being informed that we aren't looking after the planet, that all the trees will disappear and people will die. When pressed by Dr Mack, he asked if this was something she had thought before the experience or if it only occurred to her during the 'visit'. She said it was during.

In the years since, the children have continued to share their story, unwavering in what they saw. Many, including artist Emily Trim who was a witness in the playground, continue to focus on the eyes: the unearthly size and un-wavering glare that seemed to be almost mesmerizing. Emily says, 'There was no talking, all just images in the head.'

One theory is that many of the children were having some sort of mass hallucination, or that they somehow had conspired to tell some incredible fairytale. If this was the case, then it would stand to reason that many of the children would break from their story as they grew older. But, to this day the witnesses stand firm with what they saw that day in the playground.

At the time, the teachers varied from being dismissive of the story to acknowledging that the children may have witnessed 'something', but they were unsure what. With time, several of the teachers, including the head teacher Judy Bates, have come to believe that on that day alien beings did indeed pay a visit to the children of Ruwa, Zimbabwe. Judy admits that at the time she was 'selfish' to not listen or pay attention to the children, in what was a distressing incident, one that had profound effects on many of them as they have grown.

Dr Mack suffered professionally for his work in speaking to the children of Ruwa. The ridicule of his colleagues over his involvement in such a contentious topic was damaging to him, his profession and to Harvard. The legacy of his work, however, has lived on and remains valued in the UFO community long after his untimely passing in 2004.

So, what did the children of Ruwa, Zimbabwe see on that day in 1994? Given the sheer weight of testimony, it seems that a simple misidentification of something more mundane is unlikely. To read, to see, to hear the testimony of the children, and understand their confusion and fear at the time certainly lends credence to the view that an incredible, almost unthinkable event took place on that day. Why them, why children to pass on that message? Maybe this was a seed being planted, not for the story at the time to have its lasting impact, but for decades later ,when the children would become adults and continue to share their story at a time when technology, social media and documentaries are abundant and can reach a global audience.

In that case, children may be the very best way to get a message out there over time.

LEFT TOP: A drawing of the craft by Brian Robins, one of the children who witnessed the landing.

LEFT BOTTOM: Ruwa is a quiet, rural area of Zimbabwe.

| *Voronezh Oblast, Russia* | 51.4151° N, 39.1135° E |
|---|---|

# VORONEZH

An otherworldly experience in a Russian park

In 1586, the city of Voronezh was founded by the then expanding Russian state, as a way of guarding the southern borders from raids carried out by Tatar-Mongol forces during a period of Mongol domination. To fight against the Ottoman Empire, it was used by Peter the Great as a shipbuilding base in the late seventeenth to early eighteenth centuries, cementing the city as a naval stronghold and centre of industry. Then, in the Second World War, it suffered extensive damage as it was a fierce battleground and had to be built again in the years after the war. Safe to say, it is historically significant in the Russian history books. Located only 500km (around 300 miles) from Moscow, today it is a major industrial centre, with many industries based there, including electronic manufacturing, food production and chemical manufacturing. Culturally important, it is home to many universities and schools popular with students from Russia and other countries, with Voronezh State University one of the most respected educational establishments in the country. Its international airport sees many domestic and external flights take off each day from its runways, servicing many of its estimated population of two million.

UFOlogy's interest in the city began in 1989, while the city and its people were still under Soviet rule, the dissolving of the Soviet Union still a little over two years away. It was around 6.30 p.m. on the evening of 27 September, and one of the wildest accounts of a UFO sign by many witnesses was about to unfold, near a small park. Children were still playing as the sun was beginning to set, their parents talking, winding down the last daylight hours before returning home and beginning bedtime routines. Suddenly, against the dimming sky, an emerging light, incredibly bright, caught the attention of those in the area. It was an orb, around 10m (30ft) across, so bright it changed the colour of the sky around it. The orb came closer, hovering as the onlookers were staring, watching in awe and fear, anxious as to what was happening, parents worried for the safety of their children. Witnesses noted the sky first turning pink, then the object circled for a few minutes before seeming to leave. It then returned, descended, coming down slowly over another park with children playing in it close by, Levoberezhny Park. A craft was now visible as the light diminished and the children noticed a door opening and, to their amazement, like the stuff from a science fiction movie, a being emerged. This figure is described by witnesses as standing 3–4m (10–13ft) tall, with

BERJOZOVAJA ROSCHA
Ulitsa Shishkova
Voronezhskiy Tsentral'nyy Park Kul'tury I Otdykha
Severnyy Most
Voronezh
River
Voronezh
RUSSIA
Ulitsa Kol'ts ovskaya
Prospekt Revolyutsii
VORONEZH
PRIDACHA
R298
Voronezh State University
Local Voronezh district police station
Sighting
Ulitsa 20-Letiya Oktyabrya
CHIZHOVKA
Ulitsa Gramshi
N
2,000 yards
1,000 meters
Levoberezhnyy Park
Sighting

a small head, no neck and three eyes, the middle of which swivelled around like a sort of radar. Unlike many close encounters of this sort, where beings are plain, with large heads, few to no features, this had several striking features, including clothing with various symbols on its chest whichglowed, and a belt. A second figure emerged with a 'shield' on its chest, wearing silver clothing and bronze-coloured boots, along with a small robotic looking device which was activated by touch. Reports by those who were up close said the aliens seemed to communicate with each other, one stating that one of the beings shone a light from its chest that illuminated the ground with triangular lights that soon vanished. There was even a report of a tube-like object, nearly half-a-metre (2ft) long, which some thought was a gun, in the hand of one of the figures.

# Text of Tass account of UFO landing in Voronezh

The Associated Press

Following is the English-language text of the account on Monday by the official Soviet news agency Tass, distributed in New York, of what Tass reported was an alien landing in the Soviet Union. It bore the following headline:

"Confirmed UFO Landing in Voronezh, Witnesses Frightened."

VORONEZH — Scientists have confirmed that an unidentified flying object recently landed in a park in the Russian city of Voronezh.

They have also identified the landing site and found traces of aliens who made a short promenade about the park.

Aliens visited the place after dark, at least three times, locals report.

A large shining ball or disk was seen hovering above the park, it then landed, a hatch opened and one, two or three creatures similar to humans and a small robot came out.

The aliens were three or even four meters tall (just under 10 feet to slightly more than 13 feet high), but with very small heads, witnesses say.

They walked near the ball or disc and then disappeared inside. Onlookers were overwhelmed with a fear which lasted for several days.

"We identified the landing site by means of biolocation," Genrikh Silanov, head of the Voronezh Geophysical Laboratory said in an interview.

"We detected a circle 20 meters in diameter. Four 4-to-5-centimeter deep dents, each with a diameter of 14 to 16 centimeters were clearly visible. They are situated in the four points of a rhomb. We found two mysterious pieces of rock."

(A centimeter is 0.4 inches and one meter equals 3.3 feet).

"At first glance they looked like sandstone of a deep-red color. However, mineralogical analysis has shown that the substance cannot be found on Earth. However, additional tests are needed to reach a more definite conclusion."

Silanov used biolocation to trace the earthly trails of the aliens.

Witnesses were not informed about the experiment, but the route along which the aliens walked as described by the onlookers and the one established scientifically coincided.

Many also claim to have seen a banana-shaped object in the sky and a characteristic illuminated sign, as described in the *U.S. Saga* magazine.

It is unlikely that residents of Voronezh could have read the magazine.

## UFO

creature, she said, had "only a small knob instead of a head."

Stanton Friedman, a consultant who lectures on the topic "Flying Saucers Are Real" and has examined Soviet studies of UFOs, said in Secaucus, N.J., on Monday that Soviet scientists tended to treat the subject more seriously than American scientists. Last June, the Soviet publication *Soviet Military Review* included an article on "UFO's and Security."

The Tass report, which did not give the date of the purported "landing" in Voronezh, said onlookers were "overwhelmed with a fear that lasted for several days."

Genrikh Silanov, head of the Vo-

probably caused by the landing of a UFO.

Not so, Tass reported. Firefighters think a haystack simply caught fire and scorched the ground.

Russians have long been fascinated by the weird and the occult, but formerly they could glean their information only from rumors and underground copies of everything from palmistry guides to books on Eastern mysticism.

The Kremlin's economic reforms, with their emphasis on each enterprise paying its own way, have also given the official press more incentive to cater to readers' tastes in order to increase circulation.

Kurtz's committee has a UFO

LEFT Witness schoolboy Alyosha Panin shows the site of the mysterious landing site in Levoberezhny park.

ABOVE: The sighting made international news: here *The Clarion News* from Pennsylvania, USA reports on the event.

As the beings moved around the park, some noted that they appeared to fade out and fade back into existence at times, one of them raised the gun-like tube, pointing it at one of the children, a boy who screamed in terror which drew the attention of the being; the boy then disappeared in front of their eyes. This happened mere minutes after the beings had appeared, and as quickly, they got back into the craft and left. The boy re-appeared, much to the astonishment and relief of those around, who had watched in horror. He was said to be confused and disorientated, but seemed unharmed. There were many witnesses to this event, not only civilians but military, including Lieutenant Sergei A. Matveyev from the local Voronezh district police station. He was interviewed by telephone by the *New York Times* in an article in the immediate aftermath of the event, as it was a story that went international. He told a journalist: 'It was not an optical illusion . . . it was certainly a body flying in the sky.' He himself had not seen the aliens, not being right there at the scene but had watched the object in flight, describing it as moving noiselessly at high speed. He went on to say of the event: 'I thought I must be really tired, but I rubbed my eyes, and it didn't go away. Then I figured, in this day and age, anything is possible.'

Director of the regional health department, Vladimir Moiseyev, confirmed that none of those who were in close proximity to the object or beings had applied for medical help of any kind, but said that the children would be examined, particularly the child who was vanished by the gun-like-tube, and another who was paralysed, either by design or by fear. One local correspondent for press agency Tass, Vladimir V. Lebedev, treated the whole event very seriously and with respect, speaking with dozens of

witnesses. He told journalists over telephone at the time that Genrikh Silanov, who was head of the Voronezh Geophysical Lab, had met the children and asked them to draw on paper what they had seen, much like the other events in Wales, Australia and Zimbabwe (see pages 156, 186 and 190, respectively).

The drawings were all broadly similar, with the children drawing a banana-shaped object. The Soviet Army got involved and checked out the landing site, also sending scientists to investigate. They found high levels of radiation, scorched grass and several strange rock samples that were taken for further analysis.

What did those people see in the park that day? There is so much to it for misidentification to be the conclusion, surely? Huge entities, advanced technology, a child being de-materialised and re-materialised in front of a crowd. Sceptics claimed mass hallucination or hysteria was to blame. Or, perhaps, a foreign nation or shadowy government entity was using some sort of top-secret tech to fool the people? That, however, seems a dangerous risk to take so publicly in the light of day. The witnesses from the day would not be convinced that they had had anything but a truly otherworldly experience that day.

LEFT: Located 500km (around 300 miles) from Moscow, Voronezh is a major industrial city with cultural and educational importance.

| *West Lothian, Scotland* | 55.5492° N, 3.3259° W |
| --- | --- |

# DECHMONT WOODS

Forestry worker abducted by spiked aliens

The Dechmont Woods incident, from 1979, is unique in UFOlogy, particularly in the UK as it is one of the few to result in a criminal investigation. The location isn't far from the town of Livingston, Scotland, and as well as being called Dechmont Woods, can also be known as Dechmont Law. Like much of rural Scotland, it is noted for its naturally scenic landscapes, greenery, natural bodies of water and woodland trails, and is often visited by tourists, bird watchers, hikers and those looking to capture some of nature's wonders on camera. Dechmont Law itself is a hill in the woods, and once scaled, it offers some spectacular views of the landscape around. Those with an interest in ancient history can take in the remnants of old settlements still untouched by modern amenities. A little further along the A89, to the east is the town of Livingston, better known today for its shopping centre and football team.

UFOlogists know this location better as the site of a close encounter, and not a particularly pleasant one. The unfortunate victim of this incident was Robert Taylor, at the time of the incident sixty-one years old. He had been a gardener until the outbreak of the Second World War, when he took up a position as a tank driver in 1939, being part of the war efforts in France, Belgium and the Netherlands. It was 9 November 1979, and Robert was a forestry worker, heading out for the morning to inspect a particular area which was a routine part of his job, which included tree inspection, damage assessment and the like. Around 10.30 a.m., he was walking with his dog towards a particular clearing in the woods of Dechmont. Upon arriving, as he turned a corner, he noticed a huge craft in front of him. Unable to move from shock, he just stared at the alien-looking ship. He described the object as dome-shaped, dark grey in colour, approximately 6m (20ft) in diameter, and 3.5m (12ft) tall with a rough exterior finish like sandpaper. He described arms going all the way around the object, with what he could only make out as blades sticking out from them. It appeared to be trying to fade out or make itself invisible. As he stood there, two objects came out of the UFO, one from either side, two spheres with spikes sticking out of them, and began to tumble their way towards him, looking like 'sea mines'. Things at this point took a turn for the worse for Robert, as the spikes stopped either side of him, and attaching onto him by his trousers, began to drag him towards the domed craft, which hadn't moved. In his struggle, he began to lose consciousness, but before doing so, he recalls a strong, overpowering smell like something burning.

Dechmont
N
600 yards
500 meters
A899
Main Street
Craiglaw
DECHMONT
A89
Robert Taylor's route
North Woods
M8
A89
Deer Hill
Landing site
M8
Reservoir Covert
DECHMONT WOODS
UFO trail
Golf Course Road
Dechmont Law
Woodlands Park
Herd Green
Deans Community High School
Anderson Green
KnightsridgeWest Road
Dechmont Moss Wood
Dechmont Gorse
Camps Rigg
Raeburn Rigg
KNIGHTSRIDGE
Deans North Road
Waverley Crs
Houstoun Road
Newyearfield Strip
DEANS
SCOTLAND

Somewhere around 11.10 a.m., Robert Taylor began to regain consciousness, but did not recover his wits completely. His dog was panicked, the object had gone, he found it difficult to speak or shout for any help. Still unable to stand, he crawled the 90m (300ft) along the woodland floor back to his vehicle. As he pulled himself up into the car, he reached for his radio to try get in touch with someone, to come to his aid. Finding his voice had deserted him, the radio wasn't an option. Mustering the strength to drive, he got his car started but ended up reversing into a ditch; the rest of the journey home would have to be on foot.

At 11.45 a.m., Robert arrived home, shaken and upset, and his wife, Mary, was shocked at his appearance. She greeted her husband, first thinking he had had an accident in his truck. The last thing she expected was to be told that he had been attacked by, in his words, a spaceship. Disbelieving in such things, she noticed that his trousers were muddy and ripped, and his face had a long red mark across it, running down under his chin. Mary wanted to get in touch with the police immediately and report this, as her husband had clearly been attacked, but by what she was unsure. Robert wasn't immediately comfortable with this, instead insisting

they call his boss, Malcolm Drummond, who made his way to their home to check up on his staff member. Malcolm was told Robert's version of events, then accompanied Mr Taylor back to the location of the incident, which had taken place only an hour or so prior, to see if there was any sign of what had just taken place. Indeed, on the ground were markings of something which had left an impression, around forty small holes, potentially from the spiked spheres that had rolled towards Robert. The indentations indicated that the objects that left the markings had a considerable weight to them.

At this time, Mary, concerned for her husband's health and welfare, called their family doctor, asking for a house call to check over Robert, reporting that he had been attacked by what Dr Gordon Adams recalls was a 'flying saucer'. He made his way to their home that afternoon, once Robert and Malcolm had returned from the woods. A routine examination

ABOVE: Dechmont Woods is a scenic stretch of woodland on the edge of Livingston.

LEFT: Robert Taylor was on his way to inspect a piece of woodland when he came across the craft.

RIGHT: An illustration of the craft and the orbs that attached themselves to Robert Taylor.

checking vital signs, temperature and such, indicated everything seemed to be fine, but the doctor did find two marks on Roberts legs which matched where he reported his trousers had been torn by the attacking spheres.

Malcolm Drummond called the police, believing that Robert had at least been assaulted; that seemed a certainty.

The task of investigating the assault landed at the desk of Detective Constable Ian Wark. His first port of call was to get to the area of the reported incident to check it out, and upon arrival he saw the markings in the ground, noting they were around 9cm (3½ in) in diameter. Accompanying those were caterpillar marks, the sort you would expect to be left behind by a bulldozer or other heavy equipment. However, an inspection of similar equipment kept in local yards found nothing to match what had been seen in the woods. What is even more interesting is that the marks didn't appear to lead anywhere, there was no path to follow or retrace, consistent with being made by something that dropped down and then went straight back up! Continuing the investigation, Robert Taylor's trousers, torn in the attack, were sent for forensic analysis, which could only conclude they had been ripped by some sort of 'hook'

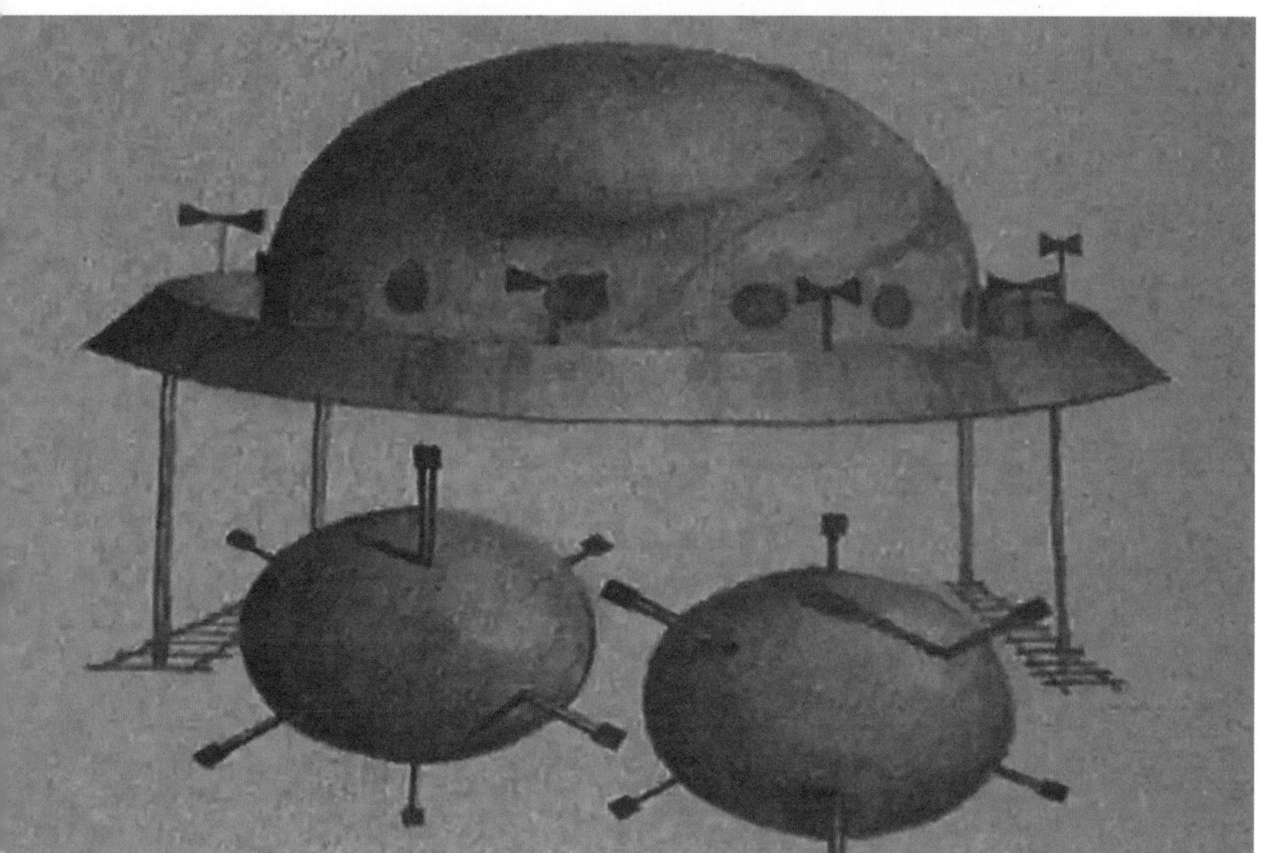

attaching on and ripping them in an upwards motion. Today the trousers are in the possession of Scottish UFO researcher and author, Malcolm Robinson, who has done some of the most extensive research on this case in the world.

Many sceptics have theories as to what may have happened to Robert, that don't involve anything of a non-human origin. Some have put forward that a stroke would account for the burning smell, the loss of consciousness and his mistaking a nearby water tower for the dome-shaped object. However, his own family doctor confirmed no history of fits before or after the event. Others suggest that perhaps he had been, knowingly or un-knowingly, under the influence of mushrooms, though no evidence or past behaviour would support this theory. Some even suggested that an astronomical mirage, of the planet Venus, could have been the reason of the sighting; this doesn't, however, explain the markings, the struggle, the collapse.

Sadly, Robert Taylor passed away in 2007, never getting the answers to what happened to him on that day in 1979. His legacy of the day he was attacked by something he believed to be from another planet lives on. Those involved in the early investigations until the time of Mr Taylor's passing, insist the story told never changed and that Robert had no reason to make this up or lie, being a man of great integrity. Researcher Malcolm Robinson's book about the subject, *The Dechmont Woods Incident – An ordinary day, an extraordinary event*, is perhaps the best research around what happened on the day and the subsequent investigations from various parties. In it, Malcolm says: 'As a man who has spoken to hundreds of UFO witnesses over many years, none has convinced me so much as Bob Taylor.'

| *New Mexico, USA* | 34.0239° N, 106.5521° W |
| --- | --- |

# SOCORRO

Otherworldly vehicle interrupts car chase

It was around 5.45 p.m. on 24 April 1964, and Police Sergeant Lonnie Zamora was engaged in a high-speed pursuit of a car along US Highway 85 (now Interstate 25). It was just on the outskirts of Socorro, New Mexico, a small rural town around 120 km (75 miles) south of Albuquerque with a modest population of around 6,000 who were involved mainly in mining, farming and other agricultural activities. At this time, Lonnie Zamora had been an officer in Socorro for around five years and had a good reputation among his colleagues for being reliable and trustworthy; this is important to note, given the incredible turn his day was about to take.

While chasing the speeding car, Zamora's pursuit was interrupted by a huge bang and he noticed a bright light in the distance, which slowly dropped to the ground. Concerned it could have been some sort of aircraft in distress, or an explosion that may have required his assistance, he made his way to the location.

The large object at Officer Zamora's first glance looked perhaps to be a car that had overturned, but as seconds went by and the scene became clearer, he realised this was no automobile. He could see it was a long, egg-shaped structure, metallic in texture, off-white in colour and mounted on four legs. It was startling, and he tried to take in any details he could to give him a clue as to what it could be. When he was less than 185 metres (about 200 yards) away, something caught his attention just next to the 'egg'. Two beings, who he later described in interviews as small adults or even children, and wearing white overalls, appeared, one seemingly noticing Lonnie as he looked over at them. Another interesting detail was an insignia on the side of the craft, a bit like an arrowhead inside a red arc.

He wanted to get a closer look, but some loud bangs like a car door being slammed shut, rang out, causing Zamora to scramble back towards his car for cover, fearing the craft may be about to explode. It didn't appear to be in trouble, however, and glancing back, he could no longer see the two beings. With a roar, the object began to emit a blue-orange flame from its underside and it rose into the air, hovering for a moment before darting off at rapid speed. It was soon gone from sight. Recalling the moment the object left in interviews afterwards with authorities or researchers, Lonnie said that the sound was like a roar, but not like that of a jet, and the strange flame left no plumes of smoke or vapour trail behind it.

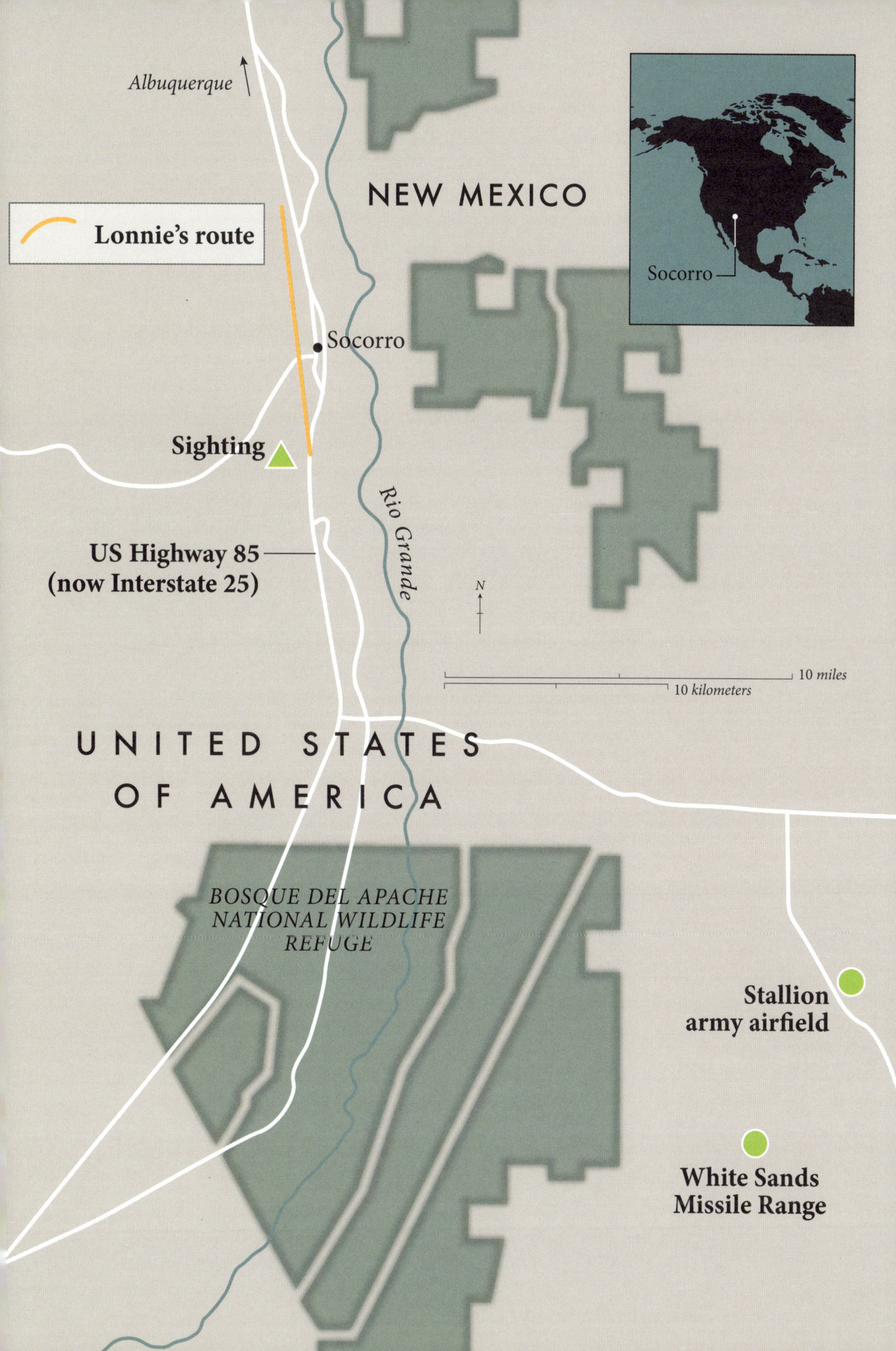
Albuquerque
NEW MEXICO
Lonnie's route
Socorro
Socorro
Sighting
US Highway 85
(now Interstate 25)
Rio Grande
N
10 miles
10 kilometers
UNITED STATES
OF AMERICA
BOSQUE DEL APACHE
NATIONAL WILDLIFE
REFUGE
Stallion
army airfield
White Sands
Missile Range

Next on the scene was Sergeant Sam Chavez, who had heard Zamora's radio call to the sheriff's department for back-up moments after the object had left the scene. It was around 6 p.m., and on arrival Chavez could see his colleague was shaken and in a state of shock, which alerted him that something out of the ordinary had happened. The two colleagues moved to inspect the area where the egg-shaped craft had stood just minutes before and could see four impressions where the legs of the weighty object had marked the ground. Around them were are some signs of burning in the vegetation close enough to have caught the flames from the 'exhaust' of the object as it left. As time passed, further law enforcement personnel began to arrive on location to examine the site. They noticed that underneath where the egg had stood, the sand had in parts turned to glass, likely due to being heated to an extreme temperature by the blue-orange flame. As the night drew to a close, the FBI was informed of the situation, with agent Arthur Byrne becoming one of the first to speak to Lonnie Zamora, questioning him on his experience that day. There were a few reasons the FBI were brought in: they wanted to rule out any national security issues such as whether a foreign adversary was operating on home soil, and whether there were military installations nearby, as the mention of flames and explosions put them on alert and they deemed it best to check things out.

The days that followed for Lonnie Zamora must have seemed a blur, his head still filled with the events of that evening playing over in his mind. He was visited by famed researcher Dr J. Allen Hynek from the air force's Project Blue Book. Civilian investigators and other groups got wind of the close encounter and also sent their own people to try to speak to Lonnie. Audio recordings of his interviews are available from different sources, since he spoke both shortly and many years after the event. He didn't court publicity, and his story never wavered or became sensationalised with the passage of time.

Many individuals from the air force, local authorities and private citizens from around the country visited the site in the days and weeks after the landing. Samples were collected, pictures taken and statements made, but the mystery of the egg-shaped craft has never been solved. Many theories have been put forward, including one suggesting that local students from a high school where Lonnie Zamora had worked played a prank on him with fireworks. It seems incredibly unlikely that an experienced police officer, well thought of by his peers, would mistake something as trivial as that for a potential alien craft. The lack of evidence, however, does have to be acknowledged. It is a fascinating case and one that remains unsolved in the Project Blue Book case files, with Dr Hynek himself stating the case 'had no obvious conventional explanation'.

ABOVE: The site where Lonnie Zamora saw the metallic object is examined.

RIGHT: Officer Lonnie Zamora was pursuing a vehicle when he observed the egg-shaped craft.

| *Yamanashi Prefecture, Japan* | 35.6500° N, 138.5500° E |
| --- | --- |

# KOFU

## Two schoolboys meet an alien being

The Japanese city of Kofu in the middle of Yamanashi Prefecture is located around 130km (80 miles) west of Tokyo, in a basin surrounded by stunning mountains. In the mid-1970s, when the events described here took place, it was already a well-known economic and political hub in the region. Home to a fascinating cultural mix, capturing the country's financial upturn and embracing modern conveniences, it still held on to its rich roots and history in a time of rapid modernization, with new meeting old. The iconic Mount Fuji looms in the distance, overseeing a sprawl of open fields and other farmland.

At about 7 p.m. on the evening of Sunday 23 February 1975, two eight-year-old friends, Yamahata Katsuhiro and Kuwahara Masato had been playing on their roller-skates near their school. As they were finishing, Katsuhiro and Masato, (in Japanese culture surnames are written first with first names last) felt their eyes being drawn to two strange orange-red lights in the darkening sky. The lights were high up in the east, and while the boys stood in awe, the larger of the lights moved off quickly towards the north of the city, but the smaller light moved over towards them. Descending from above their heads, it settled next to the vineyard behind the school, and they heard it making a sound that resembled the ticking sound of a Geiger counter. Some reports suggest the boys then ran to a graveyard and hid, but as is often pointed out, this detail wasn't in the original press or police reports and is likely a result of both mistranslations of 'vineyard' and years of re-telling leading to embellishment. This ambiguity is a feature of the reporting of this particular case in various articles, documentaries and retellings.

Cautiously, Katsuhiro and Masato made their way over towards where the object had slowly come down; there they reported seeing a disc-shaped craft, about the size of a large family car, perhaps a little bigger. They later drew pictures, showing that it had three or four oval-shaped protrusions on its underside, in some places reported as potential landing gears. As in similar incidents from around the globe, the boys when interviewed later told of a faint glow or aura around the craft, too. The event was to become even stranger, as the boys both reported seeing a being emerge from the craft. It was only around 1.2 metres (4 foot) tall, with a wrinkled brown face, brown hands and fangs rather than teeth sticking out of its mouth. The being was allegedly wearing a metallic jumpsuit or overall, and they

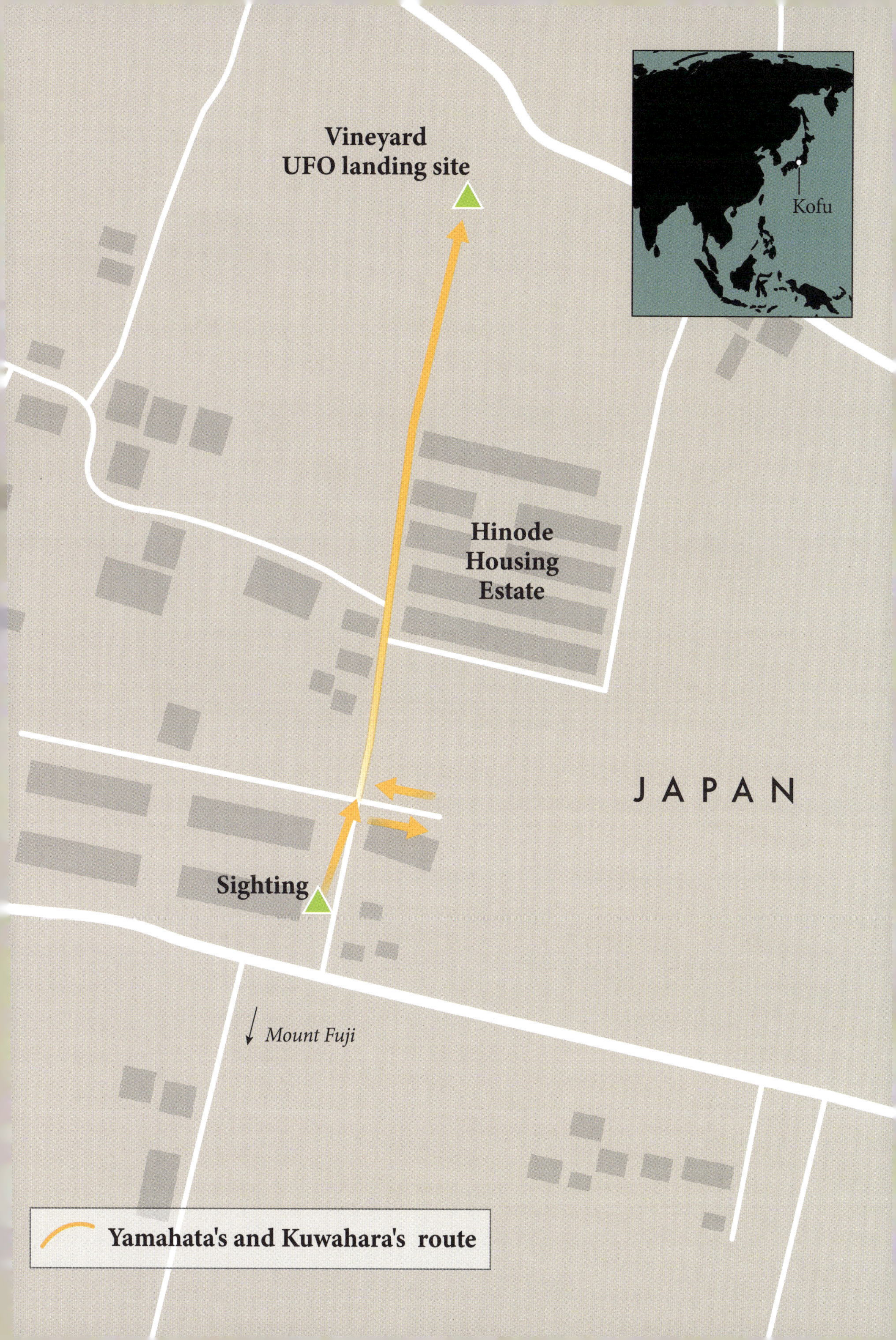

Vineyard
UFO landing site

Kofu

Hinode
Housing
Estate

JAPAN

Sighting

Mount Fuji

Yamahata's and Kuwahara's route

could see another being who remained inside the craft the whole time. The one who had emerged looked at the surroundings, reached out and tapped Katsuhiro on the shoulder and made sounds, perhaps in an attempt to communicate. When relaying back the incident, the children said the being made a sound 'like a tape-recorder running backwards'. The contact made Katsuhiro fall to the ground, frozen in fear according to Masato, but could this state have been deliberately brought on by the being? It is too hard to tell. Masato reached down to his friend, pulling him up and helping him make his way away from the immediate surroundings of the craft and being.

They then fled to their homes, immediately telling their mothers about what had happened; some reports say that the parents witnessed the craft in the distance when they checked. However, this is likely misreporting, as witnesses who reported lights in the area around the same time appear to have been unaware of what had happened to the boys. The families, believing the boys had at the very least seen something strange but unsure what it was, reported their tale to the police, who agreed to investigate. The next morning in the light of day the police visited the area where the boys had reported seeing the alien visitors in their craft. The officers found some strange markings on the ground where the disc-like object had reportedly settled. They may even have been from the being itself, made when it had approached young Katsuhiro.

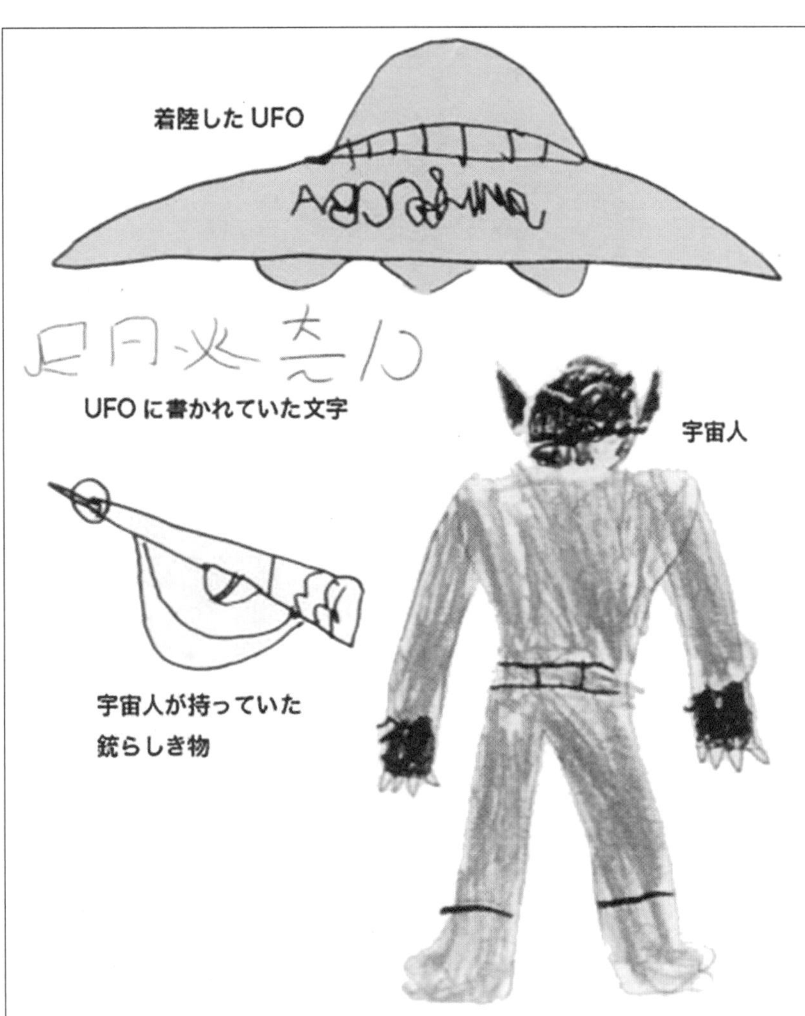


Several people, including local reporters, teachers and authorities, interviewed both the boys. Their answers included impressive detail for children so young, and stayed consistent. As the days went on, the story gained some notoriety and began to spread to local and national media. Throughout 1975 the story was reported, usually in rather small excerpts in journals such as *Flying Saucer Review* and MUFON's newsletter, 'Skylook'.

Ultimately, the Kofu case rests on the credibility of two young children and our willingness to trust their accounts. Like the Westhall School and Ariel School incidents (see pages 186 and 190, respectively) – where young witnesses also reported extraordinary events – the innocence of childhood raises an important question: why would they make this up? While we may never know exactly what Katsuhiro and Masato saw on that February evening, the fact that other witnesses reported strange lights in the sky around the same time adds weight to their story. Whatever it was, it remains one of Japan's most intriguing UFO encounters.

LEFT: Yamahata Katsuhiro and Kuwahara Masato in the vineyard.

ABOVE: The boys' drawings of the craft and the fanged creatures.

RIGHT: Kofu sits in a basin surrounded by mountains. It is covered in vineyards growing the Kōshū grape. The boys observed the craft in one of these vineyards.

# PICTURE CREDITS

p.11 Courtesy of National Archives, Records of Headquarters U.S. Air Force [Air Staff]; p.16 Courtesy of Getty/Interim Images; p.17 Courtesy, Fort Worth Star-Telegram Photograph Collection, Special Collections, The University of Texas at Arlington Library, Arlington, Texas; p.23 © Arizona Daily Star; pp.24-25 Jon Arnold Images Ltd/Alamy; p.28 Courtesy of Wikipedia; p.29 Courtesy of Associated Press/Alamy; p.33 above Courtesy of Fagner Martins/Shutterstock, below Courtesy of James Fox; pp.36-37 Courtesy of Chris Howes/Wild Places Photography/Alamy; p.43 Courtesy of TopFoto/Fortean; p.44 Courtesy of GPNaturePhotos/Alamy; p.48 above © The Church of Jesus Christ of Latter-day Saints, below © Travis Walton; p.51 © The National Enquirer; pp.52-53; p.56 Courtesy of NB/ROD/Alamy; p.59 TopFoto/Fortean; pp.60-61 Courtesy of Halbergman/Getty; pp.64, 65 Courtesy of Terry Lovelace; pp.68-69 Minden Pictures/Alamy; p72; p.73; Ken Howard/Alamy; p.73 Courtesy of Bettmann/Getty; p.74 Courtesy of Charles Walker Collection/Alamy; pp.76-77 Courtesy of Cappi Thompson/Getty; p.80 Courtesy of Pheasantry/Allied Vision/Kobal/Shutterstock; pp.82-83 Courtesy of Ultima_Gaina/Getty; p88 Courtesy of Stocktrek Images/Getty; p.91 Courtesy of MediaPunch Inc/Alamy; p.94 © The Cedar Rapids Gazette; p.95 Air Staff / National Archives, Records of Headquarters U.S. Air Force; p.97 Courtesy of Lya_Cattel/Getty; p.100 Courtesy of Taras Young/Wikipedia; p.101 Courtesy of Geogphotos/Alamy; pp.102-103 Courtesy of Clynt Garnham/Alamy; p.106 Courtesy of The Canadian Press/Alamy; pp.108-109 Courtesy of All Canadian Photos/Alamy; p.113 , p.114 Courtesy of Patrick Maréchal/Wikipedia; p.115 Courtesy of Paul Hermans/Wikipedia; pp.116-117 Courtesy of Friedrich Stark/Alamy; p.120 Courtesy of Richard I'Anson/Getty; p.122 Courtesy of Parviz Jafari; p.123 © Andy Wu; pp.126, 127 Operação Prato documents, courtesy of The National Archives of Brazil; pp.128-129 Courtesy of Odyssey Images/Alamy; pp.132-133 Courtesy of Yadid Levy/Alamy; p.138 Courtesy of Mary Evans Picture Library; pp.140-141 Courtesy of Hemis/Alamy; p.144 Courtesy of China Daily; p.145 Courtesy of MNXANL/ Wikipedia; p.148 Courtesy of George Rose/Getty Image; p.149 left Courtesy of Chronicle/Alamy, right Courtesy of Wikipedia; pp.152, 153 Courtesy of Wikipedia; pp.154-155 © Robert Powell and Glen Schulze; pp.159, 160 © Mirrorpix; pp.162-163 Courtesy of DV Aerial/Alamy; p.167 Courtesy of Wikipedia; pp.170–171 Courtesy of alexhitrov/Adobe Stock; pp.174–175 Courtesy of Zirui Wu/Alamy; pp.180, 181 Courtesy of the Intercontinental U.F.O. Galactic Spacecraft Research and Analytic Network Archives; p.182 Courtesy of Wikipedia; pp.184–185 Courtesy of John McAdorey/Shutterstock; p.188 Courtesy of World History Archive/Alamy; p.189 © Clarion Ledger – USA TODAY NETWORK via Imagn Images. Courtesy of The State Library of Victoria; p.192 Courtesy of TopPhoto/Fortean; p.196 Courtesy of Sputnik Media Bank; p.197 © The Clarion Ledger; p.198 Courtesy of Vladimir Zapletin/Getty; pp.202–203 Courtesy of Almondvale Photography/Alamy; p.204 Courtesy of Mary Evans Picture Library/Steuart Campbell; p.205 © ITV; p.209 Courtesy of Mary Evans Picture Library; pp.202, 203 © Leonard Stringfield/ International UFO Registry; pp.214–215 Courtesy of Getty/Sean Pavone.

# ACKNOWLEDGEMENTS

I would like to thank several people for helping me get this project over the line. Firstly, I would like to thank the team at Quarto, Richard and Jenny, for having the faith to ask me to do this in the first place. It has been tough, but they supported me every step of the way.

A massive thank you to Charlotte, who guided me through the process. Countless emails and calls were exchanged to ensure I had what I needed to stay on the right track – sorry for the awful timekeeping on my part!

Special thanks to one of the best historians and authors on the UFO topic, Graeme Rendall, whose incredible eye for detail was invaluable in making sure the cases were as accurate as possible. Truly, a talented gentleman.

Finally, to everyone who has played a part in shaping my involvement with the UFO topic through conversation, debate and interactions since 2020: thank you. I hope this book plays a small part in bringing forward some incredible stories of interactions with a phenomenon that I believe holds the answer to the greatest question of all: 'Are we alone?' The answer is no.

# INDEX

Page numbers in *italics* refer to illustrations.

# ABOUT THE AUTHOR

Andy McGrillen is the host and creator of That UFO Podcast. This podcast has an international reach, through Apple, Spotify, and YouTube reaching over 5 million audio downloads in only 2 years, with almost 2 million YouTube views.

The podcast started off during lockdown in May 2020, but quickly rose up the podcasting charts to secure regular places in the top 10s in Science charts around the globe. In the Summer of 2022, the podcast was also recognised at the British Podcast Awards in the listeners choice top 20. It continues to grow in stature & reputation as the UFO subject explores its place in the mainstream news cycle. Its mix of highly credible guests, news conversations & discussions are produced on a regular basis to a loyal audience, which has grown into a community now via various social platforms.

Quarto

First published in 2025 by Ivy Press
an imprint of The Quarto Group.
One Triptych Place, London, SE1 9SH
United Kingdom
T (0)20 7700 9000
www.Quarto.com

EEA Representation, WTS Tax d.o.o., Žanova ulica 3, 4000 Kranj, Slovenia
www.wts-tax.si



A catalogue record for this book is available from the British Library.

ISBN 978-1-83600-602-2
EBOOK ISBN 978-1-83600-603-9

10 9 8 7 6 5 4 3 2 1

Art Director: Paileen Currie
Book Designer: Ben Ruocco
Editorial Director: Jenny Barr
Illustrator: Lovell Johns
Publisher: Richard Green
Senior Editor: Charlotte Frost
Senior Production Manager: Alex Merrett

Printed in Malaysia PC062025